O9-AIE-829

More "tremendous good fun"* from the creator of *The Commitments*

THE VAN

RODDY DOYLE

This return visit with the family of Roddy Doyle's acclaimed first novel and hit movie finds Jimmy Rabbitte, Sr., unemployed and under-appreciated. When his best friend is sacked, they buy a rusty old fish-and-chip van and set out to feed the masses—with hilariously unpredictable results.

"There was Joyce's Dublin and now there's Roddy Doyle's: wholly contemporary, extremely funny and wonderfully and energetically delinquent. Irresistible to the modern spirit." —FAY WELDON

"Invites comparison with the best of 20th-century Irish literature." —*Publishers Weekly*

Don't miss *The Snapper,* Doyle's second novel of the Rabbitte family, now available in Penguin paperback!

Illustration: Alan Baker

VIKING   **At bookstores now**

ON THE HEIGHTS OF DESPAIR

E. M. CIORAN

Translated and with an Introduction by Ilinca Zarifopol-Johnston

This is the first work by "the most distinguished figure in the tradition of Kirkegaard, Nietzsche, and Wittgenstein" (Susan Sontag). "Cioran, at twenty-two, in his first book, is already *wholly* Cioran. Here is his tonic cynicism, his religious passion at war with itself, his extravagant honesty, his sensuality, his lyricism. . . . We need, all of us, to understand, before it is too late, the paradox of his celebratory bitterness." — Andrei Codrescu

Cloth $18.95 160 pages

THE UNIVERSITY OF CHICAGO PRESS

5801 S. Ellis Ave., Chicago, IL 60637

Sons and Lovers

One of the greatest novels of the twentieth century, is published in its unexpurgated form for the first time, as D. H. Lawrence wrote it. The novel is freed from interference and distortion with this complete, authoritative text. **$24.95**

Now in paperback...
D. H. Lawrence
Volume 1: The Early Years, 1885-1912
John Worthen
"Mr. Worthen has written an exciting first volume and an indispensable record."

—*New York Times Book Review*
$18.95

Available in bookstores or from

SONS AND LOVERS

The unexpurgated text

D. H. Lawrence

CAMBRIDGE
UNIVERSITY PRESS

40 West 20th Street, New York, NY 10011-4211
Call toll-free 800-872-7423. MasterCard/VISA accepted.

BIOGRAPHY

41

Editor: Bill Buford
Deputy Editor: Tim Adams
Managing Editor: Ursula Doyle
Editorial Assistant: Robert McSweeney
Contributing Editor: Rose Kernochan

Managing Director: Derek Johns
US Associate Publisher: Anne Kinard
US Financial Comptroller: Margarette Devlin
Publishing Assistant: Louise Tyson
General Assistant: Kirsten Wille

Picture Editor: Alice Rose George
Executive Editor: Pete de Bolla

Subscription and Advertising Correspondence in the United States and Canada: Anne Kinard, Granta, 250 West 57th Street, Suite 1316, New York, NY 10107. **Editorial Correspondence:** Granta 2–3 Hanover Yard, Noel Road, Islington, London N1 8BE, England. All manuscripts are welcome but must be accompanied by a self-addressed envelope and international postal money order for return postage from England or they cannot be returned.

Granta, ISSN 0017-3231, is published quarterly for $29.95 by Granta USA Ltd, a Delaware corporation. Second class postage paid at New York, NY and additional mailing offices. POSTMASTER: send address changes to GRANTA, 250 West 57th Street, Suite 1316, New York NY 10107.

Granta is printed in the United States of America. The paper used in this publication meets the minimum requirements of American National Standard for Information Sciences—Permanence of Paper for Printed Library Materials, ANSI Z39.48-1984. ∞

Granta is available on microfilm and microfiche through UMI, 300 North Zeeb Road, Ann Arbor, MI 48106-1346, USA.

Granta is published by Granta Publications Ltd and distributed by Penguin Books Ltd, Harmondsworth, Middlesex, England; Viking Penguin, a division of Penguin Books USA Inc, 375 Hudson Street, New York, NY 10014, USA; Penguin Books Australia Ltd, Ringwood, Victoria, Australia; Penguin Books Canada Ltd, 2801 John Street, Markham, Ontario, Canada L3R 1BR; Penguin Books (NZ) Ltd, 182–190 Wairau Road, Auckland 10, New Zealand. This selection copyright © 1992 by Granta Publications Ltd.

Cover by Senate.
Extracts from Boswell's journal are reprinted by kind permission of Yale University Library.

Granta 41, Autumn 1992
ISBN 0-14-014055-7

It's not homework.

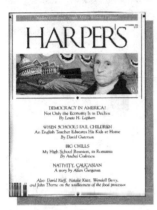

HARPER'S

DEMOCRACY IN AMERICA?
Not Only the Economy Is in Decline
By Lewis H. Lapham

WHEN SCHOOLS FAIL CHILDREN
An English Teacher Educates His Kids at Home
By David Guterson

BIG CHILLS
My High School Reunion, in Romania
By Andrei Codrescu

NATIVITY, CAUCASIAN
A story by Allan Gurganus

Also: David Rieff, Natalie Kusz, Wendell Berry,
and John Thorne on the senselessness of the food processor

Just because a magazine is intelligent and challenging doesn't mean reading it has to be hard work.

On one side, there are the general media magazines filled with the usual hype. They spoon-feed their readers the same old easy-to-digest mush. And on the other side are the stodgy, long-winded intellectual magazines. You can find some good reading in them – if you have the time and energy to search for it.

Then there's Harper's Magazine. Smart, but always concise and to the point. Every issue is loaded with gems of thought, opinion, wit and humor. Harper's is a pleasure to read. But that makes it no less serious. You'll find articles, essays, letters and fiction that consistently challenge conventional perceptions.

Harper's presents facts objectively, allowing you to draw your own conclusions. And speaking of facts, how about "Harper's Index"? It's a statistical tapestry, a minefield of unpredictable information. Try to stop reading it once you've started. You can't.

Harper's Magazine is original and inspiring. It's truly exceptional.

And right now you can take advantage of a special introductory deal; a full year of Harper's Magazine–12 issues–for *only* $12. That's 66% off the regular newsstand price. Not only that, it's risk-free, because if at any time during your subscription you're not completely satisfied, you can simply cancel for a full refund on all unmailed copies.

Fill out and mail the attached postage-paid card. And get ready – soon you'll be enjoying your first issue of Harper's.

☐ Yes, please send me Harper's at the special introductory rate of 12 issues for $12.

☐ I prefer two years (24 issues) for $22.

Name

Address

City

State _____ Zip

☐ Bill me later. ☐ Payment enclosed.

Mail to: Harper's Subscription Department, 666 Broadway, New York, NY 10012.

Please allow 6-8 weeks for your first issue. Canada $21 (CDN funds), includes postage. All other countries $38 (U.S. dollars only), includes special delivery.

HB115

"The American short story from 1944 to last Thursday"

THE GRANTA BOOK OF THE AMERICAN SHORT STORY

RICHARD FORD, EDITOR

That's how Richard Ford, himself the author of an award-winning story collection, describes the contents of this volume. By choosing "simply stories I like," he has produced one of the most comprehensive anthologies of contemporary writing available today.

Included are stories by Robert Penn Warren, Eudora Welty, Paul Bowles, Grace Paley, James Baldwin, Jayne Anne Phillips, John Cheever, Joy Williams, Joyce Carol Oates, Jean Stafford, Stanley Elkin, T. Coraghessan Boyle, John Updike, Tobias Wolff, Barry Hannah, Ann Beattie, Amy Tan, Jamaica Kincaid, William Gass, David Leavitt, and many more.

VIKING
Penguin USA

At bookstores now   GRANTA BOOKS

CONTENTS

VOICE LITERARY SUPPLEMENT

VLS

10 YEARS THAT SHOOK THE WORLD

In 1981 a magazine was born: *VLS*, a literary review that breaks the rules. For a decade, the *Voice Literary Supplement* has been provoking, informing, and delighting readers. It has won hearts and minds, not to mention literary prizes, with its bold mix of essays, reviews, cultural criticism, reporting, and new fiction. Every month, *VLS* introduces fine writers to the readers they deserve, while keeping an eye on the vagaries of the publishing world and the world at large.

VLS moves you beyond the mainstream. You'll get rigorous insights and flights of fancy from Kathy Acker, Dorothy Allison, Russell Banks, Blanche McCrary Boyd, Angela Carter, Sandra Cisneros, Susan Daitch, Jewelle Gomez, Gary Indiana, Karen Karbo, Walter Kendrick, Harry Mathews, Patrick McGrath, Bradford Morrow, Michael Musto, Geoffrey O'Brien, Greg Tate, Lynne Tillman, Edmund White, and many others.

To subscribe call toll-free:
1-800-562-1973

VLS: MAKING TROUBLE, MAKING SENSE

SAUL BELLOW
MEMOIRS OF A
BOOTLEGGER'S SON

BOLLONS

'*Gott meiner*,' said my father to my mother. 'Again no money? But I gave you twelve dollars at the beginning of the week. What have you done with it?'

'I don't know. It went away.'

'So quickly . . . by Thursday? Impossible.'

'It couldn't be helped. Some of it I used to pay old bills. We've owed money to Herskovitz for I don't know how long.'

'But did you have to pay him this week?'

'He's right in the block. For two months now I've been coming home the long way around. I gave him three dollars.'

'How could you! Haven't you any sense? And what did you do with the rest? Joshua,' he said, turning to me furiously. 'Take a pencil and write these things down. I have to know where it all went. I bought eggs and butter on Tuesday.'

'Seventy-five cents to the milkman,' said Ma, earnest and frightened. She must have believed she had done something wrong.

'Write it,' he said.

I had taken a piece of Ma's checkered stationery and placed the figures carefully within the tiny boxes. I was shaken, too, and eager to escape condemnation

'Willie had a tooth out. It cost fifty cents.'

'Fifty?' he said.

'Yes, it's usually a dollar an extraction. I sent him up alone and told him to say it was all he had. And after he was done, I waited for him downstairs. I was ashamed to show my face to Dr Zadkin.'

About forty years ago I tried my hand at a novel called Memoirs of a Bootlegger's Son. *When some 200 pages of it had been sketched, roughed out, I put it aside. A few of these recollections are to be found in* Herzog, *but when I wrote that novel, I had virtually forgotten* The Bootlegger's Son *and was reminded of it only recently by Mr James Atlas who exhumed it from a midden of discarded manuscripts. The editors of* Granta *evidently believe that the vanished world of its setting may interest contemporary readers. S. B.*

Opposite: Abram and Lescha Bellow with their children (clockwise) Zelda, Morris, Sam and Saul.

'Did it have to come out?'

'There was nothing left of it but the walls. Do you want to look at it? The child was in pain . . . Then there was fifty cents to have the boys' hair cut.'

'I'm going to buy a pair of clippers and do it myself,' Pa said. He was always resolving to do this.

'Fifty cents for the gas meter. Twenty cents for a coal shovel. Twenty-five cents to the insurance man. Twenty cents for a flat-iron handle. Forty cents to the tinsmith for relining my copper pot. Leather mittens for Bentchka cost me thirty cents. I haven't even started on the bigger things yet, such as meat.'

'We have meat far too often,' Pa said. 'We don't need it. I prefer milk soups anyway.'

'Don't expect me to stint on the stomach,' my mother said with determination. 'If I do nothing else, I'm going to feed the children.'

'They don't look starved,' said Pa. 'Especially this one. I never look at him but what he's chewing.'

My appetite was large and I seemed never to have had enough. I ate all the leftovers. I chewed down apple parings, gristle, cold vegetables, chicken bones.

'If I knew how to do things more cheaply,' said Ma, as though she now consented to take the blame.

'You don't bargain enough,' my father said to her harshly. His accusation always was that she did not accept her condition and was not what the wife of a poor man ought to be. And yet she was. She was whatever would please him. She made over our clothes. On the table there often appeared the thick Russian linens she had brought, but on our beds were sheets that she had made of flour-sacks.

'Like your sister Julia?' said my mother.

'Yes, Julia. That's why they're rich. It was she that made him so.'

I had been with Aunt Julia to the farmer's market and knew how she worked. 'How much'a der han?' she would say when she seized a rooster. 'Oh, *trop cher*,' she'd cry at the Canadian farmer, and she'd say to me in Yiddish, 'Thieves, every last man of them. But I will beat them down.' And in her Russian shawl, with her sharp nose jutting, she would shuffle to another wagon, and she always did as she promised.

'A wife *can* make the difference,' said Pa. 'I am as able as Jomin, and stronger.'

'They have grown children.'

'Yes, that's so,' said Pa. 'Whereas I have no one to turn to.'

He would often repeat this, and particularly to me. 'You can turn to me,' he'd say. 'But to whom can I turn? Everything comes from me and nothing to me. How long can I bear it? Is this what the life of a man is supposed to be? Are you supposed to be loaded until your back is broken? Oh my God, I think I begin to see. Those are lucky who die when their childhood is over and never live to know the misery of fighting in the world.'

When he flew into a rage, he forgot himself altogether and lost his sense of shame.

'Aren't you taking money for your brother?' he once shouted at Ma. 'Aren't you saving to send him . . . ?'

He meant her brother Mordecai in Petersburg. Her brother Aaron had recently died. The Bolsheviks had come to his house and slashed open the beds and the furniture in their search for jewels and gold. They had taken everything from him and he was dead.

'No, no,' Ma cried, and it was obvious to me that she was not telling the truth. 'How can you say it?'

She greatly loved these two brothers. On the day she received the news of Aaron's death, when she had been doing a Monday wash, she sat sobbing by the tub. Except to mourn, Jews were forbidden to sit on the floor. She hung over the tub, and her arms, in grey sleeves, trailed in the water. I came up behind her to draw her from the water. My arms felt the beating of her heart through her bosom. It was racing, furious, sick and swift.

'Let me be, Joshua. Leave me alone, my son,' she said.

'Aha! You do save money for him, and for your mother,' said my father.

'And if I do?' said Ma. 'Think, Jacob. Did they do nothing for you?'

'And did they do nothing *to* me?' Pa was beside himself.

'If I do put aside a little money now and then, it's less than

13

you spend on your tobacco.'

'And do you know how much money I'd have now if it weren't for you and the children?' he roared at her. 'I'd be worth ten thousand dollars. Ten thousand, do you hear? And be a free man. Do you hear what I say?' he glared with a strained throat. In his rage his face wore an expression that resembled hunger. His eyes grew huge, like those of a famished man. 'I say I might have had ten thousand dollars.'

'Why don't you leave then?' My mother wept.

'That's what I will do!'

He hurried out. It was night. He was gone for about an hour, and then I saw his cigarette glow on the front step, and he said to me, meekly, that he had only gone to buy a package of Honeysuckles.

'Will you please save the package for me, Papa?' said Willie, and Pa said to him, 'Of course, my boy. I'll remember this time and not throw it away.'

Pa was a mercurial man, and very unlucky. He had the energy to be a millionaire but nothing came of it except poverty. From Aunt Julia, I knew the story of the dowry. In less than a year, Pa had lost the ten thousand roubles and went to Ma's brothers to ask for more. One of them, Uncle Mordecai, was very rich. He had run away to South Africa as a boy and made a fortune among the Kaffirs and later he sold cattle to the Russians during the Japanese war. When they lost they didn't settle their debt, but he made a fortune nevertheless. He came back to Russia after this, and until the War led the life of a rich man. According to Ma, he was princely, dashing, brave and open-handed. By Pa's account, he drank too much and spent his money on women and neglected his respectable wife. Pa would sometimes frown at me and say that I reminded him of Mordecai. He saw the faults of my mother's family embodied in me. In my own mind I came to accept this, and was not ashamed of it even when Pa would say, 'There's insanity in your mother's line. Her Uncle Poppe was a firebug, and he was very dangerous. He used to set the curtains afire. These things are inherited. There's no taint like that on my family.'

'Not if you don't count hard hearts and bad tempers,' Ma would occasionally, but too rarely, answer. Only occasionally, because she loved him. When he was away she'd say to the children, 'If you told Mordecai that you needed something, he put his hand in his pocket and gave you what was in it, without looking.'

In Petersburg, Pa had made a handsome living. He dealt in produce and travelled widely. He was the largest importer of Egyptian onions and Spanish fruit. And it was evident that he and Ma had been people of fashion. She still owned black taffeta petticoats and ostrich feathers, now out of fashion, and some jewelry, while Pa had a Prince Albert in the trunk, and a stove-pipe hat, a brocaded vest and a fox-lined overcoat. Ma's fur coat was made over for Zelda and she wore it for four years at the Baron Byng school, complainingly. 'Over there, we had everything we needed,' Ma said. There were photos of Zelda in silk dresses, and of me in velvet pants, with long hair, like Rasputin. But every minute of this prosperity was stolen. Bribes made it possible. Then Pa was seized by the police for illegal residence. My uncles got him out of prison, and we escaped to Canada.

Within a year, the money he had brought from Russia was almost gone. The last of it he put into a partnership with three other men who owned a bakery. He had to drive a wagon, and he wasn't used to rough labour then. He had never before harnessed a horse. Over there, only coachmen and teamsters knew how to harness. Pa had to learn to do it by lantern light in the cold Canadian nights, with freezing hands which he would try to warm by the lantern-glass or against the horse's belly. His route lay in Lachine and Wilson's Pier, along the St Lawrence, by the Lachine Canal, around Monkey Park and the Dominion Bridge Company. Across the river, in Caughnawaga, the Indians lived in their old cottages. At this time Pa smelled of bread and his hair was somewhat floury. His partners were quarrelsome and rough, they swore obscenely and held Pa for a dude, and as the misery of his sudden fall was too much to hide they gave him a hard time. Why should it be so terrible to have become one of them? Ma said they gave him all the worst things to do.

The bakery was a shanty. The rats took refuge from the winter there, and were drowned in the oil and fished out suffocated from the jelly barrel. The dogs and cats could not police them, they were so numerous. The thick ice on the Saint Lawrence did not float leisurely, it ran in the swift current. In March and even April the snow still lay heavy. When it melted, the drains couldn't carry off the water. There were grey lagoons in the hollows of old ice; they were sullen or flashing according to the colour of the sky.

The partners had fist fights. Pa was no judge of the strength of others, and as he was very proud and reckless he usually got the worst of it. He came home with horrible bruises on his face and his voice broke as he told how it happened. Eliahu Giskin was the one with whom he had most trouble. Huge and stout, Eliahu had a shaved head and a tartar moustache. He drove one of the skinny, rusty wagons of the firm. The very rust was fading deeper, into a mauve colour, and on it was spelled in a circle of blind letters *Pâtisserie de Choix Giskin*. He was a bawling and clutching kind of man. He bullied the horse so that it put forth the best speed for him. Scared of him, it turned its head sidewards from the whip and galloped with heavy, hairy ankles through the streets. On the ground, Giskin himself was awkward and moved with hampered steps because of the size of his belly and his enormous boots. Pa also walked in a certain peculiar smart style; he put more weight on the left heel than on the right and marched as he went. He almost limped. It was an old Jewish way of walking, with his hands held at his back.

He and Giskin had their worst fight one day in the yard of the bakery when my mother and I were there. Exactly why they were fighting I couldn't tell you. They grappled and Pa's shirt was torn from him. It was a Russian style of fighting. Each tried to carry the other down and there was no idea of self-defence, but just one desperate body squeezing the other. Pa was burned up with violence, and he was a strong muscular man in his young days. Giskin clawed and scratched his white back as they clinched while Pa struck him with his elbow and fists. They fell on the rutted ground. A baker and one of the helpers ran out from the shack and pulled them apart.

'How can this go on?' said Ma at home where she helped him to undress and washed the dirt from him.

Pa admitted that it couldn't. He might kill Giskin or Giskin him, he said. And Ma insisted that he should withdraw from the partnership, and he did so although he did not know what to turn to next.

He tried the junk business, at which my uncle Jomin had grown rich, and with the string of jingling junk bells stretched across the wagon he drove along the St Lawrence shore and up and down the shanty streets, the little brick streets, and put in at farms and monasteries to try to buy rags, paper and metal. He spoke ten words of French and not many more of English, then.

'*Might you could sell me iron, gentlemann?*' was what he said. I was often on the wagon-seat, and watched—the eldest son, though ten years old, the *b'chor* as I was called, I was supposed to go into the world with him. He was not submissive, though he appeared to be so. At least he was not submissive to men. It was to necessities that he hung down his head and not to the farmer or the Brother or housewife. He had hard matter in him. He smoked as he drove, with keen eyes. We wrapped burlap about our knees when fall weather blew. The cold little bells clinked. '*Gentlemann?*' Pa would begin, and something both anxious and bold played through him. To weigh paper, he had a scale in the wagon; his purse was in his hand to pay, a steel-billed leather purse. The term for it was also the slang word for the scrotum. The money in it was poor, seedy money, dark copper, bleak silver and a wrinkled green paper or two.

He left this business soon, never having earned more than a few dollars a week at it. In the winter it was too much for him. With Uncle Asher, Aunt Taube's husband, he went into the bag business. They rented a loft and some machines, and hired two women to operate them. It looked as if they might make good as manufacturers. Somehow Asher got an order for munitions-bags during the War. However, the contract was cancelled because the first batch was not up to

17

specifications. When this happened, there was a big family quarrel. Everyone got into it. Aunt Taube was very haughty. Uncle Asher had great respect for Ma and was always civil to her. In fact, he was meek and good-tempered, not very clever. He boasted about his teeth and never ate candy. He was apt to repeat this too often, about candy. It was she, his sister, who said the worst things against Pa.

Ma told her, 'Don't be ungrateful, Taube.'

She meant that Taube and Asher owed their being in America to Pa. He had given them the money to marry, in his prosperous days.

'A great favour you did me,' said Taube, although her love affair with Asher was famous. The son of a mere stationmaster, he was not considered a match for her. She had seen him from a train-window while he stood idle on the platform. He was placid, and handsome because of it. My cousins, three small girls, were like him. Aunt Taube always wore a smile, but it was a shrewd smile. At the left corner of her mouth a few of the nerves were ailing and she could not govern her expressions well. She was the brainy one and wore the pants.

'It was Asher's fault,' Pa declared. 'He tried to save money on the material. That was why we lost the contract.'

'Jacob,' said my Aunt, 'you must always blame someone else.'

'Well, what good does it do to fight about it now,' said Ma. 'That's what I'd like to know.'

Neither quarrelling nor peace made a difference. Pa had no trade, he would have found no work if he had had one, for there wasn't any to be found after the War. He was ready for any humiliation, even that of serving a master, and to him that was one of the deepest. He had come into the world to do business, and there was no limit to the strength and effort he would expend in this. His pride was beaten, or almost beaten, when he was ready to labour for another man.

'A beggar!' said Pa, describing himself. 'A *bettler*!'

The ragged old country *bettler*, hairy, dirty and often crazy, were to be seen then in the yellowish streets of Jewish Montreal. They carried burlap sacks in which were old rags and scraps of food. What they couldn't finish when you fed them they clutched with their beggar's fingers from the plate and stuffed into the sack: stew, bread, crumbs of sugar. Then they blessed, they mumbled insane things, and shouldered their sacks and went away. They were supposed to be like this.

Ma therefore smiled when Pa said that. 'Not yet, by any means,' was what she answered.

'Not far from it. How far do you think?'

He had gone into innumerable enterprises: jobbing, peddling, storekeeping, the produce business, the bottle business, the furniture business, the dairy business, the insurance business, matchmaking. There was no corner into which he didn't try to squeeze himself.

At one time we thought of becoming farmers. I say 'we' because my parents discussed their projects over the kitchen table. Matters of business were always brought into the open. The children had to understand. If Herskovitz the grocer or Duval the landlord came to ask for their money, the children couldn't say that Pa or Ma were at home. We grasped these necessities very quickly.

Pa had heard of a farm out beyond Huntington that was for sale or rent, and we went to see it. It was an excursion. We put on our best. Ma was very happy; she was not a city-woman by upbringing. We went down to the Grand Trunk Station on the trolley, buying some half-spoiled Bartlett pears on the way. Pa said they had their best flavour when they were like that and peeled them for us with his penknife in his neat way. Some of his habits were very trim. Tobacco made two fingers of his left hand dark brown.

There was a soft gloom in the station. The city air was heavy that day. But as we were crossing the ponderous black bridge the sun opened up on us. Beneath the funnel hole in the toilet the St Lawrence winked. Quick death should we fall in. Then the stones of the roadbed, scratched by much speed. It was bright and hot at the station when the short trip ended. We were picked up in a buggy by the farmer, an old man. Ma mounted the step with her pointed, black, button shoes, and Zelda next, with her straw hat on which cloth roses were perishing. The kids wore pongee suits

19

with short pants, and I a pair of heavy serge knickers that made me sweat. They were picked out for me from a job lot Pa had once acquired. Blue flowers grew in the long, station-side weeds. A mill-wheel was splashing in the town.

'Ah,' said Pa. 'It's good to stand under that. It knocks your bones into place. Best thing in the world for you.'

Bentchka had a habit of dropping his head and dreaming at things with one eye. His hair was still long then. Ma would not let it be cut though he was nearly five. On her other side sat Willie with his bated-breath look; he stared at the hay, then lying over the stubble to dry. The old farmer, Archie, described the country with flaps of his whip. Ma's face softened with all the country pleasure, the warm sun and the graceful hay, and fragrance, the giant trees and hoops of birds that went about them, the perfect leaves and happy sun. She began to have smooth creases of enjoyment about her mouth and chin instead of her often sober and dark expression.

We arrived at the house. It was like silver with age, the wind had polished it so long. The old wife with her seamed skin came to the door and called in a clear voice, 'Arrrchie—the hens are in the garrrden.' Willie ran to shoo them. Pa and Ma inspected the long doors, went through the house and then down toward the yard. Ma said, 'It just revives you to smell this air.' From the tone she took, Zelda and I knew that this was just a holiday in the country. And I had been imagining great things and let my mind build hopes that I could be a farmer's son and walk on those gold stubble fields from one horizon to another and not as a timid, fleshy city boy with these meek shoes, but in boots. But look! It was obvious. We couldn't live here. Glancing at me as if I would be the most prone to it, Ma said, 'We can't have children growing up ignorant and boors.' I couldn't hide my disappointment. It filled my face.

'I don't see why they should,' said Pa.

But Ma said it was plain enough. No synagogue, no rabbis, no kosher food, no music teachers, no neighbours, no young men for Zelda. It would be good for the health of the younger children, that was true, but she wasn't going to have us grow into cowherds, no finer feelings, no learning.

'Ach, too bad,' said Pa with gloom, but he nodded. He was sizing up the beast-world of the barnyard, and I don't doubt but that he was thinking what hardship it had been for him to learn to harness a horse. And our mother had strange ideas about association with animals. If I stroked a cat she'd occasionally warn me against it. She'd say, 'You'll be cat-witted.' Or a dog, the same. 'You'll be dog-souled.'

'No, no,' she said to my pleading. Zelda was on her side; Pa was not wholeheartedly on mine.

And when we were ready to leave, we had to search for Willie. He had wandered off to the river to watch the blackbirds plunge through the bulrushes and to try to catch toads in his handkerchief. This was enough for Ma. She was in a panic. A river! Small children wandering away. There was no more discussion of farms. The farmer drove us back to the station toward night, when a star like a chopped root flared in the sky.

Pa would often say afterwards that he still wished he owned a piece of land. Losing his temper he'd exclaim against my mother, 'There could have been bread. All we needed. But you had to have your city. Well, now we've got it. We've got bricks and stones.'

The next business he tried was a dry goods store in Point St Charles, not a prosperous district. The streets ran into nothing after blocks of half-empty slum and goat-tracked snows. The store was in a wooden building. Stairs led down to it from the sidewalk. When you got down to the bottom, where the wood underfoot was shredded with age, you found a door in which there was a little pane, and when you opened it you encountered Pa and Cousin Henoch. They were setting up shop. Railroad overalls and ladies' drawers hung on exhibit, stockings, gloves, wool headwear, layettes, silk shirts and Hudson Bay blankets, and a lot of army goods. There was an odour of smoke from some of these articles; Pa had bought them at salvage sales. The business had no credit as yet and could not lay in an entirely new line. Pa got job lots wherever he could. Cousin Henoch had brought a little money into the partnership, and Pa had borrowed some from his sister Julia and her husband, who had plenty of it.

21

I participated in this, too. Pa, you see, thought that I was stupid and backward. He had a biased and low opinion of me and he was anxious for me to take shape, and quickly. He couldn't stand for me to remain boyish. He would say to me, 'You'll be a man soon and your head still lies in childish things. I don't know what will become of you. At twelve, thirteen, fourteen, I was already a man.' Oh, he was very impatient of childhood. One must not remain a child but be mature of understanding and carry his share of difficulty. He wouldn't have me studying magic or going to the baths with Daitch, or hiding in the free library.

Catching me there, he'd drive me into the street. When his temper was up, he thought nothing of gripping me by the ear and leading me away. Back from unseriousness. Back from heathen delusions. Back from vain and childish things. We'd march together while he gripped my ear.

'Do you know what you are?' he'd say full of rage. 'A chunk of fat with two eyes staring from it. But I'll make something of you. A man. A Jew. Not while I live will you become an idler, an outcast, an Epicurus.'

I was frightened and begged him to let go. I wasn't entirely a submissive son. But I didn't dare try to free my ear, though my voice went deep and hoarse when I said, 'Don't do that, Pa. Don't do that!' I yelled, 'Oh, let go!' while he gripped me and led me home. He made me look like a fool in the eyes of the old lady at the library. To him such things didn't matter. He kept his eye on the main business of life: to provide for us and teach us our duty.

After a family conference he often said, when it had been decided what to do, 'And you'll come with me.'

So I was with him when he went to make a loan of Aunt Julia and Uncle Jomin.

Aunt Julia was his eldest sister, a very shrewd and sharp-minded woman, and rich, and her attitude toward many things was condemnatory. She had a thin face and a pinched nose, very unfeminine to my way of thinking; her colour was flushed and it made her look threatening sometimes. Yet she was witty, also, and often kept you laughing; and when you were laughing and out of breath, then came something that took the ground from under your feet. When she said something about you, you were criticized to the heart. It was merciless, for she was a harsh judge of character. Her face, I said, was thin, but her hair was heavy and glossy. She wore it in a single stout braid down her back. Her body was also heavy, in contrast with her face, and at home she wore a few unusual and choice garments—a man's undershirt, a pair of voluminous green bloomers and over them a scarlet crêpe de Chine wrapper, wool stockings and fleece slippers. She sat heavily or, cooking, cleaning, she stood and moved with heaviness, and at all times, in that unvarying nasal tone, she uttered the most damaging and shrewd remarks conceivable: a sort of poetry of criticism, fault-finding and abuse. She was always ingenious and there were very few offences that she forgave.

Though she oppressed me, I was crazy about her. She was a great show-woman and she said whatever she pleased with utter frankness, and she and Uncle Jomin, that mild person, were extremely salty. Because, you understand, they were outstanding people; they had a right and nobody would contest it. My Uncle Jomin was a brown man and slender. His beard was tight, short and black; it surrounded the broad teeth of his smiling mouth, of which one was gold. The bridge of his nose had an intense twist, and then the cartilages broadened—it became a saddle nose. He had the brown eyes of an intelligent, feeling, and yet satirical animal. He had a grim humour about him. The odour of his breath was tart and warm. I always found it agreeable to be near him. He enjoyed playing the hand-slapping game with me, a homely game that went like this: you laid your hands on his palms and were supposed to snatch them away before he could slap them. If he missed, it was your turn to try to slap his. Despite his slight trembling—he was not well, he had an enlarged heart—he was quicker than me. With a bent head that shook slightly he would hide a deep smile and gaze at my reddened hands. His crisp beard itself made a slight sound. My hands smarted. I would laugh, like the rest of them, but be angry at heart.

23

My cousins, grown men and all in business, stood watching.

'Faster, you duffer,' said Cousin Abba. He was nearest to me in age and already had an enterprise of his own; in summer he operated a fruit stand. Abba subscribed to *Chums* and *Magnet*, British schoolboy magazines. He talked continually of Bob Cherry and Tom Merry and Billy Bunter and hamptuckers, and mixed 'jollies' and 'eh what's with the fantastic Yiddish they all spoke, a French-Russian-Hebrew-British Yiddish.

'Faster there, Houdini, you *golem*. Stay with it, now. Stiff upper lip does it. That's the spirit my man. Ay, what a *frask-o*. Burns, eh? Good for the circulation, I'll be bound.'

He whinnied when I cried out. He was all right, Abba. Not more open-handed than the rest of them. They didn't exactly have that reputation. But we were fond of each other and he often gave me good advice.

Jomin's business was junk. He was one of the biggest junk dealers in Montreal. In his yard there were piles, mountains of old metal shapes, the skeletons of machines and beds, plumbing fixtures. A deep, scaly red-brown beautiful rust shone like powdered chicory and dry blood to the sun. Cobwebs floated from it. I went around in the loft and tried to read funnies on the faces of paper bales or looked for locks that I could study, as Houdini had done. In the office swung chandeliers and pricey metals. Long-armed and stooped in his cocoa-coloured sweater, Uncle Jomin stood in the middle of the yard and sorted scrap. He examined a piece of metal, classified it and threw it to the top of the appropriate pile. Iron here, zinc there, lead left, brass right and babbitt by the shed. Boys, Indians, old women, half-wits and greenhorns who did not know a word of English, arrived with junk in little carts and coasters. Junk men with wagons and plumed horses came. During the War Uncle Jomin did a vast business. The junk was needed at the shipyards and on the Western Front.

My aunt bought real-estate, and my cousins went into business. Moneywise, they were among the first families. They lived simply, and they were known as hard dealers. In the synagogue, they rated very highly and had seats against the eastern wall, the best because the nearest to Jerusalem. The dark man and his sons, with other leading Jews, faced the rest of the congregation. Of these, most were meek immigrants, peddlers, factory workers, old grandfathers and boys. From the women's gallery Aunt Julia, thin-nosed, looked down. Her Hebrew was good and she prayed as well as any man. She wore glasses and read steadily from her book.

She'd say to me, 'What do you think of Tante Julia? Your old *Trante* is no fool.'

She could not let a word go by without giving it a twist. She had a great genius with words.

One winter afternoon we came to make a touch for the store in Point St Charles. Naturally enough, Pa was a little scared of such a woman. Ma said, 'It will be hard but you have to do it. They can give you the money, and Jomin doesn't have a bad heart. Not even she can refuse her brother.'

Pa shrugged and turned his hands outward. He had been tramping the town, making his stops: he covered miles daily in his hunt for business opportunities, and did it in his outward-pointed stride, favouring the left heel, always, and his hands behind his back and his head dropped to one side. 'We'll see,' he said. He had stopped at home to get me to come with him, and so didn't take off his fox-lined overcoat—the orange fur was bald in places—and his scarf, the colour of creamed coffee, was wound thickly under his chin; it sparkled with melted frost, and so did the moustache that covered his handsome mouth. He diffused an odour of cigarettes; his fingers were dyed with the brown colour. Ma helped me into my sheepskin. She wasn't well that day, she suffered with her teeth and was heating buckwheat on the stove to apply to her cheek. Bentchka was ailing, too. He sat and looked through the bars of his bed at the sparrows as they ruffled on the wires and on the glass clusters of the telephone poles and dropped down to peck in the horse-churned, sleigh-tracked snow. You could leave him alone; he'd amuse himself for hours.

We changed cars at Place d'Armes; the snow stung like rock salt, and then we travelled another half an hour on the Notre Dame car and arrived at Aunt Julia's at sunset. Ribbons of red colour were buried in the dry snow. The sun seemed snarling, the moon pearly cold and peaceful. We went in. The stoves were hot and there was a bearskin on the sofa. The curl-tailed bitch barked. Her teeth were sharp, curved and small. My face smarted with heat and cold, and my mouth watered at the smell of gravy. Meat was roasting.

Tante Julia was thinking, as I took off my coat, how chunky I was. I knew. In her eyes this was not a bad thing, but meant I had a lot of good hard work in me.

Her floors were highly polished and gleamed with darkness, with stove lights and the final red of the roaring cold Canadian day. While she watched us take our outdoor clothes off her face judged us in a very masculine way. She knew what Pa was here for. Trust her for that.

'Come in the kitchen and have something,' she said nasally. She was not stingy with food; she always fed you well. 'The lad must be hungry.'

'Give him something, yes,' said Pa.

'And you?'

'I'm not hungry.'

'Too worried to eat, ah?'

Nevertheless, Pa also ate several slices of delicious dry roast meat with carrots and tart grape jelly. We drank tea. Uncle Jomin was a slow eater. For every piece of bread he recited a blessing. Then he sliced away the crust and bent to the plate with a slow shake of his broad head.

'Tuck in, old top,' said Cousin Abba. 'Joshua is a *gefährlicher* trencherman.' All my cousins laughed. Everyone was present this evening. I laughed, too.

I was in an odd way a favourite with them all, although they were also sardonic with me and gave me hell. I caught it from Cousin Moses because I tracked tar one summer day into his new Ford. He had bought it to court a girl—a rich girl related to Libutsky the bottle man.

I crept into Moses's car with tar on my shoes, and he lost his temper and whacked me on the head—a favourite place; perhaps everyone felt that it was thick and hard and I would take no harm there. I cried and said I would get him for that, and for a while we were enemies. At Huntington, where Aunt Julia had a summer house, Cousin Moses slapped my face once and I picked up a piece of wood and tried to kill him. I would have brained him; I was in a rage. It swept me away and I no longer knew or cared what I was doing. He was sitting on the swing with his fiancée; he was swarthy and she pale. He was grinning. A vine wove fiercely around the lattices; it grew a kind of cucumber, full of prickles and inedible. Moses teased me out of the side of his mouth. I gave him an angry answer because I couldn't bear to be ridiculed before the girl, and I suddenly felt a spirit of murder in my blood and ran at him with the piece of firewood. He knocked me over and picked me up by the collar, choked me with the neckband and beat some sense into me. He slapped me till I tasted blood in my saliva and then booted me in the tail. He told Aunt Julia he wouldn't have me around. He said I was a goy, an Ishmael, and that I'd have to go back to St Dominique Street. It was a holiday, you see. They would rescue each of us a few days at a time and give us some country air at the cottage. So back I went and Willie was sent down.

I made it up afterwards with Moses. Maybe it weighed on his conscience that he had beaten me so hard; I felt ashamed, too, that I had tried to murder him. Anyway, I got along better with him than with my cousin Philip. Philip was a law student at McGill and behaved very slyly toward me. They were all my seniors and dealt with me more as uncles than as cousins. Cousin Thelma, two years older than I, was fat and huge and had a bold savage temper. Her hair was hugely frizzy and her teeth obstinate and white.

Well, my brother,' said Aunt Julia when everybody was present. 'I gather that things are going badly again.'

'They never went well,' said Pa. 'But I may be doing better soon, God willing.'

'Why, do you have something new in mind?'

'Yes,' said Pa.

'And why don't you stick to one thing,' his sister said. 'You jump from this to that, and here and there. You have no patience.'

'I have little children,' said Pa, in a lowered but not patient voice. 'I have to put bread on the table. I am no coward and I'm not idle, and I'm learning the language and the ways. I'm all over the city every day and digging in the cinders for a bone. I thank you for your good advice. When a dog is drowning, everyone offers him water.'

'Yes, yes,' said my Aunt Julia. 'You don't have to tell us what it is to be poor immigrants. We know the taste of it. When Jomin came over he dug ditches. He worked with pick and shovel for the CPR and he has a hernia to this day. But I, you understand me, knew how to manage and I never thought I was a grand lady from St Petersburg with rich brothers and a carriage and summer house and servants.'

'She doesn't have them any more,' Pa said.

'You didn't know anything of such things either, before you met her,' said Aunt Julia, 'and don't pretend to *me* that you were born with a golden spoon in your mouth. In a silk shirt.'

'Yes, but what of it?'

'You cry because you've fallen so. And how humiliating it is. In Petersburg common people couldn't see you, your windows were so high.'

'I never snubbed you, or anyone,' said Pa. 'My door always was open and my hand was too. I tasted prosperity once but I know something else now. Eliahu Giskin beat my bones, and *I haven't a piece of tin/To stop up my hole, or cover my skin*, as they say. I often feel as if I was buried alive.'

'My children had no pianos and violins. They knew they were poor. You have to know, and be, what you are. Be what you are. The rest is only pride. I sent them out to earn a penny. They collected bottles and bones and ran errands. They had no time to be musicians. Now, thank God, things have gone better. They will hire musicians when they marry. *Then*,' she said, 'we'll dance. And I hope you'll be there to share our joy.'

The Jomins owned the house we were sitting in, and other properties around town.

'A wife has a duty to her husband not to make him a slave to the children,' said Aunt Julia. 'If you saved the dollars that you spend to make Kreislers of your boys and a princess of your daughter you wouldn't have to dig in the cinders like a dog, as you say.'

The blood had risen to her face, which never was pale, her eyes were angry and her voice high and hard. As Pa had come to confess failure and ask for aid he was obliged to listen. Also, he may not have disagreed entirely; perhaps he wanted to hear Ma blamed. He was an influenceable man and sometimes said these very things himself. Pa didn't have a constant spirit. Depending on how he felt, he changed opinion. One night he'd sit and shed tears when Zelda played Beethoven, his heart touched; another time, he'd stamp his feet and say we were ruining him: 'Food! That's my duty. Shoes!—Shoes I'm obliged as a father to put on your feet. Whatever a father should do, I will do!' he'd shout at us all. 'But I will not lay down my health and strength for luxuries and nonsense.'

Aunt Julia said, sternly, with fierce eyes turned to me, 'Children have their part to do, too.'

'Oh,' said my father, 'he's a pretty good lad.' He put his hand on my head gently. I almost burst into tears at this. A moment before I was indignant with him because he said nothing in defence of Ma. I, you see, knew what she was up against. Fear of Aunt Julia and my other hard elders kept me from speaking. It was no time to have a burst of temper and hurt Pa's chances of a loan. But now when he touched me and said I was pretty good, I wanted to take his hand and kiss it, and say how well I understood what was happening, and how much I loved him. The roof of my mouth ached, and my throat closed. I didn't dare move or open my mouth.

'He should be that,' said Aunt Julia. 'He's got a good father —a father who watches over his children. He's old enough to understand the difference.'

I was old enough, certainly, to understand.

'What's this new business you have gone into, Uncle?' said Cousin Moses respectfully. It came hard, because Pa was an immigrant, all but a pauper. Also, like everyone else, Pa was subject to mockery, probably, as soon as his back was turned. I had seen all the Jomins take turns at mimicking acquaintances. I

29

had seen them put an entire Sunday afternoon on the porch into this wicked vaudeville—how so-and-so walked, stammered, wiped his nose on his sleeve or picked bones out of fish. My sister Zelda also had a great gift for this game. She didn't spare anyone. And I am positive that Pa was often taken off in Aunt Julia's house. And perhaps he had just done something typical, and they were barely able to hold back their laughter. However, respect for elders was drummed into all of us. Pa was Moses's uncle and Moses had to speak to him with consideration and civility. It was quite a thing to watch, for a man like Moses had a strong spirit of satire. He smiled at the side of his mouth. He had a powerful, swarthy face, and passed air loudly through his nose to punctuate what he said.

His engagement to the Libutsky girl, now broken off, was the result of Pa's matchmaking. My parents had tried that, too, as a sideline, and had brought Moses and the girl together. Uncle Jomin read matrimonial notices aloud to his sons from the Yiddish paper. Widows with fortunes were the chief interest, and young women with large marriage portions from the Far West who needed Jewish husbands. My Aunt Julia told her children, 'Don't hold yourselves cheap. Marry rich.' The Libutsky girl had money, but it didn't work out. Ma thought well of Moses. However, she said, the girl was too gentle for him. He would need a bolder one.

'What is this business?' Moses said.

'A little dry goods store in Point St Charles.'

'Not a bad idea,' said Moses, 'Is it a good location?'

'Yes, we can make a living there. If the Lord will send a little luck. You know I've never been a lazy man. I've had money, and I'll have it again, as surely as we're alive this day in the world . . . '

'With God's help, it happens,' said Uncle Jomin.

'It was hard for Sarah to get used to the life here, but . . . '

'You have a good wife,' said Uncle Jomin. 'I feel for her. And it is a strange country. But you have to keep your head. That's the main thing about strangeness.'

Aunt Julia interrupted, saying, 'I don't see what's so strange. You had to make your way over there, too. Would you want to be in Russia now? A fire!' she said. 'A destruction! Millions of corpses.

Ploughing with cannon. Typhus. Famine and death. Didn't you have a taste of it? Don't you thank God that you escaped from those madmen?'

She told Pa this sternly, and glared at him that he could be so weak-minded, so forgetful, so ignorant as to talk loosely about the strangeness here. She showed you how the old country was sealed up in doom and death. She spoke strongly, and as though it was a credit to her to have come here. Escape? No it was more like a triumph.

Melba the fox terrier sat in Uncle Jomin's lap and cunningly reached for scraps on his plate. She extended her head sidewise under his arm. Melba was privileged and the reason was that one night she woke Uncle Jomin when the house was afire. She pulled the blanket from him and saved the family. Therefore she had the run of things. She escorted Jomin to the junkyard in the morning and then she came home to accompany Aunt Julia to the market. They seemed to me exceptionally lucky in their dog. We could not have one. I brought a terrier in and he gave us fleas. We had to be treated with Paris Green. Pa went out and brought it home in a paper sack, mixed a paste and smeared it on our bodies. Another time an English bulldog followed me home. I fed him peppermint hard-balls, the red and white kind. However, he ran away. I ran after him all the way to Peel Street but couldn't get him back. We had cats, instead, many of them. They belonged to Bentchka.

Then, too, Aunt Julia had pictures on the wall that seemed to me of a high degree. Of these, the best was Queen Victoria with a veil and diadem, her flesh very fair and pure. She had her elbow on the table and her chin rested on her wrist. In addition, there was a painting of a basket of fruit. A peach sliced in half with a very rich red stone was in front. Another picture was of a faithful collie who had found a lamb in the snow and wouldn't abandon it. These were powerful and influential pictures. It wasn't any old thing that turned up in the junkyard that Aunt Julia would hang on her walls. At home we had only one picture, of Moses holding up the tablets.

'I have a partner for the Point St Charles business,' said Pa.

31

'A partner! Why a partner?' said Aunt Julia. 'Why are you afraid to do anything by yourself? And who is this partner?'

'Henoch,' he told her.

'*Gottenyu!*' Aunt Julia raised her sarcastic eyes to heaven. She clasped her hands and wrung her fingers. Her long upraised nostrils were tense with laughter and horror at Pa's idiocies.

'That one?' said Cousin Moses.

Aunt Julia cried out, 'You poor beggar. You everlasting fool.'

'Is this,' said Philip, 'the Henoch who left his wife?'

Henoch was my mother's cousin, and he had brought his wife and family over, but then there had been a divorce. No one approved of that.

'I didn't want a partner,' Pa explained. 'But I had to take in someone. I couldn't do everything myself.'

'Not if you took Joshua out of school?'

'No, not even.'

Jomin said, 'What happened to Henoch's fish store?'

'Gone,' said Pa.

'Well, that's a fine omen,' said Aunt Julia. 'He ruined his own business, and now you want to give him a second opportunity in yours.'

'They say he's living with another woman,' said Moses.

Moses had a passion for gossip. He'd come and tell his mother things. That very evening, I heard him say to her in an undertone, 'Max Feldman, you remember . . . '

'Yes.'

'Was caught.'

'With another woman?'

'His own mother-in-law.'

'No!' she said, turning her fine sharp head to him, with hypocritical alarm. 'Woe-to-us-not! Those wasters! Where?'

'Where do you think,' said Moses. 'In bed, of course.'

She gave a little scream of horror and satisfaction. 'What a beast of a woman, to do this to her daughter.'

'Well,' Pa said in reply to Moses's question about Henoch. 'I don't know where he's living.' His answer was uneasy, for it wasn't truthful.

'And such a sport yet,' said Aunt Julia, 'with his little

moustache, and his crooked eyes and fat lips, and his belly, and that coat he wears with a split in the back, like a Prussian.'

She was a deadly observer. Cousin Henoch's coat did bear a resemblance to the Prussian military overcoat.

'And he stinks of fish,' she added. 'And he's rotten to the bone, and lazy, and he probably has syphillis. And if you think I am going to throw away money on a business like . . . '

'I'll give you my own note,' said Pa. 'Not his, mine.'

' . . . If you think we are going to throw away hard-earned money,' she said, 'you can go out in the woods, and find a bear, and pick up the bear's apron, and kiss the bear,' she said, fiercely nasal and high, 'right under the apron.'

The mirth of the Jomin family was a curious thing—it had a devil of a twist to it. They were dark, and they were all clever and subtle, and laughed like wolves, pointing their faces.

The kitchen walls were hot. The stoves were bursting with heat. Where old pipe-holes entered the chimney there were circular asbestos plugs with flowers painted on them.

The Jomins laughed at Aunt Julia's wit, but Pa said angrily, 'You are heartless people! Hard people! One schleps himself out to earn a living for his wife and children, and another mocks him. You have it good in America. While my face is being ground.'

The hot kitchen filled with high, wrathful voices. The cries mounted.

'America is all yours, my dear brother,' cried Aunt Julia. 'Go and do as Jomin did. Work with a pick and shovel, as he did. Dig ditches and lay tracks. To this day he wears a truss.'

That was a fact. An elaborate truss with a cushion for the groin hung in the bathroom. I found it behind the bathroom door and tried it on. The pad pushed uncomfortably into the belly.

'He'll never be the same man. Don't expect me to waste his money on your wife's relatives.'

'A coarse, cruel character you have,' Pa shouted. 'Your brother's misery does you good, you devil, you.'

'You grudge me my good luck,' she cried. 'You're envious. You have the evil eye.'

33

'And you would murder people in the street, with your arrogant heart. And you are brazen. And you don't know what it is to pity. You're not a woman at all. I don't know what you are.'

They raged and shouted at each other. It was a lifelong quarrel of nearly forty years' duration, which now and then flared. Pa blamed her for his ruin in Canada. He called her a witch. He said she could have saved him any time she chose but preferred to see him struggle and go under.

Her face was red as Chinese paint. I am sure she knew of more sins and dooms than he could imagine if his anger lasted a month. She cried out, 'Why do you throw yourself on people. You fool! And don't you think I know better than to try to soak up the sea by flinging loaves of bread into it.'

It was Pa's outrage that she found intolerable.

'You may kiss my—!' she told him.

'You may lie in your grave before then,' he shouted, 'and not a penny will you have there.'

Melba barked at him so shrilly that Abba finally took her away, and it appeared as if her barking had incited Pa and Aunt Julia, for when her dog-shrieks ended, they both grew calmer. I too was susceptible to dogs' barking.

And Uncle Jomin on his own lent Pa 150 dollars to go into business in Point St Charles, and took Pa's note for the amount. He sternly warned him against his partner. Uncle Jomin had a pair of eyes of gloomy strength; they had great power to warn and threaten. But what good does it do to threaten a desperate man?

For one brief year we had the feeling of a family that owned a business. It was a store. People went everywhere else to buy their dry goods—if the French and Irish families in this sparse slum bought anything at all. But there was a little store, nevertheless. The partner, as predicted, was no good. He put his entire trust in Pa, and so did nothing. Every afternoon he took a nap on an old bench at the back of the store, which must have come out of the waiting-room of a station. He flirted with the Ukrainian and French women who came, and Pa said we had to keep an eye on him, he might give things away. All the men in Ma's family had this weakness for women, he told me. Henoch snoozed, during vacant summer afternoons when the air was warm and grey. Pa went out to hunt bargains, job lots, and to check on prices in other stores. I read books and practised tricks, and tried to discipline my body. I was ambitious to learn to tie knots with my toes. Houdini could both tie and untie them. I studied the books of spiritualists, too: Oliver Lodge, A. Conan Doyle, and a book called *The Law of Psychic Phenomena*, by Hudson.

The dry goods store soon went on the rocks.

PENGUIN • THE BEST IN PAPERBACKS

TUVA OR BUST!

RICHARD FEYNMAN'S LAST JOURNEY

"Readers who enjoyed the collaborative efforts of Feynman and Leighton in *Surely You're Joking, Mr. Feynman!*, and *What Do You Care What Other People Think?* will undoubtedly cherish this poignant account of Feynman's last escapade."
— *Library Journal*

RALPH LEIGHTON

Where on earth is Tannu Tuva?

Nobel Prize-winning physicist and prankster Richard Feynman, who remembered Tuva from his childhood stamp collecting, set out on a ten-year quest to discover the mysterious country with his good friend Ralph Leighton.

"Chock-full of boundless enthusiasm, wacky humor, and gleeful determination."—*Booklist*

"A tale of adventure, heart-break, and rare friendship."
—*Publishers Weekly*

At bookstores now

Interview

Just an all-American BBQ
in your all-American magazine

Subscribe! 1-800-247-2160 (in the U.S.)
010-1-212-941-2900 (outside U.S.)

LYPSINKA PHOTOGRAPHED BY HUGH HALES-TOOKE

James Atlas
Starting Out
in Chicago

'I was, in 1937, a very young, married man who had quickly lost his first job and who lived with his in-laws. His affectionate, loyal and pretty wife insisted that he must be given a chance to write something.'

But what?

In 'Starting Out in Chicago', originally delivered as a Brandeis commencement address in 1974, Saul Bellow provides a portrait of his beginnings as a writer that, more than anything he ever wrote, captures the early stage of that momentous confrontation in which 'American society and S. Bellow came face to face.' If the year is wrong—it was 1938—the details are painfully accurate.

The job he'd lost was a stint in his brother's coal yard on Carroll Avenue, and he was fired for absenteeism. Maurice, not unreasonably, expected his brother to keep regular hours; Bellow had other ideas about how to spend his time— he wanted to write.

He was living in his mother-in-law's apartment, a block from the North Shore Channel in Ravenswood: drab, anonymous, one of the thousands of identical dwellings, mustard- and burgundy-coloured brick flats that sprawled, mile upon mile, across a dull, orderly grid of streets. While his wife Anita attended classes at the University, where she was working towards a degree in social work, Bellow sat at a bridge table in the back bedroom:

> My table faced three cement steps that rose from the cellar into the brick gloom of a passageway. Only my mother-in-law was at home. A widow, then in her seventies, she wore a heavy white braid down her back. She had been a modern woman and a socialist and suffragette in the old country. She was attractive in a fragile, steely way. You felt Sophie's strength of will in all things. She kept a neat house. The very plants, the ashtrays, the pedestals, the doilies, the chairs, revealed her mastery. Each object had its military place. Her apartment could easily have been transferred to West Point.
>
> Lunch occurred at half past twelve. The cooking was good. We ate together in the kitchen. The meal was followed by an interval of stone. My mother-in-law took a nap. I went into the street. Ravenswood was utterly

Opposite: Saul Bellow, 1947.

Photo: Daniel Broten/Bostonia

empty. I walked about with something like a large stone in my belly. I often turned into Lawrence Avenue and stood on the bridge looking into the drainage canal. If I had been a dog I would have howled.

William Faulkner emerged out of the somnolent town of Oxford, Mississippi; Hemingway was brought up in the bland suburb of Oak Park, just a few miles from Ravenswood itself; Sinclair Lewis was from Sauk Center, Minnesota. American writers were largely self-made. They 'simply materialized,' as Bellow put it; he, too, would have to invent himself. But even by the folkloric standards of American literary childhood, his isolation was extreme. In Chicago, during the Depression, culture didn't matter:

> What did, what could Chicago have to do with the mind and with art? With the steel-making dinosaurs just to the south and the stockyards, the slaughter-rooms blazing with aerated blood where Negro workers sloshed in rubber boots, right at your back, and the great farm machinery works and the automobile assembly lines and mail-order houses, and the endless railyards and the gloomy Roman pillars of the downtown banks, this was a powerful place, but the power was something felt, not shared. What Chicago gave to the world was goods—bread, bacon, overalls, gas ranges, radio sets, telephone directories, lightbulbs, tractors, steel rails, gasoline . . .

Everything but novels.

'The first writer I ever met,' Bellow recalled in a 1967 lecture, 'was an elderly neighbor in Chicago, a tool-and-die maker who turned out pulp stories.' He lived in a bungalow across the street from Bellow's father and wrote for *Argosy* and *True Confession*. Bellow dreamed of writing for *Transition*. But he and the old man typing across the street shared a common fate. They were the only able-bodied men in the neighbourhood during the day. Everyone else was off at work.

'People see me hanging around and think I'm sick or loafing, but I'm not a loafer,' the tool-and-die maker complained to Bellow. 'I'm a writer.'

It was not a claim one could comfortably make. Bellow liked to quote Wyndham Lewis's observation that a young person contemplating an artistic career might just as well be an Eskimo as an American from a Midwestern city. 'A man's duty was to get up in the night, wait on the corner at daybreak for the streetcar, go to the plant'—not to sit at a card table writing short stories.

In his relatives' eyes, Bellow was an eccentric, 'a crazy scribbler.' He dressed 'like a Canadian hick' and went around with a briefcase full of foreign books. Why couldn't he act more American? His two older brothers, Maurice and Sam, were sleek, well-barbered businessmen; his brother-in-law Jack, Anita's brother, wore a straw hat, was a member of the American Legion and read the *Saturday Evening Post*. Bellow's cousin Arkady, a travelling salesman with Old Country manners, was so determined to be American that he wanted his name changed to Lake Erie (in the end, he settled for 'Archie').

But in his own way, Bellow was also becoming Americanized. He didn't go to the public library to read the Talmud, he often said; he went to read Poe and Melville, Dreiser and Sherwood Anderson. Even as a boy, he thought of himself as 'a Midwesterner and not a Jew.' If he wasn't Chicago-born, like Augie March—Bellow was born in Lachine, Quebec; his family moved to the city in 1924 when he was nine—he was still practically a native. His mandate, as he later defined it, was clear: 'to write about American life, and to do with Chicago or Manhattan or Minneapolis what Arnold Bennett had done with the Five Towns or H. G. Wells with London.'

What was Bellow writing at the card table in the back room of his mother-in-law's house? He claims that he can't remember, though 'it must have been terrible.'

Whatever it was, the results were insufficiently compelling to persuade him that he had discovered his vocation. By the fall of 1938 he and Anita had returned to Hyde Park, where he had been a student in the early thirties, attending classes and living the dilatory life of a University of Chicago graduate. That winter he was registered in Introduction to Linguistics, but failed to complete the course. The following summer he signed up for History

329—Economic History of the Middle Ages—and an anthropology course in Aztec and Mayan cultures. He got a C and an 'Incomplete'.

Student life was entertaining, Bellow wrote in a memoir of the period, 'but when you had your degree and were a student no longer, and when your friends had gone to take up their professions, moving to New York, to California or North Africa, your life became difficult to justify.' Alone for most of the day, assailed by the dolorous odours of cooking and the gurgle of the toilet down the hall, he would go out into the empty street in the middle of the day on the pretext of an errand—buying a newspaper, picking up the laundry. Lunch was at one of the coffee shops on 63rd Street, beneath the elevated tracks. Bellow's underwear was so tattered, he joked, that he didn't know which hole to put his foot through. Anita, meanwhile, had given up on graduate school and got a job as a social worker, delivering welfare cheques. Her salary was twenty-five dollars a week.

Like Joseph, the unemployed Hyde Park intellectual in *Dangling Man*, Bellow was oppressed by the 'narcotic dullness' of his existence. He was 'on detached service,' he recalled, employing the military term, 'but drawn by powerful and vivid longings and sympathies, hungry for union and for largeness, convinced by the bowels, the heart, the sexual organs and, on certain occasions, by the clear thought that I had something of importance to declare, express, transmit.' Just what that message was had yet to be revealed. One day Bellow encountered a professor on the street, a European scholar renowned for his great learning. 'And how is the *romancier*?' the professor asked with wry condescension. The *romancier*, Bellow admitted, still smarting decades later from this sarcastic inquiry, was 'not so hot'. There were times when he believed himself to be the only full-time *romancier* in Chicago, a humiliating thought: 'He was angry, obstinate. The *romancier* was *dans la lune.*'

In the summer of 1940, Bellow unexpectedly came into some money. His mother, who died in 1933, had taken out a life insurance policy, and now, seven years after her death, the company had paid its premium: 500 dollars. The policy turned out to be in Bellow's name. Bellow's father Abram insisted that the money was his, but Bellow refused to hand it over. Instead he and Anita decided to spend it on a trip to Mexico. Bellow, deeply immersed in D. H. Lawrence, had been especially moved by *Mornings in Mexico*, with its celebration of the cleansing primitivism of Mexican culture, its instinctual, nihilistic sensuality.

Bellow and Anita left Chicago in mid-June, travelling by way of New York and arriving in time to hear the news that the Germans had entered Paris —'a devastating event.' They then boarded a Greyhound bus for the long journey down. Bellow had never been in the Deep South before and was stunned when the bus was briefly held up by a chain gang doing road repairs. 'I sat in a window seat holding a copy of Stendhal's *The Red and the Black*,' he recalled. 'Outside, a green landscape; the freshly turned soil was a deep red. The shackled convicts were black, the stripes they wore were black and yellow. My suitcase in the overhead rack contained more books than clothing.'

They stopped overnight in Augusta, Georgia, to visit Bellow's Uncle Max, who had moved there from Canada and gone into business selling second-hand clothes to black sharecroppers. The next day they continued on to New Orleans and El Paso, then crossed the border to Mexico. When they got to Mexico City, they checked into a small hotel at 25 Calle de Uruguay that came with a high recommendation; Lawrence himself had stayed there. (So would Augie March, who described it, under the name of La Regina, as 'quiet and modest-looking, unusually clean, with a skylight over the center.') Lawrence had omitted to mention that the hotel was 'a house of assignation,' as Bellow primly referred to it. During the day he and Anita had the place to themselves; at night traffic was heavy up and down the halls.

His fellow anthropology student Herb Passin and his wife Cora arrived a few days later by car, and in July the two couples headed further south, first to Cuernevaca, then on to Taxco—cobbled streets, red-tiled roofs, iron-grilled balconies hung with jasmine, a baroque church dominating the main square.

Going about town in a sombrero and sarape, Bellow adapted quickly. He was proficient at languages and picked up a fair amount of Spanish. Before long he and Anita were part of the crowd that made its headquarters at Paco's, the local *cantina*. The town was full of expatriates, 'escapists', according to Graham Greene, who had been there two years earlier, 'with their twisted sexuality and their hopeless freedom.' Among the regulars were the eagle trainers Daniel and Jule Mannix; the publisher Joseph Hilton Smyth and his black girlfriend, the cabaret singer Hazel Scott; and D'arcy Lyndon Champion, an Australian who wrote pulp fiction for *Black Mask* and *Dime Detective*.

During the mornings Bellow wrote in a desultory way—the two couples had rented a villa on a hill overlooking the town—but he was getting nowhere: 'I was groping.' In the afternoons he went horseback riding in the mountains, and the evenings were generally spent in the *cantina*. 'We'd get so drunk,' Herb Passin recalled, 'we had to crawl up the hill.'

Towards the end of August, Bellow and Passin drove to Mexico City, where an associate of Trotsky's had arranged an interview. Trotsky was a significant figure for Bellow. Forced into exile in Mexico, struggling to maintain his power from afar, the Old Man represented the triumph of the intellectual over history—even in defeat. While the revolution degenerated into mass terror, Trotsky managed to preserve its original ideals, a romantic revolutionary vindicated by his charisma. Trotsky enjoyed wide support among American intellectuals, and Bellow had been persuaded by his argument that the impending war in Europe would be an imperialist war, not a war to save democracy. By 1940, after Trotsky defended Stalin's annexation of Finland, Bellow no longer viewed the great revolutionary as a hero. But he was still eager to meet him.

It wasn't to be. On the afternoon of 21 August, Bellow and Passin read in the newspaper that Trotsky was dead; the day before, he had been murdered at his fortress in Coyoacan, smashed over the head with an ice-axe wielded by Ramon Mercador, the mysterious assassin known in Trotsky's circle as 'Jacson'.

Bellow and Passin hurried off to the house, then proceeded to the funeral parlour on Calle de Tecuba. Thousands of people were milling in the street. They pushed towards the door; the police, assuming they were American journalists, waved them through. They walked up a flight of stairs, Passin recalled, 'and there, by God, was Trotsky.' His coffin was open, and the corpse lay inside, surrounded by a crowd of photographers on ladders. The morticians had done a good job: the bandaged head looked more like a bust of Trotsky than a corpse. 'We finally got to see the Old Man,' said Passin ruefully—'a little late.'

By September they were back in Chicago.

'Until I was twenty-five I had little success,' Bellow wrote on his application for a Guggenheim fellowship in 1943. For years he had sent his stories out to magazines and had them returned with depressing regularity. He had tried large-circulation journals like the *Saturday Evening Post* and little magazines like *Kenyon Review*; but the magazine that counted when you were trying to break in as a writer—the magazine that Bellow read faithfully every month—was *Partisan Review*. For American intellectuals of the thirties and forties, *Partisan Review* was *the* journal. Its circulation was around three thousand, but its readers were its writers and included just about everyone of importance in contemporary literature. T. S. Eliot, Edmund Wilson, Lionel Trilling, Delmore Schwartz, John Dos Passos and James T. Farrell appeared alongside Arthur Koestler, Gide, Silone, even a posthumous work by Kafka. Trotsky himself, the subject of much heated discussion in the magazine's pages, contributed an essay, 'Art and Politics', an eloquent manifesto on behalf of the artist's autonomy.

If *Partisan Review* was read with close attention in the precincts of Greenwich Village, it was read with perhaps even greater avidity in Hyde Park, where, in addition to its progressive influence, the magazine was a synecdoche for New York, the centre of the literary world, the place where reputations were made. Among the contents of the May/June 1941 issue—an issue that included one of T. S. Eliot's 'Four Quartets' plus contributions by Clement Greenberg, Allen Tate and Paul Goodman—was a story entitled 'Two Morning Monologues'. Its author was identified in a terse author's note at the back: 'Saul Bellow is a young Chicago writer. This is his first published story.'

The monologues were competent if undistinguished sketches. The first, entitled '9 a.m. Without Work', recounted the plight of a young man named Mandelbaum who is unemployed and waiting to be called up by the draft board. His father hounds him to get a job—'You're a teacher, aren't you? Five years in college. The best'—and puts an advertisement in the newspaper on his son's behalf. The other monologue, '11.30 a.m. The Gambler', featured an early version of Bellow's low-life types, the small-time mobsters and con artists and touts he'd observed hanging around Freifeld's pool hall or Brown and Koppel's restaurant on Division Street, where there was always a card game in progress upstairs.

Over the next year, Bellow published two other stories, 'The Mexican General' in *Partisan Review*, and 'Mr Katz, Mr Cohen and Cosmology' in an obscure quarterly called *Retort*, edited out of Bearsville, New York.

On the strength of the stories, Bellow acquired a literary agent, Maxim Lieber, a card-carrying member of the Communist Party; among the writers he represented at one time or another were Erskine Caldwell, Howard Fast and Josephine Herbst. Several months later Lieber was able to submit Bellow's first novel. *The Very Dark Trees*, written in the first person, concerns an English professor named Jim who teaches at a Midwestern university—'an enlightened Southerner' who, on his way home from teaching, is struck as if by a bolt of lightning and finds himself turned black. When he gets home, his wife doesn't recognize him at first, then locks him in the basement in order not to alarm the neighbours. The novel was both a fable about the tenuous nature of identity and 'a caustic tale of a liberal Southerner confronted by the reality of prejudice,' remembered Bellow's friend Nathan Gould. It was also, Gould said, very funny. Bellow's friends referred to it as *White No More*.

Lieber submitted the book to Vanguard Press. Established in the late 1920s as a charitable foundation sympathetic to progressive causes, Vanguard had got its start publishing cheap editions of Hegel, Veblen, Marx, Lenin and other classic thinkers in the radical tradition. Its publisher was James Henle, a former newspaper reporter and editor at *McCall's*. Henle was determined to turn the company into a genuine publishing house while preserving its left-wing flavour. In the thirties, the Vanguard list featured muckraking biographies of J. P. Morgan and Andrew

Carnegie, books with titles like *Graft in Business* and *The Public Pays*, an account of the Sacco–Vanzetti case, and fiction by Nelson Algren and James T. Farrell.

The readers' reports on what came to be known around the house as 'that Negro manuscript' were mixed. *The Very Dark Trees* was 'an extraordinary tour de force,' wrote one editor. 'In spite of the fantastic turn the plot takes, it seems to me the writer shows an original style and real ability.' But the editor didn't see how Vanguard could market the book without testimonials from 'big names'—and even then it would be a hard sell. Another editor, Evelyn Shrifte, who would eventually become the firm's president and publisher, found the novel 'provocative' and 'absorbing', but she was also worried that no one would buy it, 'unless we could get it started by snob appeal—a strange, different kind of book.' A third editor had a different problem: the book just wasn't believable. 'The Trotsky episode,' he objected, 'is just too fantastic.' As for the protagonist's racial transmogrification, he couldn't understand 'why Jim didn't have himself examined by a reliable physician.'

The Very Dark Trees continued to make the rounds, 'wandering around in the desolate sticks of the industry,' until the spring of 1942, when William Roth of the Colt Press wrote to Bellow after reading 'Two Morning Monologues' in *Partisan Review* and asked if he was working on a novel. Roth, the scion of a wealthy San Francisco shipping family, published elegant gardening books and works of literary merit that hadn't found a home elsewhere, including Henry Miller's *The Colossus of Maroussi*, Edmund Wilson's *The Boys in the Back Room* and Paul Goodman's early novel, *The Grand Piano*. Bellow submitted 200 pages, cautioning Roth that it was a first draft, but urging him, with a characteristic mixture of arrogance and humility, to 'attend to it speedily (for better or for worse),' as the Army was 'hot on [his] heels.'

Six weeks later, he got an answer: Roth wanted to publish *The Very Dark Trees*. He offered an advance of 150 dollars—payable upon publication in November.

'Your letter bowled me over,' Bellow replied on 3 April. 'I am neither too shy nor too hardened to admit it freely, and I wish I could frame a very special kind of "thank you". The occasion certainly calls for it.'

Excited by the prospect of publication, Bellow threw himself into the work of revision, writing the whole book over in a frenzy; he was to be inducted on 15 June. When he showed up at the draft board, having stayed up half the night to put the finishing touches on his manuscript, he was deferred until mid-July. By then he had no money, and 'an incomeless month' lay ahead unless Roth could advance him something. Roth answered with bad news: he himself had been drafted by the Office of War Information and was about to be shipped off to Alaska. All publishing activities of the Colt Press were suspended for the duration of the war. Enclosed was a cheque for fifty dollars.

Bellow was devastated. His book had finally found a publisher; after years of disappointment, he was about to make his debut. He had even alerted the editors of *Partisan Review* to mention the novel's imminent publication in his contributor's note for 'The Mexican General'. Now he had no publisher, no prospects and no money.

Whether or not *The Very Dark Trees* deserved publication will never be known, for soon afterwards Bellow decided that the book wasn't very good after all and, to forestall posterity's judgement, tossed it down the incinerator chute.

Yet even as his first novel was going up in flames Bellow was informing the editors of the *Partisan Review* that he would be instructing his agent to send along a story entitled 'Juif!' He also informed them that he was at work on a new novel: *Notes of a Dangling Man.*

For intellectual sustenance Bellow regularly went to New York, a forty-eight-hour ride from Chicago on the Greyhound bus. Any Chicagoan with ambitions was destined to head for New York 'and live in some room with bedbugs in Greenwich Village,' as Bellow put it. He usually stayed with the Chicago writer Isaac Rosenfeld and his wife Vasiliki on the Upper West Side, where the Rosenfelds had a cramped apartment in the West 70s with a bathtub in the kitchen; then on Christopher Street after they moved down to the Village in 1942.

New York was vibrant; it breathed possibility. One of the most captivating documents of the period is Alfred Kazin's *New York Jew*, which opens: 'One dreamlike week in 1942 I published my first book, *On Native Grounds*, became an editor at the *New Republic*, and with my wife, Natasha, moved into a little apartment on Twenty-fourth Street and Lexington.' Careening around Grand Central in a taxi at dusk, Kazin recounts being intoxicated by 'the sudden opulence of wartime, when the incomparable autumn light of New York still hung over the buildings that would soon be shadowed by the faint wartime brownout . . . ' At the weekly lunches held in the *New Republic*'s private dining-room above Madison and 49th Street, Kazin found himself in the company of Edmund Wilson and Van Wyck Brooks; as the magazine's book review editor, he got to know Rosenfeld and Delmore Schwartz— and Bellow; they were introduced through Rosenfeld. Vasiliki was Kazin's secretary. 'As I walked him across Brooklyn Bridge and around my favorite streets in Brooklyn Heights, he looked my city over with great detachment,' Kazin wrote of Bellow.

> He had the gift—without warning, it would follow a seance of brooding Jewish introspection—of making you see the most microscopic event in the street because *he* happened to be seeing it. In the course of some startling observations on the future of the war, the pain of Nazism, the neurotic effects of apartment-house living on his friends in New York (Chicago was different; it was a *good* thing to grow up in Chicago), he thought up some very funny jokes, puns, and double entendres. It was sometimes difficult to catch the punch line, he laughed with hearty pleasure at things so well said. And they were well said, in a voice that already shaped its words with careful public clarity. He explained, as casually as if he were in a ball park faulting a pitcher, that Fitzgerald was weak, but Dreiser strong in the right places. He examined Hemingway's style like a surgeon pondering another surgeon's stitches. Then, familiarly calling on the D. H. Lawrence we all loved as our particular brother in arms, he pointed to the bilious and smoke-dirty sky over the

Squibb factory on Columbia Heights. Like Lawrence, he wanted no 'umbrella' between him and the essential mystery. He wanted direct contact with everything in the universe around him.

Kazin was impressed by the large scope of Bellow's ambition. He had only published a few stories in *Partisan Review* and was virtually unknown, yet he spoke with proud serenity about the significant career that lay in store: 'He had pledged himself to a great destiny. He was going to take on more than the rest of us were.'

New York was only a temporary domicile, and by the summer of 1943 Bellow was still in Hyde Park, waiting, like Joseph in his novel, for a summons from the draft board. In the meantime, he was putting the final touches to *Dangling Man*, as the novel was now called, the Dostoyevskian 'Notes' having been dropped from the title. Earlier that summer, he had submitted it to James Henle, the publisher of Vanguard Press who had turned down *The Very Dark Trees* but continued to express interest in his work. On 7 July Bellow received a telegram from Henle: AM DEEPLY IMPRESSED BY DANGLING MAN BUT WANT TO GET ANOTHER OPINION. Two weeks later they had a deal. Henle offered a 200 dollar advance—half upon signing. Bellow was jubilant. By November the book was in proofs, and he was enjoying the luxury of quibbling over minor points: the word 'nooky', for instance. Henle was concerned that it would offend readers; Bellow defended it, citing the profanity of *Ulysses*. Then there was his use of the word 'darky'—it was vernacular, Bellow insisted, and had nothing to do with his stand on the Negro question. 'I can't make the changes,' he declared flatly, invoking Luther's *Ich kann nicht anders*, but he conceded on grammatical matters, confessing that he couldn't tell a predicate from a pickle: 'I usually guide myself by sound and meaning and leave the rest in the hands of God.'

That winter Bellow carried on a busy correspondence with Henle, absorbed in a flurry of publication details. Vanguard was badgering him for a photograph; he sent two, one by himself and one with Anita: 'You can black her out, if you like it,' he suggested, but didn't recommend it: 'Anita's really far more beautiful than I.' He also wanted to dedicate the book to her: 'She's a deserving wife.' Asked for a biographical sketch, he noted that he was Canadian-born, had lived most of his life in Chicago and attended various local schools which he dutifully enumerated: 'If you need more information I shall send you a second thrilling installment of my life-story.'

*D*angling Man was published on 23 March, during the darkest days of the war. Hitler had just invaded Hungary; the gas chambers at Auschwitz had become public knowledge; American pilots were bombing Berlin. 'There is no personal future any more,' Bellow's protagonist declares in the novel—a plausible sentiment in the spring of 1944.

The war was a subtle but ubiquitous presence in his book. Written in the form of a journal, it chronicles four months (December 1942 to April 1943) in the life of a young intellectual by the name of Joseph. Out of work, having been laid off from his job at a travel bureau, he awaits induction—as it turns out, a protracted business. A Canadian and thus a British subject, Joseph is required to undergo an investigation of his background before he can be classified 1A, ready for active service. In the fall of 1942 his induction is postponed because of a new regulation exempting married men. Thus Joseph dangles.

Outwardly his life is empty. His wife works during the day while Joseph wanders about the neighbourhood, has lunch alone in restaurants, smokes, does errands, listens to the radio, reads the paper. Most of his friends have gone off to the war. So uneventful is his life that he commemorates 'the day I asked for a second cup of coffee' or 'the day the waitress refused to take back the burned toast.' He has trouble reading; books fail to hold his attention. He toys with the idea of going back to work, but doing nothing has become a moral test: 'I am unwilling to admit that I do not know how to use my freedom and have to embrace the flunkydom of a job because I have no resources—in a word, no character.'

From the first page, *Dangling Man* sounds a brashly declamatory note that prefigures the famous opening of *The Adventures of Augie March*:

Do you have feelings? There are correct and incorrect
ways of indicating them. Do you have an inner life? It is
nobody's business but your own. Do you have emotions?
Strangle them. To a degree, everyone obeys this code.
And it does admit of a limited kind of candor, a close-
mouthed straightforwardness. But on the truest candor, it
has an inhibitory effect. Most serious matters are closed
to the hard-boiled. They are unpracticed in introspection,
and therefore badly equipped to deal with opponents
whom they cannot shoot like big game or outdo in daring.

If you have difficulties, grapple with them silently, goes
one of their commandments. To hell with that! I intend to
talk about mine, and if I had as many mouths as Siva has
arms and kept them going all the time, I still could not do
myself justice.

The primary example of this 'era of hardboiled-dom,' as no
contemporary reader of the novel needed to be told, was Ernest
Hemingway; the oblique reference sets the novel's literary tone.
From beginning to end *Dangling Man* is a 'highbrow work,' as
Bellow himself characterized it. Not only the allusions to
Shakespeare and Goethe, the mystic Jacob Boehme and
'Burckhardt's great ladies of the Renaissance,' but the structure
itself identifies it as a work aware of its antecedents: as literature.
The reviews were mixed—but only one counted. Writing in the
New Yorker, Edmund Wilson praised the novel as 'well written and
never dull,' and pronounced it 'one of the most honest pieces of
testimony on the psychology of a whole generation who have
grown up during the Depression and the war.'

*D*angling Man had made a Bellow a writer, but it hadn't
changed his situation. The very week of publication, he
learned that he had been turned down for a Guggenheim,
and the early reviews, while for the most part favourable, hardly
amounted to a triumph. Wilson's review pleased him, but he was
still smarting from Diana Trilling's disparaging assessment of the
novel's sterility and lack of 'grandeur' in the *Nation*. 'She made the
worst possible estimate of me, the one I fear most,' Bellow

admitted to Henle, offering his own candid assessment of the book:

> Plainly she has such an antipathy to 'small sterile' books
> that if she thinks she has one before her she is incapable
> of giving it a dispassionate reading. Yes, *Dangling Man* is
> bitter. I wonder if Diana thinks one could write 'an
> affirmation of life' (damned phrase) upon such a theme.
> But the book is square and honest. It is probably not
> great, but it is not 'small'. It is too genuine for that. As
> for the accusation that my physical world lacks
> dimensions, that is just nonsense; she hasn't read the book
> if she says that. She's swept away by her initial antipathy.
> But if I thought I were merely talented and clever in a
> small way I would give up writing tomorrow and never
> write again, not so much as a letter.

Still, he had begun to attract attention. An agent named
Jacques Chambrun wrote offering his services, and Henry
Volkening of Russell & Volkening, who only a few weeks before
had returned a story of Bellow's called 'On the Platform' with a
curt dismissal, wrote urging him to send new work if he could
'forgive the wham we gave the short story.' He also got a call from
Metro Goldwyn Mayer—but not for an option on the novel's
movie rights. A studio executive had seen Bellow's photograph in
the *Chicago Sun* and offered to make him a star. Bellow wasn't an
Errol Flynn type or a George Raft type, the man from Hollywood
explained—that is to say, he wasn't handsome or tough in the
conventional sense. But he could have a great screen career in the
sensitive role, the guy 'who loses the girl to the George Raft type or
the Errol Flynn type.'

Bellow stuck with literature, but making a living at it wasn't
easy. He had got a job at *Encyclopaedia Britannica* as an indexer of
ideas, but it interfered with his writing, and he was thinking of
quitting if the book sold well. Henle counselled prudence. *Dangling
Man* had launched Bellow as a novelist, he acknowledged, but 'as
for living on what you earn as a writer, I have to warn you that
there are very few human beings in this world who are able to do
this IF THEY WANT TO PRODUCE HONEST WORK.' Henle's advice was
sound; the first edition of *Dangling Man* sold 1,506 copies.

In the summer of 1944, Bellow was at last called up for a physical, only to be diagnosed as suffering from an inguinal hernia. The medical examiner arranged for an operation at Michael Reese Hospital in August. It was minor surgery; Bellow was given a local anaesthetic, and chatted with the surgeon while he worked. But recovery was slower than he'd anticipated, and he was in constant pain for weeks. By October he was classified 2A, even though he had made it clear that he wasn't requesting an exemption. 'I don't want to dodge,' Bellow explained to Henle, 'but if they don't want me I'll go on writing. That's much more important, of course, but I didn't want to take it on myself to decide. Let *them* do that.'

Meanwhile, he was at work on a novel and stories, writing daily. 'The new book is inching along,' he wrote his publisher in October 1944: 'I haven't had the courage to look back at what I've written; I might turn into a pillar of salt.' Bellow wrote copiously and threw away what didn't work out. Better to stop after a few chapters than to be tied down by characters who weren't what you intended them to be—'unwanted and delinquent children,' Bellow called them. Book-length projects were abandoned as casually as short stories. 'My new book (no title as yet) has hit a fresh snag—no. 883,' he wrote Henle that winter. 'But I think I can dislodge it by the usual method of going to the movies every night for a week.' The book was called *The Adventurers*, perhaps an early version of *The Victim*, perhaps the novel about 'a middle-class individual, Victor Holben,' that he described to the Guggenheim Foundation (no trace of it remains).

Bellow also carried on a busy correspondence with friends and writers, often dashing off several letters a day. To Jean Stafford, a promising young novelist he had met on one of his trips to New York, he wrote an admiring fan letter that revealed in the first sentence how modest his reputation still was in literary circles (and in the second, how generous he could be):

> You remember me, I think; Bellow, the man who never called you back because he was desperately busy elsewhere. My purpose in coming forward now is to tell you how very happy I am to find you a fine writer. I

haven't read the book [*Boston Adventure*], just the chapter in P.R. It is heartening to read such writing. I reserve the right to criticize on some heads, but the writing, the writing I acknowledge with all my heart. I say it who should know by virtue of having slaved at it, if by no other.

I've had no occasion to use Pepto-Bismol again, but I own a large bottle. It was all I had remind me of you until the last P.R. arrived.

It was apparent from his decorous reference to past debauchery that Stafford was already embarked on the hard-drinking life that would wreck her career.

In April 1945, fed up with the Army's delays, Bellow volunteered for the Merchant Marines. Stationed in Sheepshead Bay, he was released to inactive status on 15 September 1945, a month after Truman dropped the Bomb on Hiroshima. That same day he wrote to James T. Farrell.

I'm putting in for a Guggenheim (Jim Henle says my chances are better this time) and I'd appreciate it greatly if you would once more consent to sponsor me. I'm putting on one of my annual drives to get out of Chicago. It grows more like Siberia all the time. I come in, petition the Czar to free me from banishment, he refuses and I get into the Pacemaker [the New York -Chicago train] with the other condemned and return. Seriously, Chicago oppresses me in a way only another Chicagoan can understand. It terrifies outsiders— Wilson, for instance in his piece on Jane Addams in 'Travels in Two Democracies'—but it haunts the natives.

Bellow's impatience with Chicago was a measure of his ambition. He was thirty years old, and his one book had achieved a *succès d'estime*; he could claim a certain renown among the circle of writers he had read in *Partisan Review* back in his boarding-house days. Yet he was still a Hyde Park intellectual with a closetful of ill-fitting suits, a wife and now a child to support, and a

postmark that read Stock Yards Station—in effect, nowhere. The
essay by Wilson that he referred to, 'Hull-House in 1932',
accurately described the grim, almost ominous place to which
Bellow had returned in the autumn of 1945, 'one of the darkest of
great cities,' a mass of skyscrapers and warehouses, 'black factories
and long streets, with rows of lights that stretch away into
darkness'—a scene that had left Wilson 'amazed, desolated,
stunned.' It didn't hold Bellow for long. At the end of September,
he packed up his family, stored their furniture in the Shoreland, a
grand hotel on the Hyde Park lakefront that his brother Maurice
owned, and boarded the Pacemaker for New York. 'As a
Midwestern provincial, I had the obligation of going to the Big
Town and taking it on,' Bellow said many years later, invoking with
retrospective bravado 'the immemorial pattern of young hicks.'

They had nowhere to stay and arrived on the doorstep of
Arthur Lidov and his wife Victoria, another University of Chicago
boy who had migrated to New York. Lidov was a painter who
earned a living doing illustrations for magazine ads and feature
stories in *Life*. He was a big, powerful man with an ample stomach
and a full beard—'kind, large, oracular,' as Alfred Kazin
remembered him. The walls of his fifth-floor walk-up in Brooklyn
Heights were covered with his big oil paintings, sensuous Jewish
nudes and concentration camp victims staring out from the canvas
with baleful black eyes—his 'real work,' Lidov insisted, 'not the
money work I do for Luce.' Bellow playfully depicted him in *The
Adventures of Augie March* as Basteshaw, the Chicagoan who ends
up in a lifeboat with Augie after their ship is torpedoed in mid-
Atlantic, a garrulous, Shelley-quoting autodidact built like a
'human fortress'.

Lidov, on his way up to a farmhouse he was renting in
Patterson, New York, invited the Bellows to live there free. They
accepted on the spot.

It was a happy arrangement, although no one had any money.
The Lidovs were so poor that whenever Arthur got paid by a
magazine, his wife drove to New York to pick up the cheque
instead of waiting for it to be sent through the mail. Bellow
contributed unsigned reviews to the back pages of the *New York
Times Book Review* and the *New Republic*, and wrote readers'

reports for Victor Weybright, the British publisher, who was starting up the American imprint of Penguin Books. Bellow showed up once a week at Weybright's office and carried off a shopping bag full of books. The pay was five dollars for novels and ten dollars for non-fiction. The night before his report was due, Bellow would be up until all hours, but he made enough —just—to support his family.

It was a warm autumn until Thanksgiving, when the weather turned fierce. By the end of November, the house was freezing. The coal furnace went out every night, and no one knew how to keep it going until the coal delivery man showed up and gave a demonstration on how to start a fire. Bellow complained that he 'nearly froze his nuts off,' and it wasn't long before the pleasures of communal living began to wear thin. With the Lidovs' two cats and a dog and the Bellows' son Gregory—and one bathroom between them—the house felt crowded. In December, Bellow found another farmhouse, in nearby Holmes, and moved the family once again. No sooner had they settled in than Anita and Greg had to go back to Chicago; her brother Jack was dying of a brain tumour. 'I'm holding down this eight-room house, a servitor to the pipes and heaters,' Bellow wrote Henle on 12 January. 'My nearest friends are ten miles away.'

He was lonely for Anita and wrote her often. But he was also capable of finding company elsewhere. 'There were women; there were always women,' said Vicki Lidov. When he went into New York on the train to see Victor Weybright or to pick up an armful of review copies at the *New York Times Book Review*, storing his manuscript in the freezer in case the house burned down, he often stayed over with one girlfriend or another. Anita apparently knew about and tolerated his *amours*, but the situation was hard on her. Bellow went his own way, in his domestic life as in everything else. He doted on Gregory, bestowing affectionate nicknames on him—'Jemby' and 'Hirsch', diminutive for Herschel, 'a fine old Yiddish name'—but he didn't knock himself out doing household chores. For Bellow, his indifference to such matters was traditional. 'There hasn't been an honest workingman on either side of the family as far back as can be known,' he confessed to Henle. 'Most of my forefathers were Talmudists. My maternal grandfather had twelve children and never worked a day in his life. You see what a tradition we have to live up to.' Bellow often said he would have been a rabbi in the Old Country; and in truth, there was a rabbinical element in his vocation. Like the *talmid khokhem* of his distant shtetl past, wise men revered for their learning, he spent his days and nights—most of them—hunched over books.

By the spring of 1947, the Bellows were back in Chicago—at his mother-in-law's again, where, a decade before, Bellow had fought off the impulse to howl like a dog as he wandered the empty neighbourhood after his morning's stint at the card table in the back bedroom. 'With all this bucking back and forth from east to west to east, I'm astounded that anything gets written,' he wrote Henle. 'But, amazingly, it does.' He was 'in a high state of excitement' about his work-in-progress, which he'd given a new title: *The Victim*.

In the meantime, weary of freelancing, Bellow was looking for a job. Herbert McCloskey, an assistant professor of political science at the University of Minnesota who had met Bellow through his Chicago friend Sam Freifeld, had heard of his plight and managed to procure an invitation from the university's newly founded Department of the Humanities. The salary was 2,500 dollars—for Bellow a huge sum.

The University of Minnesota was a giant land-grant college with a rah-rah fraternity life and a flourishing agricultural school, but it also had a distinguished English department, a sort of northern outpost for gentlemen scholars—men like Henry Nashe Smith and Joseph Warren Beach and Samuel Holt Monk, whose tripartite names certified their gentility. It also had Robert Penn Warren, banging away at his typewriter in a room on the top floor of the library the fall that the Bellows arrived, finishing up *All the King's Men*. Warren had scholarly credentials—he had done graduate work at Yale, been a Rhodes Scholar and served as an editor of the *Southern Review*—but he was more a writer than an academic. He and Bellow became fast friends. They often had lunch together at the Faculty Club, and Warren read *The Victim* in manuscript.

Bellow set up shop on the third floor of Nicholson Hall,

'where I have a desk in something that looks like the complaints department of Commonwealth Edison in Chicago,' he reported to James Henle in October. His residential quarters, in a Quonset hut on the Agricultural School campus, weren't much better. 'We're in a kind of paper walled hutch that looks like something wasps make—I know that rabbits live in hutches, but this isn't a hive either. But hutch or hive, it has no running water and no dividing wall or partition.' The only heat was from a kerosene stove.

That autumn his father came up for a visit. The Bellows had no room for him in their Quonset hut, so he stayed with the McCloskeys. Dignified in a suit and tie, Abram wouldn't eat in the McCloskeys' house because they weren't kosher, but he sat at the kitchen table drinking coffee and pouring out 'a threnody of complaint.' What was his son doing in Minneapolis? Why didn't he go into the family coal business, where he could make a good living? Why did he have to live this way? 'He was heartbroken,' Herb McCloskey recalled. 'He really thought Saul was a failure.' Bellow was teaching Advanced Composition that term, an experience he likened to classes in manual training. But he was hard at work on his book, which he hoped to get done by Christmas, if he could stay put for once. 'This bounding from place to place, though it comes about through my own fault, exasperates me when I start to write. I feel like a man trying to sign his name in the last seat of a roller-coaster.'

Even so, Bellow was putting in five or six hours a day on the novel, rewriting the entire manuscript. He was a compulsive reviser, but with Bellow revision was less a matter of Flaubertian sentence-polishing than of rewriting the manuscript from start to finish—a process he went through on every book. On 27 January he sent Henle a 'first draft'—which meant that he was just getting down to work.

Ten days later, he heard back from his publisher. It wasn't the enthusiastic response he'd expected. Among other things, Henle objected to two scenes involving a cafeteria *kibitzer* named Schlossberg, which struck him as 'set-pieces'. Bellow vigorously defended himself. Schlossberg was a commentator on the action, he argued, a figure whose impassioned discourse on what it means to be human indirectly points up the meaning of the book. 'The moral act is the human one and implies humanity on all sides,' Bellow explained 'But the conditions of life make the humanity of others difficult to discern.' Schlossberg stayed.

Bellow was more hopeful than Henle about the book's prospects. Robert Penn Warren had read *The Victim* and liked it, he stressed: 'He predicts that it will sell widely.' But he was clearly wounded by Henle's lack of enthusiasm. In January, acknowledging various acts of generosity, Bellow had thanked Henle for his 'kindness', but, three months later, a note of testiness was creeping into his correspondence. Responsibility for the novel's success rested in part with the publisher, he suggested: 'And you have made no commitments or promises. Perhaps it is not businesslike for you to volunteer such things, but I have not guided myself by business standards in my relationship with you. You haven't mentioned that you have any particular plans for the book, and I wonder why that is.'

Henle was more than a little annoyed. He scrawled in the margin, 'This guy is just an author after all,' and dashed off an irate reply. Vanguard had done all it could for *Dangling Man*, he maintained. No one had ever claimed that literature was a profitable enterprise. He was sorry Bellow had taken off his 'philosopher's robe' and meddled in matters of commerce that he knew nothing about.

Bellow's response was conciliatory, but he was obviously still aggrieved. 'I've given a lot of thought to your letter,' he replied on 15 March:

> What I said may have appeared to you unmotivated and unjust but there was no intention on my part, I assure you, to hurt or to anger. But what you say about the philosopher's robe is not apropos. The only thing you can accuse me of is distrust of providence, since I give up half my freedom in the effort to save the remaining half. This philosopher's robe, as you call it, is put on and taken off with great frequency. I shed it when I start for the

university. I'm often a little guilty and uncomfortable in it
when I come home and sometimes am only able to wear it
in defiance . . .

You say 'the better a book is, the less effect advertising
has on its fortunes.' It's of course true that some books
can only be sold by plugging, like canned soup. But
Dangling Man was well reviewed and didn't sell out its
first edition. There must be a mean. I'll most respectfully
hand over my robe when I write a book full of snares and
bait, boudoirs and glitter. I'm not looking for the
maximum. As I say, I may be upbraided for playing a
double game and making my way smoother, or trying to,
with assistant professorships, but it's not in order to be on
the best-seller lists that I banish myself to Minnesota. And
I've never asked for more than your assurance that you
would do your damndest—as I do mine. But I have asked
for that assurance and I think I was not unjustified.

He was still feverishly revising *The Victim* and 'living on
benzedrine tablets,' Bellow confessed to Henle. He was convinced
the novel was greatly improved, but 'weary to the bone of it.' Plans
for the following year were up in the air, as usual. He wasn't sure if
his contract at the University of Minnesota would be renewed, and
the landlord of their St Paul house had put it on the market. 'The
Son of Man still hath no place for his head, and even the fox has
lost his hole,' Bellow wrote his publisher on 13 May.

In the event, he was invited back, and by September, the
Bellows were installed in a large old house in Prospect Park, a
pleasant residential neighbourhood near the campus, although
to make ends meet, they took in two boarders. Anita had spent the
summer going over proofs of *The Victim;* the publication day was 6
November. The proprietors of the Minnesota Book Store had
commissioned a photographer to come and take Bellow's picture. 'I
had it taken today, *sans* pipe, to the disgust of the photographer
when he learned I was an author.' Bellow received his first copy
that week. He thought it was 'extraordinarily handsome,' especially
the jacket, which had 'what Aristotle used to call magnificence.'

61

'You've outdone yourselves,' he wrote excitedly to Henle: 'I only hope it's received as handsomely as it's presented. It should be; it's good, honest, solid work, but the world's so mad!'

Solid work it was. 'I labored and tried to make *The Victim* letter perfect,' Bellow testified, noting that he had 'accepted a Flaubertian standard.' Like its predecessor, it was a quiet book, though it had more of a plot: an ordinary New Yorker, a sub-editor on a trade journal, is harassed and pursued by a man he barely knows, who accuses him of having been responsible, through some obscure causality, for the loss of the man's job. In fact, the novel is less Flaubertian than Kafkaesque. The main characters, Asa Leventhal and his tormentor Kirby Allbee, are allegorical, and the novel's few events unfold with hallucinatory intensity. Allbee shows up uninvited at Leventhal's apartment and follows him to a crowded park, where he confronts him on a park bench; and then doggedly shadows his prey, hounding him at all hours of the night. Allbee, evicted from his boarding-house, persuades Leventhal to put him up; the more Leventhal acquiesces, the more importunate Allbee becomes. Arriving home to find his door chained, Leventhal breaks it down and discovers Allbee in his own bed with a woman. In a final, climactic outrage, the aggressive intruder tries to kill himself in Leventhal's kitchen, putting his head in the oven and turning on the gas.

Bellow later disparaged *The Victim* as a 'victim' novel—a well-mannered, 'repressive' book that reflected his upbringing as a child of Jewish immigrant parents uncertain of his status in the New World and lacking the confidence to write in his own voice. 'I was still learning, establishing my credentials, proving that a young man from Chicago had a right to claim the world's attention,' he once told an interviewer, 'so I was restrained, controlled, demonstrating that I could write "good".' *Dangling Man* was his M.A., Bellow liked to say; *The Victim* was his Ph.D.

Yet he never set out to be a Jewish novelist—certainly not in the sense that Abraham Cahan, Henry Roth and Daniel Fuchs were Jewish novelists. Bellow was no stranger to this life; he, too, captured the subtle tonalities and cadences of Jewish speech—the women prattling on about doctors, the banter of men around the pinochle table at a family gathering. But he was after something deeper: the moral life of man.

Bellow was grateful for the effort Vanguard was making to publish the book—he was delighted to see an advertisement for it in the *New York Times Book Review*—but was realistic about its prospects. 'I'd like to make it clear to you that I understand perfectly well that the sale of a book depends on a great many imponderables and that I don't expect to make bales out of The Victim and as a matter of fact don't want to make bales,' he assured Henle in mid-November, stating with remarkable objectivity what he thought he had accomplished and where he had failed:

> I fully realize that many people will be alienated by the theme and will find the characters disagreeable. People who liked the Dangling Man because of its writing will be disappointed in The Victim. In writing it I deliberately renounced 'style' and sought for transparency because I think the distinction between poetry and fiction has, from Flaubert to Virginia Woolf, been greatly weakened to the detriment of both and of fiction particularly. So I will have to write a few more books before people begin to see what I was after in The Victim.

His peers were already beginning to see it. Robert Penn Warren, who had admired *The Victim* when he read it in manuscript, insisted that it read even better the second time around, and supplied Vanguard with a quote praising Bellow as 'a vivid, compelling, and serious writer, destined to occupy an important position among the novelists of our time and place.' Alfred Kazin found the book 'amazing in its completely authentic and personal recreation of Dostoyevsky.' *The Victim* was 'one of the few really distinguished books published by an American of my generation,' he wrote to the Guggenheim Committee, to which Bellow had once again applied for a fellowship.

The reviews were mostly good. Diana Trilling, in her column for the *Nation*, reversed her low opinion of Bellow. *Dangling Man* had been too 'small' for her, but *The Victim* she pronounced 'morally one of the furtherest reaching books our contemporary culture has produced,' a work 'hard to match, in recent fiction, for brilliance, skill and originality.' The indefatigable Robert Penn Warren, writing in the *Chicago Daily News*, proclaimed it 'a timely wrought, compelling and important book, a book that ought to place Bellow squarely in the literary picture of our day.' Elizabeth Hardwick concurred, predicting in *Partisan Review* that 'it would be hard to think of any young writer who has a better chance than Bellow to become the redeeming novelist of the period.' The one wholly negative review, buried on page twenty-nine, was in the *New York Times Book Review*, where the book was disposed of in a few grudging paragraphs, by a Princeton man, Alan Downer, who objected that it was 'at once overcontrived and undercontrived,' and that Bellow had failed 'to make clear what the novel is "about".'

Bellow was disappointed, but bore what felt to him like a mixed reception with equanimity. The reviews had been 'singularly stupid; the one in the Times particularly,' he complained to Henle. But Bellow had doubts of his own about the novel. *The Victim* was too harsh, he wrote Alfred Kazin; he had been too constrained by the bonds of naturalism, unwilling to go beyond 'probabilities' and acknowledge that the book was a fantasy. To Henle he also confessed that *The Victim* had fallen short. 'I don't myself think that the execution of the novel is equal to the scale of its conception,' Bellow admitted. 'I do however draw satisfaction from my first real success with character and feel I have completed one of the difficult stages of my apprenticeship.' It was a courageous—and correct—assertion. Whatever its virtues or defects, *The Victim* was more than promising; it completed Bellow's literary education. If the novel was his Ph.D., he had graduated with high honours.

Bellow continued to be vigilant about the progress of his book, urging his publisher to send review copies to local booksellers and complaining that it hadn't been properly distributed in bookstores around the University of Chicago: 'In '44 a lion in Hyde Park, in '47 a nonentity.' He vacillated between ironic acceptance of its fate—'I don't suppose the sales of The Victim will shoot up because Commentary reviewed it well,' he observed wryly—and grandiosity: 'Is there much of a chance for the Pulitzer Prize?' he inquired. 'I'd feel foolish getting it when writers like Faulkner, Jim Farrell etc. have never made the grade.' But not that foolish.

The book was a mild critical success and a commercial failure. It sold 2,257 copies—only a few hundred more than *Dangling Man*. When Bellow learned of these figures from Henle, the bantering tone of his correspondence abruptly vanished. 'Dear Jim,' he wrote on 9 February:

> Surely you don't mean that the total sales of the book come to 2000! Why, you wrote last November that it had an advance-sale of 2300. Is the two thousand you speak of in addition to the advance-sale? That would be little enough for a novel that has been reviewed like mine. And if you mean that the *total* sale is 2000 I hardly know what to say after two years of wringing to pay bills and fighting for scraps of time in which to do my writing. Have I nothing to look forward to but two years of the same sort and a sale of barely two thousand for the next novel I write? And can it be worth your while to continue publishing books which sell only two thousand copies? I don't understand this at all; I feel black and bitter about it, simply.

Henle tried as best he could to placate his anguished author, reiterating his earlier admonition that writing novels had never been a lucrative profession, but Bellow was inconsolable. 'I never expected things to be easy,' he replied, 'but neither did I expect such a sharp disappointment.' A week later, he wrote again, appending an epigraph from *The Duchess of Malfi*: 'Miserable age, where the only reward/Of doing well is the doing of it.' For the first time Bellow sounded a note of mild reproach. It was true that Henle had supported *The Victim*, but he could have done more with it in Chicago 'and in the college towns where I have some kind of reputation.' However, that was 'spilt milk.' Bellow was already plotting his third and fourth novels. 'Well, these are rough days,' he signed off. 'All I need now, and I shall probably get it, is a third rejection from the Guggenheim.'

Henle was loyal to his authors, and especially to Bellow. He had taken him on when no one else would; he had commended him to the Guggenheim Committee as 'the most gifted, the most intelligent and the most sincere' young writer he had come across in years; in an internal memo circulated to his staff after the publication of *Dangling Man*, he had stressed that Vanguard 'should do everything possible to keep Mr Bellow happy—for he is a writer of distinction and we shd. feel proud to publish his book.' But like many independent publishers who put up their own money, Henle was also tight. He had advanced Bellow 500 dollars for *The Victim* and kept close accounts; when all the sales figures were in, he duly noted, Bellow owed him 170 dollars. It was Henle's fixed belief that there was no money in literature. Bellow's accountant agreed: apprised of his client's debit on the novel, he recommended going into another line of work.

But it was too late for that. 'I never thought about doing anything else,' Bellow said later. 'What else could I have done?' Writing wasn't a career he'd chosen; it was an involuntary act. That winter he was ten thousand words into a short novel about a diver, tentatively entitled *Who Breathes Overhead*—an echo of Schiller's line, 'Who breathes overhead in the rose-tinted light may be glad.' He was also meditating two other 'novelettes'. The first, inspired by Luke 16:8—'the children of this world are in their generation wiser than the children of light'—was entitled *The Children of Darkness*. The second was based on the life of Croesus, not as a historical figure but as 'an ex-man-of-property.' A 'devaluation of man' had occurred over the last two centuries, Bellow explained to the Guggenheim Committee: 'The scope of the mind has, through science, been immensely extended while that of the personality has shrunk.' Modern man was 'an object of slender importance,' he wrote in his 'plans for work,' quoting de Tocqueville. Democracy, for all its advantages, was a threat to the individual; it levelled distinctions between people.

On 1 April 1948, Henry Allen Moe, the director of the Guggenheim Foundation, informed Bellow that he had been appointed to a Fellowship. The stipend was 2,500 dollars. Two days later, Bellow acknowledged the award with a brief letter of thanks, dating it 3 April 1943—the year he'd first applied.

Three weeks later, Henle learned from 'an unimpeachable source' that Frank Taylor, an editor at Random House, was courting Bellow.

His source was accurate. Taylor *had* approached Bellow. So had Monroe Engel, an editor at Viking. Vanguard had an option on his next novel, but at the end of April, Bellow asked Henle to release him from his contract. 'It isn't easy to make this request,' he wrote contritely. 'I know I won't have another publisher I can like personally as much as you or one whose judgment I respect half as much as I respect yours. But I've come to the conclusion that I'm not the kind of writer that Vanguard can do much for.' He was determined not to resume teaching when his Guggenheim expired, and he needed more money than Henle could offer.

In a follow-up letter, Bellow enumerated his grievances. To begin with, there was the letter in which Henle had accused Bellow of taking off his philosopher's robe when he dared to seek assurances that his publisher was committed to the book. Then there was the lack of aggressive marketing; in Chicago, Bellow's hometown, *The Victim* wasn't to be found in the stores. And finally, there was the matter of money: if Truman Capote could hit it big (*Other Voices, Other Rooms* had just come out), why couldn't he? 'I know it is unpleasant to receive such letters,' Bellow summed up his position,

> but it's better for me to speak out than, like Job, to sin not with my lips when I am angry. You know, after four years, that I am not a prima donna and do not cast longing eyes upon the golden ladders and the big money. It's only that it galls me to go on teaching when I have as full a right as anyone in America to devote myself to writing.

Henle was livid. He had launched Bellow, had supported him in times of need. No publisher could have done more:

> When you write that you are not the kind of writer that Vanguard can do much for, you imply that another publisher will be able to do more for you. That is quite possible; on the other hand, what is not possible but certain is that some publishers (and their handymen) will

    promise a great deal more than Vanguard. It will be
    interesting to see what they accomplish; much, of course,
    will depend on the nature of your next book.

At the bottom of his letter, Henle wrote: 'whether we already have
done something for you, I leave it for you to judge.' But he
graciously released Bellow from his obligation.

Two months later, after visiting several publishers in New
York, Bellow signed a contract with Viking for a new novel; its
tentative title was *The Crab and the Butterfly*. The advance this
time was 3,000 dollars—a very substantial improvement over what
he'd been getting from Henle and a fair amount of money in those
days. To Frank Taylor at Random House Bellow offered an
explanation of his decision to go with Viking that was notable for
its passive and convoluted syntax. He had 'found things so working
themselves out,' he explained, 'as to convince me that I had no
other alternative. It was all like radar acting on my instructions.'
Viking had claimed him, and he had gone.

To Alfred Kazin he reported with laconic insouciance: 'Henle
and I have broken off as of last week. He bungled both books
awfully.'

The Crab and the Butterfly would never appear. Bellow's next
book, which wouldn't be published for another five years, was *The
Adventures of Augie March*.

The author wishes to acknowledge the Jean Stafford
Collection of the Norlin Library at the University of Colorado in
Boulder for Bellow's letter to Jean Stafford; the Department of
Special Collections of the Joseph Regenstein Library of the
University of Chicago for correspondence between Bellow and
James Henle; the John Simon Guggenheim Memorial Foundation
for excerpts from Bellow's Guggenheim application; the Random
House and Vanguard Press papers, Rare Book and Manuscript
Library, Columbia University, for Bellow's letter to Frank Taylor
and for correspondence between Bellow and James Henle and to
the University of Pennsylvania for the letter to James T. Farrell.

GABRIEL GARCÍA
MÁRQUEZ
DREAMS FOR HIRE

At nine o'clock in the morning, while we were having breakfast on the terrace of the Hotel Riviera in Havana, a terrifying wave appeared out of nowhere—the day was sunny and calm—and came crashing upon us. It lifted the cars that had been passing along the sea front, as well as several others that had been parked nearby, and tossed them into the air, smashing one into the side of our hotel. It was like an explosion of dynamite, spreading panic up and down the twenty floors of our building and transforming the lobby into a pile of broken glass, where many of the hotel guests were hurled through the air like the furniture. Several were wounded in the hail of glass shards. It must have been a tidal wave of monumental size: the hotel is protected from the sea by a wall and the wide two-way avenue that passes before it, but the wave had erupted with such force that it obliterated the glass lobby.

Cuban volunteers, with the help of the local fire brigade, set to sweeping up the damage, and in less than six hours, after closing off the hotel's sea front entrance and opening up an alternative, everything was back to normal. Throughout the morning no one paid any attention to the car that had been smashed against the wall of the hotel, believing it had been among the vehicles parked along the avenue. But by the time it was eventually removed by a crane, the body of a woman was discovered inside, moored to the driving seat by her seat-belt. The blow had been so great that there wasn't a bone in her body which was left unbroken. Her face was messy and unrecognizable, her ankle boots had burst at the seams, her clothes were in tatters. But there was a ring, still worn on her finger, which remained intact: it was made in the shape of a serpent and had emeralds for eyes. The police established that she was the housekeeper for the new Portuguese ambassador and his wife. In fact she had arrived with them only fifteen days before and had that morning left for the market in their new car. Her name meant nothing to me when I read about the incident in the papers, but I was intrigued by that ring, made in the shape of a serpent with emeralds for its eyes. I was, unfortunately, unable to find out on which finger the ring had been worn.

It was an essential detail: I feared that this woman might be

Photo: Inge Morath/Magnum

someone I knew and whom I would never forget, even though I never learned her real name. She, too, had a ring made in the shape of a serpent, with emeralds for its eyes, but she always wore it on the first finger of her right hand, which was unusual, especially then. I had met her forty-six years ago in Vienna, eating sausages and boiled potatoes and drinking beer straight from the barrel, in a tavern frequented by Latin American students. I had arrived from Rome that morning, and I still recall that first impression made by her ample opera-singer's bosom, the drooping fox tails gathered round the collar of her coat and that Egyptian ring made in the shape of a serpent. She spoke a rudimentary Spanish, in a breathless shopkeeper's accent, and I assumed that she must be Austrian, the only one at that long wooden table. I was wrong: she had been born in Colombia and between the wars had travelled to Austria to study music and singing. When I met her she must have been around thirty, and she had begun ageing before her time. Even so, she was magical: and, also, among the most fearsome people I've ever met.

At that time—the late forties—Vienna was nothing more than an ancient imperial city that history had reduced to a remote provincial capital, located between the two irreconcilable worlds left by the Second World War, a paradise for the black market and international espionage. I couldn't imagine surroundings better suited to my fugitive compatriot, who went on eating in the students' tavern on the corner only out of nostalgia for her roots, because she had more than enough money to buy the whole place, its diners included. She never told us her real name; we always referred to her by the German tongue-twister that the Latin American students in Vienna had invented for her: Frau Frida. No sooner had we been introduced than I committed the fortuitous imprudence of asking her how she came to find herself in a part of the world so distant and different from the windy heights of the Quindio region in Colombia. She replied matter-of-factly: 'I hire myself out to dream.'

That was her profession. She was the third of eleven children of a prosperous shopkeeper from the old region of Caldas, and by the time she learned to speak, she had established the habit of telling all her dreams before breakfast, when, she said, her powers of premonition were at their most pure. At the age of seven, she dreamt that one of her brothers had been swept away by a raging torrent. The mother, simply out of a nervous superstitiousness, refused to allow her son to do what he most enjoyed, swimming in the local gorge. But Frau Frida had already developed her own system of interpreting her prophecies.

'What the dream means,' she explained, 'is not that he is going to drown, but that he mustn't eat sweets.'

The interpretation amounted to a terrible punishment, especially for a five-year-old boy who could not imagine life without his Sunday treats. But the mother, convinced of her daughter's divinatory powers, ensured that her injunction was adhered to. Unfortunately, following a moment's inattention, the son choked on a gob-stopper that he had been eating in secret, and it proved impossible to save him.

Frau Frida had never thought that it would be possible to earn a living from her talent until life took her by the scruff of the neck and, during a harsh Viennese winter, she rang the bell of the first house where she wanted to live, and, when asked what she could do, offered the simple reply: 'I dream.' After only a brief explanation, the lady of the house took her on, at a wage that was little more than pocket money, but with a decent room and three meals a day. Above all, there was a breakfast, the time when the members of the family sat down to learn their immediate destinies: the father, a sophisticated *rentier*; the mother, a jolly woman with a passion for Romantic chamber music; and the two children, aged eleven and nine. All of them were religious and therefore susceptible to archaic superstitions, and they were delighted to welcome Frau Frida into their home, on the sole condition that every day she revealed the family's destiny through her dreams.

She did well, especially during the war years that followed, when reality was more sinister than any nightmare. At the breakfast table every morning, she alone decided what each member of the family was to do that day, and how it was to be done, until eventually her prognostications became the house's sole voice of authority. Her domination of the family was absolute: even the slightest sigh was made on her orders. The father had died just prior to my stay in Vienna, and he had had the good grace to leave Frau Frida a part of his fortune, again on the condition that she continued dreaming for the family until she was unable to dream any more.

I spent a month in Vienna, living the frugal life of a student while waiting for money which never arrived. The unexpected and generous visits that Frau Frida paid to our tavern were like fiestas in our otherwise penurious regime. One night, the powerful smell of beer about us, she whispered something in my ear with such conviction that I found it impossible to ignore.

'I came here specially to tell you that last night I saw you in my dreams,' she said. 'You must leave Vienna at once and not come back here for at least five years.'

Such was her conviction that I was put, that same night, on the last train for Rome. I was so shaken that I have since come to believe that I survived a disaster I never encountered. To this day I have not set foot in Vienna again.

Before the incident in Havana I met up with Frau Frida once more, in Barcelona, in an encounter so unexpected that it seemed to me especially mysterious. It was the day that Pablo Neruda set foot on Spanish soil for the first time since the Civil War, during a stopover on a long sea journey to Valparaiso in Chile. He spent the morning with us, big game hunting in the antiquarian bookshops, buying eventually a faded book with torn covers for which he paid what must have been the equivalent of two month's salary for the Chilean consulate in Rangoon. He lumbered along like a rheumatic elephant, showing a childlike interest in the internal workings of every object he came across. The world always appeared to him as a giant clockwork toy.

I have never known anyone who approximated so closely the received idea of a Renaissance Pope—that mixture of gluttony and refinement—who even against his will, would dominate and preside over any table. Matilde, his wife, wrapped him in a bib which looked more like an apron from a barber-shop than a napkin from a restaurant, but it was the only way to prevent him from being bathed in sauces. That day Neruda ate three lobsters in their entirety, dismembering them with the precision of a surgeon, while concurrently devouring everyone else's dishes with his eyes, until he was unable to resist picking from each plate, with a relish and an appetite that everyone found contagious: clams from Galicia, barnacle geese from Cantabria, prawns from Alicante, swordfish from the Costa Brava. All the while he was talking, just like the French, about other culinary delights, especially the prehistoric shellfish of Chile that were his heart's favourite. And then suddenly he stopped eating, pricked up his ears like the antennae of a lobster, and whispered to me: 'There's someone behind me who keeps staring at me.'

I looked over his shoulder. It was true. Behind him, three tables back, a woman, unabashed in an old-fashioned felt hat and a purple scarf, was slowly chewing her food with her eyes fixed on Neruda. I recognized her at once. She was older and bigger, but it was her, with the ring made in the form of a serpent on her first finger.

She had travelled from Naples on the same boat as the Nerudas, but they had not met on board. We asked her to join us for coffee, and I invited her to talk about her dreams, if only to entertain the poet. But the poet would have none of it, declaring outright that he did not believe in the divination of dreams.

'Only poetry is clairvoyant,' he said.

After lunch, and the inevitable walk along the Ramblas, I deliberately fell in with Frau Frida so that we could renew our acquaintance without the others hearing. She told me that she had sold her properties in Austria and, having retired to Porto, in Portugal, was now living in a house that she described as a fake castle perched on a cliff from where she could see the whole Atlantic as far as America. It was clear, although she didn't say as much explicitly, that, from one dream to another, she had ended up in possession of the entire fortune of her once unlikely Viennese employers. Even so, I remained unimpressed, only because I had always thought that her dreams were no more than a contrivance to make ends meet. I told her as much.

She laughed her mocking laugh. 'You're as shameless as

ever,' she said. The rest of our group had now stopped to wait for Neruda who was speaking in Chilean slang to the parrots in the bird market. When we renewed our conversation, Frau Frida had changed the subject.

'By the way,' she said 'you can go back to Vienna if you like.'

I then realized that thirteen years had passed since we first met.

'Even if your dreams aren't true, I will never return,' I told her, 'just in case.'

At three o'clock we parted in order to accompany Neruda to his sacred siesta, which he took at our house, following a number of solemn preparatory rituals that, for some reason, reminded me of the Japanese tea ceremony. Windows had to be opened, others closed—an exact temperature was essential—and only a certain kind of light from only a certain direction could be tolerated. And then: an absolute silence. Neruda fell asleep at once, waking ten minutes later, like children do, when we expected it least. He appeared in the living-room, refreshed, the monogram of the pillow case impressed on his cheek.

'I dreamt of that woman who dreams,' he said.

Matilde asked him to tell us about the dream.

'I dreamt she was dreaming of me,' he said.

'That sounds like Borges,' I said.

He looked at me, crestfallen. 'Has he already written it?'

'If he hasn't, he's bound to write it one day,' I said. 'It'll be one of his labyrinths.'

As soon as Neruda was back on board ship at six that afternoon, he said his farewells to us, went to sit at an out-of-the-way table and began writing verses with the same pen of green ink that he had been using to draw flowers, fish and birds in the dedications he signed in his own books. With the first announcement to disembark, we sought out Frau Frida and found her finally on the tourist deck just as we were about to give up. She, too, had just woken from a siesta.

'I dreamt of your poet,' she told us.

Astonished, I asked her to tell me about the dream.

'I dreamt he was dreaming about me,' she said, and my look

of disbelief confused her. 'What do you expect? Sometimes among all the dreams there has to be one that bears no relation to real life.'

I never saw or thought about her again until I heard about the ring made in the form of a serpent on the finger of the woman who died in the sea disaster at the Hotel Riviera. I could not resist asking the Portuguese Ambassador about it when we met up a few months later at a diplomatic reception.

The Ambassador spoke of her with enthusiasm and tremendous admiration. 'You can't imagine how extraordinary she was,' he said. 'You would have been unable to resist wanting to write a story about her.' And he continued in the same spirit, on and on, with some occasional, surprising details, but without an end in sight.

'Tell me then,' I said finally, interrupting him, 'what exactly did she do?'

'Nothing,' he replied, with a shrug of resignation. 'She was a dreamer.'

Translated from the Spanish by Nick Caistor

Subscribe to the Leading Intellectual Journal in the US

Where can you find Garry Wills writing on the Republican Convention, and John Richardson describing the hype of the Guggenheim Museum? Only in the pages of *The New York Review of Books*, where today's best writers and scholars discuss the most important issues in current affairs, literature, history, science, and the arts.

In issue after issue, *The New York Review* publishes criticism and commentary by such celebrated writers as John Updike, Nadine Gordimer, Václav Havel, Norman Mailer, Joan Didion, Theodore Draper, E. H. Gombrich, V. S. Naipaul, Murray Kempton, Gore Vidal, Robert Hughes, Diane Johnson, Charles Rosen, and many others.

Now you can subscribe to *The New York Review* and receive: **21 Issues** at the special rate of $22.95 (a saving of almost 50% off the regular newsstand rate). **A Free Book**—*A Middle East Reader*, a collection of *New York Review* articles that provides a better understanding of the explosive politics in the Middle East and the role taken by the US. Contributors include Bernard Lewis, Arthur Hertzberg, Avishai Margalit, and Samir al-Khalil. It is yours as our gift to you. **A Risk-Free Guarantee:** a refund of any remaining portion of the subscription is guaranteed at any time—but you keep all issues received and *A Middle East Reader*.

Please return this coupon or a photocopy of this coupon to:

The New York Review of Books

Subscriber Service Department, PO Box 420380, Palm Coast, FL 32142-0380

❑ YES, you may enter my subscription to *The New York Review* for a full year (21 issues) at the special rate of $22.95. With my paid subscription, I will also receive *A Middle East Reader* at no extra charge.

* Check or money order must be made payable to *The New York Review of Books* in US Dollars drawn on a US bank. Offer good for new subscribers within the US and Canada only. Canadian subscribers, please add $16.05 for postage and GST. Please allow 6-8 weeks for receipt of your first copy. May not be used for gift subscriptions.

Name

Address

City   State   Zip

❑ $22.95 enclosed.*   Or charge my ❑ Am Ex ❑ MasterCard ❑ Visa.   ❑ Send Bill.

Acct. No.   Exp.Date

Signature

A2JGAX

BLAKE MORRISON
WHEN DID YOU LAST
SEE YOUR FATHER?

A hot September Saturday in Cheshire, 1959. We haven't moved for ten minutes. Ahead of us, a queue of cars stretches out of sight around the corner. Everyone has turned his engine off, and now my father does so too. In the sudden silence we can hear the distant whinge of what must be the first race of the afternoon, a ten-lap event for saloon cars. It is five minutes past one. In an hour the drivers will be warming up for the main event, the Gold Cup—Graham Hill, Jack Brabham, Roy Salvadori, Stirling Moss and Joakim Bonnier. My father has always loved fast cars, and motor racing has a strong British following just now, which is why we are stuck here in this country lane with hundreds of other cars.

My father does not like waiting in queues. He is used to patients waiting in queues to see him, but he is not used to waiting in queues himself. A queue to him means a man being denied the right to be where he wants to be at a time of his own choosing, which is at the front, now. Ten minutes have passed and my father is running out of patience. What is happening up ahead? What fat-head has caused this snarl-up? Why are no cars coming the other way? Has there been an accident? Why are there no police to sort it out? Every two minutes or so he gets out of the car, crosses to the opposite verge and tries to see if there is movement up ahead. There isn't. He gets back in. The roof of our Alvis is down, the sun beating on to the leather upholstery, the chrome, the picnic basket. The hood is folded and pleated into the mysterious crevice between the boot and the narrow back seat where my sister and I are scrunched together as usual. The roof is nearly always down, whatever the weather: my father loves fresh air, and every car he has ever owned has been a convertible, so that he can have fresh air. But the air today is not fresh. There is a pall of high-rev exhaust, dust, petrol, boiling-over engines.

In the cars ahead and behind, people are laughing, eating sandwiches, drinking from beer bottles, enjoying the weather, settling into the familiar indignity of waiting-to-get-to-the-front. But my father is not like them. There are only two things on his mind: the invisible head of the queue and, not unrelated, the other half of the country lane, tantalizingly empty.

'Just relax, Arthur,' my mother says. 'You're in and out of

the car like a blue-tailed fly.'

But being told to relax only incenses him. 'What can it be?' he demands. 'Maybe there's been an accident. Maybe they're waiting for an ambulance.' We all know where this last speculation is leading, even before he says it. 'Maybe they need a doctor.'

'No, Arthur,' says my mother, as he opens the door for a final time and stands on the wheel arch to crane ahead.

'It must be an accident,' he announces. 'I think I should drive ahead and see.'

'No, Arthur. It's just the numbers waiting to get in. And surely there must be doctors on the circuit.'

It is one-thirty and silent now. The saloon race has finished. It is still an hour until the Gold Cup itself, but there's another race first, and the cars in the paddock to see, and besides . . .

'Well, I'm not going to bloody well wait here any longer,' he says. 'We'll never get in. We might as well turn round and give up.' He sits for another twenty seconds, then leans forward, opens the glove compartment and pulls out a stethoscope, which he hooks over the windscreen mirror. It hangs there like a skeleton, the membrane at the top, the metal and rubber leads dangling bow-legged, the two ivory ear-pieces clopping bonily against each other. He starts the engine, releases the handbrake, reverses two feet, then pulls out into the opposite side of the road.

'No,' says my mother again, half-heartedly. It could be that he is about to do a three-point turn and go back. No it couldn't . . .

My father does not drive particularly quickly past the marooned cars. No more than twenty miles an hour. Even so, it *feels* fast and arrogant, and all the occupants turn and stare as they see us coming. Some appear to be angry. Some are shouting. 'Point to the stethoscope, pet,' he tells my mother, but she has slid down sideways in her passenger seat, out of sight, her bottom resting on the floor, from where she berates him.

'God Almighty, Arthur, why do you have to do this? Why can't you wait like everyone else? What if we meet something coming the other way?' Now my sister and I do the same, hide ourselves below the seat. Our father is on his own. He is not with us, this bullying, shaming, undemocratic cheat, or rather, we are not with him.

My face pressed to the sweet-smelling upholstery, I imagine what is happening ahead. I can't tell how far we have gone, how many blind corners we have taken. If we meet something on this narrow country lane, we will have to reverse past all the cars we have just overtaken. I wait for the squeal of brakes.

After an eternity of—what?—two minutes, my mother sticks her head up and says, 'Now you've had it,' and my father replies, 'No, there's another gate beyond,' and my sister and I raise ourselves to look. We are level with the cars at the head of the queue, which are waiting to turn left into the brown ticket holders' entrance, the plebs' entrance. A steward steps out of the gateway towards us, but my father, pretending not to see him, drives past and on to a clear piece of road, where, two hundred yards ahead, the half a dozen cars that have come from the opposite direction are waiting to turn into another gateway. Unlike those we have left behind, these cars appear to be moving. Magnanimous, my father waits until the last one has turned in, then drives through the stone gateposts and over the bumpy grass to where an armbanded steward in a tweed jacket is waiting by the roped entrance.

'Good afternoon, sir. Red ticket holder?' The question does not come as a shock: we have all seen the signs, numerous and clamorous, saying RED TICKET HOLDERS' ENTRANCE. But my father is undeterred.

'These, you mean,' he says and hands over his brown tickets.

'No, sir, I'm afraid these are brown tickets.'

'But there must be some mistake. I applied for red tickets. To be honest, I didn't even look.'

'I'm sorry sir, but these are brown tickets, and brown's the next entrance, two hundred yards along. If you just swing round here, and . . . '

'I'm happy to pay the difference.'

'No, you see the rules say . . . '

'I know where the brown entrance is, I've just spent the last hour queueing for it by mistake. I drove up here because I thought I was red. I can't go back there now. The queue stretches for miles. And these children you know, who'd been looking forward . . . '

By now half a dozen cars have gathered behind us. One of them parps. The steward is wavering.

'You say you applied for red.'

'Not only applied for, paid for. I'm a doctor, you see . . . '—he points at the stethoscope—'and I like being near the grandstand.'

This double *non sequitur* seems to clinch it.

'All right, sir, but next time please check the tickets. Ahead and to your right.'

This is the way it was with my dad. Minor duplicities. Little fiddles. Money-saving, time-saving, privilege-attaining fragments of opportunism. The queue-jump, the backhander, the deal under the table. Parking where you shouldn't, drinking after hours, accepting the poached pheasant and the goods off the back of a lorry. 'They' were killjoys, after all—'they' meaning the Establishment to which, despite being a middle-class professional, a GP, he never felt he belonged; our job, as ordinary folk, trying to get the most out of life, was to outwit them. Serious law-breaking would have scared him, though he envied and often praised those who had pulled off ingenious, non-violent crimes, like the Great Train Robbers or, before them, the men who intercepted a lorry carrying a large number of old banknotes to the incinerator. ('Still in currency, you see, but not new, so there was no record of the numbers and they couldn't be traced. Brilliant, quite brilliant.') He was not himself up to being criminal in a big way, but he'd have been lost if he couldn't cheat in a small way: so much of his pleasure derived from it. I grew up thinking it absolutely normal, that most Englishmen were like this. I still suspect that's the case.

My childhood seems to be a web of little scams and triumphs. The time we stayed at a hotel near a famous golf course—Troon, was it?—and discovered that if we started at the fifth hole and finished at the fourth we could avoid the clubhouse and green fees. The private tennis clubs and yacht clubs and drinking clubs we got into (especially on Sundays in dry counties of Wales) by giving someone else's name: by the time the man on the door had failed to find it, my father would have read the names on the list upside-down: 'There, see, Wilson. No, Wilson, I said, not Watson.' If all else failed, you could try slipping the chap a one pound note. With his odd mixture of innocence, confidence and hail-fellow cheeriness, my father could usually talk his way into anything and, when caught, out of anything.

Oulton Park, half an hour later. We have met up with our cousins in the brown car park—they of course arrived on time—and have come back with them to the entrance to the paddock. My father has assumed that, with the red tickets he's wangled, we are entitled to enter the paddock for nothing —along with our guests. He is wrong about this. Tickets to the paddock cost a guinea. There are ten of us. We're talking serious money.

'We'll buy one, anyway,' my father says to the man in the ticket booth and comes back with a small, brown-paper card, like a library ticket, with a piece of string attached to a hole at the top so you can thread it through your lapel. 'Let me just investigate,' he says, and disappears through the gate, the steward seeing the lapel ticket and nodding him through: no stamp on the hand or name-check. In ten minutes or so my father is back, in a state of excitement. He whispers to my Uncle Ron, hands him the ticket and leads the rest of us to a wooden slatted fence in a quiet corner of the car park. Soon Uncle Ron appears on the other side of the fence, in an equally quiet corner of the paddock, and passes the ticket to us between the slats. Cousin Richard takes the ticket this time and repeats the procedure. One by one we all troop round: Kela, Auntie Mary, Edward, Jane, Gillian, my mother, myself. In five minutes, all ten of us are inside.

'Marvellous,' Father says. 'Four pounds, twelve shillings and we've got four red tickets and ten of us in the paddock. That'd be costing anyone else twenty guineas. Not bad.'

We stand round Jack Brabham's Cooper, its bonnet opened like a body on an operating table, a mass of tubes and wires and gleamy bits of white and silver.

Later, Brabham is overtaken on lap six by Moss, who stays there for the next sixty-nine laps. A car comes off the circuit between Lodge Corner and Deer Leap, crashing through the wooden slatted fence along from where we're standing. My father disappears 'to see if I can help.' He comes back strangely quiet and whispers to my mother: 'Nothing I could do.'

2

She will sleep with him tonight. She worries that it is macabre, but I encourage her: she must do what she feels right. This is, she says, the last night she'll ever have him here, and she wants them to spend it together.

Round midnight, we are sitting on the bed, and she is stroking his hair and kneading his face and then tweaks his nose and says: 'Icy. But you never did complain of the cold, did you?' We have kept the window open, which is just as well because we've not been able to turn the radiator off, and from time to time I catch a whiff of something I don't much want to think about. His face, the chin propped up on its hod or golf tee or sock darner, is still perfect. He has always been a great sleeper ('I was really hard on,' he'd say when he woke from his afternoon nap or evening pre-pub *zzz*), and all this sleeping he is doing now seems his apotheosis—the hardest sleep of all. 'No, the easiest,' says my mother when I try this conceit on her: 'No dreams, no worries about oversleeping, nothing.'

She leaves the room, and I lift back the sheet. There is a deep blackberry bruise spreading across either side of the stomach scar —the skin looks papery-thin and in danger of oozing or bursting. Little red lines have appeared on parts of his bleached hands. The back of his neck, from what I can make out, has gone purple and discoloured, all the blood gathering there.

When I come in at seven next morning, she's asleep beside him. I return later and find she's been crying.

'I've just been talking to my little man.'

'What about?'

'Oh, I've been telling him he shouldn't have gone and left me alone like this—not so soon.'

'I'm sure he didn't want to.'

'No, I know, but the fact remains: he's upped and gone.'

She berates him some more, and I am reminded of Shakespeare's Cleopatra, berating Antony:

Hast thou no care of me, shall I abide
In this dull world, which in thy absence is
No better than a sty.

This is the way the world goes, the men running out on the women, running out *before* the women. A shorter life expectancy: there's one inequality men can brandish on their placards, can grumble about to women, who endure most of the others. But perhaps even in this women—as the ones left painfully behind while their husbands move beyond pain—end up suffering the most.

3

A skiing trip to Lech, Austria, 1971. Long after the time when most parents would have written off their children as surly adolescents scarcely to be endured even for a weekend, and long after the time when most children would be holidaying only with their peers, here we all are for a fortnight together, father, mother, daughter, son. Friends at university have spoken enviously of the wonderful *après-ski* life awaiting me—parties, cocktails, drugs, girls—but I can't see how I'm going to come by all this with my parents inhibitingly omnipresent and my sister, supposing I did get away from them, lumberingly in tow. On the slopes I'm tormented by glimpses of beautiful faces and long hair streaming from bobble hats. In the long waits for the lift or cable car, I dream about the evening ahead and how I will come upon her at the bar, the special one I have been waiting for. But the accommodation is a 'small family hotel'; my sister and I seem to be the only humans aged between nine and forty-nine; the disco action is somewhere else in town, not here. At least there's nothing to distract me from my work: while everyone else is sitting in the bland pine-and-whitewash meliorism of the hotel lounge, I sneak back to my bed to read a bit more Marlowe or Tourneur or Webster, blackness and murder, infinite torture in a little room.

'*There* you are,' my father says, from the doorway of the twin-bedded room I'm sharing with him, chaps-chaps/girls-girls being the way my parents—or, rather, *he*—has chosen to divide this up, instead of husband-wife/daughter-(third room or dividing curtain)-son, as other married couples might. 'Bit anti-social, wasn't it, to skip off like that? We didn't know where you'd gone.'

'I said, Dad. I've got this work to do.'

'Well, if you said, I never heard, you mumble so much. Look at you: unshaven, scruffy hair, in need of fresh air and exercise.'

'I wouldn't be getting that in the bar, would I?'

'Don't get smart with me. We're all family together. Come on, it's time to eat.'

At the next table sit a pair of middle-aged Scottish women, who when greeted by my father—'Nice day on the slopes? Snow to your liking?'—seem even bonier, pricklier and more dour than they were last evening.

'Rather puir conditions. And the queues to the chair-lift wair tairrible. We took a little lunch: would you believe it, two sandwiches and two lemon teas came to over five pounds?'

These ladies are on the same package as ourselves, and I wonder whether their relentless itemizing of the holiday's shortcomings have contributed to yesterday's sudden departure of the tour rep—a muddly fuzz-blonde from Manchester—to 'a meeting at head office.' The Scottish ladies turn disapprovingly back to their meal. I reach for another glass of *liebfraumilch*.

'Dr Morrison, I presume?'

A young woman is standing beside the table. She is tall, dark, with big sensual lips, heavy make-up, a long nose and hair down to her shoulders. She looks as if she has just stepped out of one of those plays I've been reading, or dreams I've been dreaming.

'I'm Rachel Stein, your new rep. This must be your family. I hope you're all having a good holiday.'

'Smashing, love,' says my father, pulling over an extra chair beside him and ordering her a drink before she has time to refuse. He takes it upon himself to fill her in on the hotel, the town, the best ski-lifts to use, the restaurants to avoid, the deficiencies of the laundry system. He also fills her in on where we live, what he does, what we're all called, our ages, our stages in life. When he talks proudly of me at school and now university, I wait for recognition to flare in her eyes, for her to acknowledge the feeling which I'm feeling and she surely must also feel. But she looks back to my father. A second drink arrives. The Scottish ladies, her other charges, to whom she has nodded a brief hello, look on frostily as she begins to talk. She is due to read English at Bristol University next autumn, she says, but is having a year off first —the travel company who took her on have a super scheme for reps, a month here, six weeks there, always on the move. She had Agadir in Morocco last, and it will be Greece next. She's used to moving around: her father worked abroad a lot, being uprooted by his firm every two years.

Her eyes swim suddenly: 'He died last year. My mother thought it would do me good to get away, though I miss her.'

She is on her third beer. We are on sweet and coffee. I am in love, and she has barely looked at me yet. How artful of her to seem to be so interested in my boring old dad, not me. Suddenly she's up and gone in pursuit of the Scottish ladies—'Must catch a word with them: they're sisters, you know, the Misses Laidlaw from Kirkcaldy.' We watch her flounce into the distance.

'Always a good idea to get on with the rep,' my father says. 'Nice girl—she'll look after us.'

She certainly looks after him. Over the next evenings it becomes a ritual for her to join us at the table and for my father to relate the events of the day, every little skiing feat and mishap. Even with half a bottle of wine inside me, I'm out of my mind with embarrassment at his banal chat (how does she hide how bored she must be feeling?) and veer between looking away in shame and trying to catch her eye. She speaks often of her poor little rich girl's childhood, and I want to take her away and comfort her in her pain and loss. I wait vainly for my mother to help me out by signalling some disapproval of my father's monopolizing of her. I wait vainly for my father to say: 'Why don't you young people take off for the evening?' But he's too obsessed with Rachel, even by his own obsessive standards, to let her go. Despairingly, I join my mother and sister in the television room while my Dad and Rachel sit on high stools at the bar.

Back in our room, my father's snores reverberating round the pine and whitewash, I think of how the bit of him that wants the best for me, makes things easy for me, takes pride in me, is up against a different, more competitive bit I haven't admitted to seeing before. Last June, when he came to collect me at the end of my first year at Nottingham, he insisted we play squash, which I had recently—at his encouragement, seeing my face pasted by two terms of parties and drugs and seances—taken up: 'Perfect game for busy people: short, sweet and very active. I got quite good at it myself when I was a medical student.' I anticipated a gentle, non-competitive knock-up as the best thing for both of us: I'd not slept the night before, and he hadn't (he claimed) played for twenty-five years. But after a few minutes' limbering up, he said, 'What about a game then?' He was stiff and erratic, and I let him have the first game, knowing that I'd be able to crank myself up for the next one.

What I hadn't reckoned on was his getting more confident. And as he cracked his shots low and irretrievably into the court's four corners, or sent me scrambling in nausea after one of his feinted drop shots, and the whoops and ironies echoed from the dozen or so of my friends whom he had invited into the gallery, I realized that he was simply better at this than me, that I was not going to beat him, that I was going to be trounced. He eased off a bit towards the end to make a game of it, but that only made me angrier and more wayward than ever.

Now, as his snores vibrate through me, I see this is what it's been like for at least five years now. I learned to water-ski; so did he. I invited friends down to our North Wales caravan; somehow, on those weekends, he always happened to be there. I talked them into going for midnight swims; he was the first out into the night-cold in trunks and towel. Lately I mentioned a vague plan to go to Canada to read for an MA after I graduated. 'Great,' he said: 'Gill and Mum and I will sail out and join you. We'll buy a Dormobile and get it kitted out and we can tour North America. I'll have four months off and hire a locum. Why not?' Why not, except that this was a man who, when we were small, never had time for a holiday; why not, except that the whole point of Canada is to get away from him. When is the old bugger going to admit he's old? Next thing he will tell me he's given up medicine and applied to read English at Nottingham.

Not quite: the next thing he does is to announce, when he wakes up, that he has strained his back in some way, that he thinks it unwise to ski today and in any case fancies a day off sitting on his balcony in the sun. My mother jokes, as the three of us troop off to the slopes, that he'll 'No doubt be seeing his girl-friend.' It is the kind of thing she's said before, about other women he's latched on to, as if calling them 'girl-friends' is her way of convincing herself that they aren't. I leave my mother and sister on the nursery slopes and join my own class higher up.

We're practising parallel turns, and with my father absent I seem to get the hang of it at last. After lunch, I become fascinated by the figure in front of me in the chair-lift. I can see the backs of her shoulders as she reclines languidly and unfazed, long blonde hair pouring from beneath her hat. I prepare myself as I come in behind her at the landing-stage. I'll quote Eliot, I decide, 'Here in the mountains you feel free,' and then, if she seems uncomprehending, the German bits: '*Frisch weht der Wind/ Der Heimat zu*' (terribly genteel and polyglot). She's almost into the station and I swing my bar up in readiness to leap out. Twenty yards ahead of me she alights and turns, and I see that she has a large belly and bad acne. I also see that she is a twenty-five-year-old man.

Back in the room, at dusk, my father and Rachel are sitting on the balcony: they have drinks in their hands and are smoking, and, with the mountains and ice-blue skies beyond, look like a Martini advertisement. I pour myself a whisky. My mother begins to witter about our time on the slopes, and they listen politely, like a married couple smiling condescendingly at a nanny or grandma's account of her day out with the little ones. I look at the bed—unrumpled—but they'd have had time to straighten it, so who can tell? I feel a sudden disgust, not just with him, for stealing Rachel before I could even get hold of her, but with her, for her sophistication and cosmopolitanism and orphan's wide-eyed fascination with an older man. As soon as I decently can, I flounce off to read some more of *The White Devil*.

> *To dig the strumpet's eyes out; let her lie*
> *Some twenty months a-dying; to cut off*
> *Her nose and lips, pull out her rotten teeth;*
> *Preserve her flesh like mummia, for trophies*
> *Of my just anger! Hell, to my affliction,*
> *Is mere snow-water . . .*

Whenen I wake next morning, my father's not there. I find him with my mother, in her room. My parents are giggling. There's an odd pranky collusiveness between them.

'Shall we do it now?' my father asks.

'Yes, ring her,' my mother says.

'What's this about?' I ask.

'You'll see—just keep a straight face.'

My father dials three numbers. 'Could you come to the room?' he mutters bleakly into the receiver. 'Something terrible has happened.'

Rachel is up two minutes later. She looks pale, worried, no make-up, her face the colour of a Russian winter, her lovely black hair without its sheen.

'What happened?' she asks.

'There was this man on the balcony,' my mother says, sitting on the bed, her head bowed, wringing her hands.

'When was this?'

'Last night, when I came back to my room—Gillian was already asleep, thank God.'

'What did he do?'

'He just stood there.'

'He didn't come in?'

'No.'

'But you were frightened. You thought he was going to come in?'

'More than that.' My mother looks down at her hands. 'He . . . you know.'

'You mean he exposed himself?'

'Yes, he got out his, you know, and just stood there.'

'What did you do? Did you ring reception? You should have rung reception, or screamed, or something.' Rachel is sitting on the bed beside my mother, stroking her hands.

'I was going to, but next thing he disappeared.'

'But this is terrible. You must have been horribly frightened. You didn't sleep?'

'No.'

'Right,' says Rachel, getting up from the bed. 'I'm going

92

straight down to reception to report it and to get on to the police.'
'There's one other thing you should tell them,' my father says.
'What's that?'
'That it's April the first.'
'Sorry, I'm not with you.'
'It's April Fool's day.'
'I still don't . . . '
'You've been April-Fooled,' my father says. 'We made it up, it didn't happen, it's a story, we were having you on, love.'

Rachel sits down on the bed again and bursts into tears.

They give her coffee, calm her down, say, 'There there, you've had a nasty shock, love,' themselves shocked that the joke has worked too well. She still doesn't really see it, and nor can I see why my father wanted to play it on her. For my mother to invent a tale of sexual violation makes sense: it's probably what she's been feeling for several days. But what was in it for him? Is it because he has slept with her and wanted to punish himself for it—the joke as atonement? Or that he hasn't slept with her and he wants to punish her for it—the joke as revenge?

4

Twenty minutes after his death, I'm wading in boxes and boxes of photographs. It's something I do every Christmas, but Christmas has come a little early this year. Even now I can see it's some futile struggle to resuscitate and preserve him. His face swims up from the bendy sheens of black and white, the cardboard transparencies, the tiny sepia squares—in RAF uniform in the Azores; in his wedding suit in 1946; with a litter of twelve labrador pups; with babies, with toddlers, with his leg in plaster; being carried downstairs half-drunk ('fresh') by a collection of male friends at his retirement party. There is something boyish and little in these that won't do, won't measure up to how I want to remember him. Then I find something better: a photograph of him outside our Georgian rectory, leaning dandyishly against the side of his black Mercedes and drawing on a cigarette, his beautiful wife, fortyish then, posed beside him—an image not just of wealth and health and substance to set against the poverty and sickness and insubstantiality of the body we've lived with for the past month, but also of the aspirations and even affectations death has snuffed out.

My mother comes in to say that she has rung the vicar. It is not yet eight, so he can say a prayer at matins and word will get round the village without our having to phone: the church still has its uses after all. She asks was that me who's just been in her bedroom—somebody had seemed to be walking about. This is the one haunted moment. Otherwise the house feels unspooky; my father (I know) is too much of a materialist to become a ghost, and the room in which we've watched him die is unwaveringly bright and rationalist. It isn't him but we who move about like ghosts, pale and hovery and traumatized. There he lies, solid on his bed. I touch his skin. An hour after his death, his forehead has cooled to marble already, but when I slip my hand under the covers and across his huge ribs the chest is hot.

And it is still warm when Dr Miller, the GP, comes at nine: 'Poor Arthur, you didn't deserve this,' he says. And it is not much cooler—I know, I check—when Malcolm, the undertaker, arrives four hours later. He is fortyish, remembers me from primary school, is gangly in a grey suit with a Rotary Club badge on his left lapel: 'Oh dear, oh dear, Arthur,' he says, and doesn't know where to put himself.

He asks for a bowl of water, and while my mother is out of the room uses a long tweezery implement to shove a piece of cotton wool into my father's open mouth, where it rests (visibly) at the back of the tongue—'To stop any gases coming up,' he explains. My mother returns with the warm water. Malcolm takes a razor and for the next hour or so works away at my father's week-old stubble, 'just tidying him up.' I look at my mother and see that she is thinking what I am thinking—why bother with these cosmetics? Who will see him in the coffin? And even if he were to lie open for public viewing in a Chapel of Rest, who would mind the stubble? He might, I suppose: he was always a great one for checking whether I'd shaved. But he didn't like this sort of shaving himself—used only an electric razor—and would have resented the waste of manpower: better to have got Malcolm out doing something useful in the garden. If he'd been here, *really* been here, that's what he'd have been arranging.

But my mother and I are new to all this and yield to Malcolm's sense of etiquette. And at least it gives him something to do while he chats.

'I've done forty-eight of these this year—about one a week it works out, usually. It's a sideline, really, the undertaking. My main business is joinery. But I don't get much call for that these days, and you've got to make ends meet. There's nothing special you want, is there? No? Fine. Of course some people want the works, you know, the whole waxworks. It's amazing what you can do these days—some undertakers, they inject the client with formalin by sticking this tube into the neck artery, or you can drain the blood and urine off with an electric pump, and put these caps under the eyelids to make the eyes more rounded, sleep and peace, like. I don't hold with that: making a corpse like a plum instead of a prune, it's not right. Simple and clean, that's my philosophy.'

I wait for the moment when he will nick my father's chin— do the dead bleed less or more profusely than the living?—but he does it all spotlessly. I help him roll my father on to his side, so he can remove the pads from under him, wash his bottom and put a fresh nappy between his legs: it's dirty work. 'There may be more fluids,' he says. My father's body is a little stiffer now, but his back, as I hold him, is still warm, the skin red and corrugated where the sheet has wrinkled under him. 'This is why we come in fairly sharpish,' says Malcolm, 'before the rigor mortis. After twelve hours they can be very stiff and hard to move. After four or five days they go floppy again.'

My father always said that he'd never wear a shroud in his coffin, and he would not have wanted to waste a good suit. So now I help dress him in a pair of fawn cotton pyjamas. Malcolm hasn't batted an eyelid yet, any more than my father has, but as I hold the torso upright for him, he slips the right arm in the left sleeve and realizes his mistake only after finding the pyjama buttons are underneath my father's back. We lift the body and get the pyjamas off, then on again the right way. They won't button

up over the swollen stomach and zip scar, so we leave them open.
There's one final cosmetic act: the chin support, a small white
plastic hod or T to keep the jaw from dropping too far open.
Malcolm has some trouble adjusting the length of this: it's either
too short, leaving my father dopily open-mouthed, or too long,
clamming him up, unnaturally tight-lipped. Finally he jams the
stick end into the collar bone, an awkward riving process, and I
have to remind myself that this won't be hurting. My father, at
any rate, looks better for it: peaceful, no teeth showing.

'I should have said earlier,' Malcolm remarks as we draw the
sheets back up to the chin, hiding the hod support. 'That's a
pacemaker there, isn't it? I'll have to get the doctor to remove it
or come back with a scalpel myself. We have to take it out, you
see, if he's being cremated: it says so on the form, no HPMs.
There've been cases where they exploded.'

'I'd like to have it in that case—if it's not going to be used
by anyone else.'

'I'll check with the doctor. I'm sure that will be fine.'

Once Malcolm has gone I sit with my father again and touch
the little pacemaker box in his chest and slide it about under the
skin. Still warm, that chest, though it is six hours now since he
died and for two hours he has been exposed to cold air. But the
forehead is damp and Siberian. My mother sits across from me,
holding his hand. She has not cried properly yet: with each phone
call—and as the morning wears on there are more and more of
these—her eyes water and her lips tremble, but she does not
howl. Now, finally, she throws herself across him and sobs into
his cold neck and chest.

When did you last see your father?

When did you last see your father? Was it when they burned the
coffin? Put the lid on it? When he exhaled his last breath? When
he last sat up and said something? When he last recognized me?
When he last smiled? When he last did something for himself
unaided? When he last felt healthy? When he last thought he

might be healthy, before they brought the news?

The weeks before he left us, or life left him, were a series of depletions; each day we thought, 'He can't get less like himself than this,' and each day he did. I keep trying to find the last moment when he was still unmistakably there, in the fullness of his being, *him.*

When did you last see your father? I sit at my desk in the big cold basement of a new house, the one he helped me buy, his pacemaker in an alcove above my word processor, and the shelves of books have no more meaning than to remind me: these are the first shelves I ever put up without him. I try to write, but there is only one subject, him. I've lost sight not only of his life, what it meant and added up to, but of mine. When my three children come back from school, their cries echo emptily round the house, and I feel I'm giving them no more than a stranger could give them: drinks, attention, bedtime stories. Never to have loved seems best: love means two people getting too close; it means people wanting to be with each other all the time and then one of them dying. I feel as if an iron plate has come down through the middle of me, as if I were locked inside the blackness of myself, cold and futureless. I thought that to see my father dying might remove my fear of death, and so it did. I hadn't reckoned on it making death seem preferable to life.

When did you last see your father? The question hangs about, waiting to be answered. I try to remember where I first heard it asked, or saw it written. I invent contexts for it: in some sixties film, late at night, two drop-out bikers have begun to confide in each other about their pasts, and one asks the other, their Harley-Davidsons nearby, 'When did you last see your father?' A television documentary this time, and in the horrid brightness of a police interview room a kindly woman constable is coaxing what information she can from a fourteen-year-old Geordie boy found bruised and shivering in a shop doorway near Kings Cross: 'When did you last see your father?' Or maybe it was my own father who had used the phrase. I remember him telling me, at some point in my late teens or twenties when I was drifting away from him, seeing less of him, how badly he'd taken the death of his father, and how he didn't want this to happen to me. Maybe it was then he said it: 'I used to see Grandpa every weekend. But for some reason I'd not been over to Manchester for about six weeks, and he hadn't come to Thornton, and then he had his heart attack and was dead. There were rows we'd had we hadn't really settled, and that made me very guilty after. I remember someone at the wake asking "When did you last see your father?" and me feeling terrible.'

I want to ask the question of others and warn them: don't underestimate filial grief, don't think because you no longer live with your parents, have had a difficult relationship with them, are grown-up, a parent yourself—don't think that will make it any easier. I've become a death bore. I embarrass people at dinner parties. I used to think the world divided between those who have children and those who don't; now I think it divides between those who've lost a parent and those whose parents are still alive. Once I used to get people to tell me their labour stories. Now I want to hear their death stories—the heart attacks, the car crashes, the cancers, the morgues.

Letters come. They begin: 'I know no words can help at such a time.' Words like these do seem to help, a bit. No one can live inside another's body, feel another's pain; grief, like joy, must be experienced in isolation. But the letters suggest something different, a commonality, that is both a solace and a chastening. Others have known worse: how much worse for a spouse than for a son; how much worse to die at thirty-one (as a beautiful, intelligent woman I sit next to at a dinner does, of cancer, two weeks later) than to die at seventy-five, like my father.

Beside me on the desk is a new anthology, *A Book of Consolations*. There are plenty of brisk, snap-out-of-it sorts in there, like Walter Raleigh ('sorrows are dangerous companions . . . the treasures of weak hearts'), or Dr Johnson, who thought sorrow 'a kind of rust of the soul' and recommended, much as my father would have, the healing powers of fresh air and exercise. There is plenty of speciousness about death, too: nothing to worry about, says Plato; a 'dreamless sleep', a migration of the soul; the ruins of time becoming the mansions of eternity. I hate all this lying cheeriness and evasion. I think of Larkin in 'Aubade' seeing off religion,

That vast moth-eaten musical brocade
Created to pretend we never die,
And specious stuff that says no rational being
Can fear a thing it will not feel, *not seeing*
This is what we fear—no sight, no sound,
No touch or taste or smell, nothing to think with,
Nothing to love or link with,
The anaesthetic from which none come round.

The cursor pulses on the screen in front of me. What can I say about my father that others haven't said, more memorably, of theirs? Some of my friends and contemporaries have written moving elegies for their fathers. Even when my father was in the best of health, I used to sit mooning and tearful over their words as if they were for me, as if I'd written them myself. I wanted my father to hurry up and die so that I could join the club. I wrote an elegy for a friend of his, as preparation. I ran elegiac lines for him through my head. Now he's given me my opening, and the poems won't come.

I tell the therapist this. Yes, Dad, a therapist. I know that you don't approve, that you're down on analysts, male or female (and this one's female), and that, yes, *of course*, I should have shopped around, found a cheaper one, or at least asked: 'How much for cash?' (I supinely write the cheque.) But I have to talk to someone.

There is no couch in her room, though there are bean bags, and a baseball bat to hit them with. Myself, I don't use the baseball bat, nor scream, nor weep. I sit in a white canvas chair, the sort film directors have, and play back bits of my life. She asks me how I'm feeling, where I've got to now, what my body's telling me, and I find that sure enough my stomach's taut and hurting. She tells me I don't listen enough to my feelings, that I'm all head, no body or heart. She catches me smiling at critical points of my psycho-story, and this, she says, or gets me to say, is because I'm trying to distance myself ironically from my emotions. She tells me I'm a poor communicator, that I give out ambivalent signals. All of this is true, and helpful—so helpful that soon, I think, I shall stop seeing her.

In July I go up to Yorkshire—back at the house for the first time in seven months—the wind blowing through the delphiniums and the roses not yet deadheaded. The rustic fencing you put up is starting to rot. The raspberries have mildew—they're grey and squelchy like a dead mouse and dissolve ashily in the wind.

The ashes themselves, your ashes, have been kept in a big sheeny-brown plastic jar at the bottom of the wardrobe. Today is when we've chosen to scatter them. I take the jar down the garden, unscrew the lid, dip my hand in and taste a few grey specks: a smoky nothingness on my tongue. You, or your coffin, or a crematorium pick 'n' mix, how can I tell? My mother and sister come, having waited months for this moment, and we start to pour helpings of you among your favourite bits of the garden. We take it in turns, filling the lid of the jar with fine shale (like those upturned lids we used to fill with mouse poison and leave behind the fridge), then tossing the shale to the wind. The wind blows powder back in our faces; a speck catches in my sister's eye, her good eye; my trouser bottoms are sifted in volcanic dust. You cover the flower-bed like fine spray, every leaf variegated. We keep on scattering till the jar is tipped up for the last time—empty. My mother hugs my sister. I walk off with the jar, which is like a giant pill box, and hear your voice in the wind: 'Useful container that—I should hang on to it.' I stow it in the garage between the jump-leads and a shrunken plastic bottle of antifreeze.

Back in London, the therapist asks: 'How long did you say it had been now?'

'How long has what been?'

'Since the death. When did you last see your father?'

When did you last see your father? I remember the answer then. I tell her.

6

He isn't drinking, isn't eating. He wears his trousers open at the waist, held up not by a belt but by pain and swelling. He looks like death, but he is not dead and won't be for another four weeks. He has driven down from Yorkshire to London. He has made it against the odds. He is still my father. He is still here.

'I've brought some plants for you.'

'Come and sit down first, Dad, you've been driving for hours.'

'No, best get them unloaded.'

It's like Birnam Wood coming to Dunsinane, black plastic bags and wooden boxes blooming in the back seat, the rear window, the boot: herbs, hypericum, escallonia, cotoneaster, ivies, potentillas. He directs me where to leave the different plants —which will need shade, which sun, which shelter. Like all my father's presents, they come with a pay-off. He will not leave until he has seen every one of them planted: 'I know you. And I don't want them drying up.'

We walk round the house, the expanse of rooms, so different from the old flat. 'It's wonderful to see you settled at last,' he says, and I resist telling him that I'm not settled, have never felt less settled in my life. I see his eyes taking in the little things to be done, the leaky taps, the cracked paint, the rotting window-frames.

'You'll need a new switch unit for the mirror light—the contact has gone, see.'

'Yes.'

'And a couple of two-inch Phillips screws will solve this.'

'I've got some. Let's have a drink now, eh?'

'What's the schedule for tomorrow?' he asks, as always, and I'm irritated, as always, at his need to parcel out the weekend into a series of tasks, as if without a plan of action, it wouldn't be worth his coming, not even to see his son or grandchildren. 'I don't think I'll be much help to you,' he says, 'but I'll try.' By nine-thirty he is in bed and asleep.

I wake him next day at nine, unthinkably late, with a pint-mug of tea, unthinkably refused. After his breakfast of strawberry Complan he comes round the house with me, stooped and crouching over his swollen stomach. For once it's me who is going to have to do the hammering and screwing. We go down to the hardware shop in Greenwich, where he charms the socks off the black assistant, who gives me a shrug and a pat at the end, as if to say, 'Where'd you get a dad like this from?' Back home again, he decides that the job for him is to get the curtains moving freely on their rails. 'You know the best thing for it?' he says. 'Furniture polish. Get me a can of it and I'll sort it out for you.' He teeters on a wooden kitchen stool at each of the windows in the house, his trousers gaping open, and sprays polish on the rails and wipes it over with a dirty rag. His balance looks precarious, and I try to talk him down, but he is stubborn.

'No, it needs doing. And every time you pull the curtains from now on, you can think of me.'

I ask him about the operation: is he apprehensive?

'No point in being. They have to have a look. I expect it's an infarct, and they'll be able to cure that, but if not . . . well, I've had a good life and I've left everything in order for you.'

'I'd rather you than order.'

'Too true.'

I make sure there are only two light but time-consuming jobs for us. The first is to fix a curtain pole across the garden end of the kitchen, over the glazed door, and we spend the best part of two hours bickering about the best way to do this: there's a problem on the left-hand side because the kitchen cupboards finish close to the end wall, six inches or so, and you can't get an electric drill in easily to make the holes for the fixing bracket. The drill keeps sheering off, partly because I'm unnerved by him standing below, drawing something on the back of an envelope. I get down and he shows me his plan: a specially mounted shelf in the side wall to support the pole rather than a fixing bracket for it on the end. Sighing and cursing, I climb back up and follow his instructions in every detail—not just the size of screws and Rawl plugs needed, but how to clasp the hammer.

'Hold it at the end, you daft sod, not up near the handle.'

'Christ, Dad, I'm forty-one years old.'

'And you still don't know how to hold a hammer properly —or a screwdriver.' Infuriatingly, his plan works—the shelf mounting, the pole, the curtain, all fine. I try not to give him the satisfaction of admitting it.

We bicker our way into the next room and the other job: to hang the chandelier he once gave me, inherited from Uncle Bert. At some point in the move, many of the glass pieces have become separated, and now, in the dim November light behind the tall sash-window, we spend the afternoon working out where they belong, re-attaching them with bits of wire, and then strengthening the candelabras from which they dangle. 'This really needs soldering,' he says, meaning that he will find an alternative to soldering, since to solder would mean going out and spending money on a soldering iron when he has a perfectly good one at home. I watch him bowed over the glass diamonds, with pliers and fractured screw-threads and nuts and bits of wire: the improviser, the amateur inventor. I think of all the jobs he's done for me down the years, and how sooner or later I'll have to learn to do them for myself. The metal clasps joining glass ball to glass ball are like the clasps on his King Edward cigar boxes, and like those on his old student skeleton, Janet, whom we'd joined together once, bone to bone.

'I think that's it,' he says, attaching a last bauble. 'Three pieces missing, but no one will notice.' He stands at the foot of the step-ladder, holding the heavy chandelier while I connect the two electrical wires to the ceiling rose, tighten the rose-cover and slip the ring-attachment over the dangling hook. He lets go tentatively—'Gently does it'—unable to believe, since he has not done the fixing himself, that the chandelier will hold. It holds. We turn the light on, and the six candle-bulbs shimmer through the cage of glass, the prison of prisms. 'Let there be light,' my dad says, the only time I can ever remember him quoting anything. We stand there gawping upward for a moment, as if we had witnessed a miracle, or as if this were a grand ballroom, not a suburban dining-room, and the next dance, if we had the courage to take part in it, might be the beginning of a new life. Then he turns the switch off and it's dark again and he says: 'Excellent. What's the next job, then?'

IVAN KLÍMA

MY GOLDEN TRADES

Ivan Klíma had never imagined that he would become a smuggler. But then he had also never imagined that he would be an archaeologist. Or a courier. Or a surveyor's assistant. Or a train driver (though it had been his childhood fantasy). Nevertheless, when in the 1980s he was prevented from publishing his books by the Czech communist government, these were the jobs he found himself having to do. In this – the most personal of Klíma's books – they become occasions for the trade he does best: story-telling.

Published October 1992   £13.99

GRANTA BOOKS

VIKING

TODD MCEWEN
A VERY YOUNG
DANCER

I have a snapshot of the two of us: late on a summer afternoon we're playing in an inflatable wading pool. You can see in our faces that the water has gone cold, the sun too low now. I remember the day: my sister Moira, in the risible frilled bathing-suit of 1959, had deliberately leaned on the side of the pool and let the water out. After she'd done this ten times, I tried to drown her. That night I found my bed had been filled with giant rusting nails.

Between Moira and me there is love and fear and crankiness. And always her stubbornness. Before her stubbornness unfolded, gigantic, we played happily together. She Felix and I Poindexter.

At times I had to protect her.

The O'Gradys lived next door. Loud and knockabout, they were a large share of the pool of playmates. It wasn't possible to tell what 'play' with the O'Gradys might mean. It might be lots of fun or an O'Grady might hit you in the stomach as hard as he could. You might be building a magic fort, Mighty Mouse's redoubt itself, only to watch an O'Grady suddenly run into your own house and break something on your mother's vanity table. I have a picture of Moira with a huge scarf tied round her neck (she was Mighty Mouse that day), standing on the front porch with Kelly O'Grady. Later that day Kelly's brother Joe pushed Moira down on the rough driveway. She scraped her knee open, and I socked him in the belly, and another of Mrs O'Grady's Maginot Lines went up between our yard and theirs. She made them out of clothes-line, wheelbarrows, tampon boxes and rickety laths.

Here, another picture, 1961: a portrait in a cardboard frame stamped in gold, *La Playa Dance Studio*. There were many times in Moira's life when she wanted to be a dancer. The first was when she was a chubbette—as JC would say (JC is one of those men who met my sister in the 1970s and never forgot her). In this picture, she has glitter in her hair and is wearing a black leotard and blue tights; she's holding a spray of plastic flowers; behind her is a parasol. I can see Moira is already *away from the family*. She is doing things for her own secret reasons. Moira wouldn't have danced because others did, nor would she have taken any pleasure in its physicality.

Her reasons were deep, theatrical, almost religious.

But it was after she had given up dancing for the first time
—had not danced for many years—that Moira's stubbornness
really bloomed tough and rooty. She had fallen in love with beauty.
And then she added death. Death she liked.

She was getting attention as a poet in high school. She wrote
beautiful, dark sonnets, contrasting love and pain or, really, filling
love with pain. Sonnets, however, brought praise from teachers, and
good marks brought praise from Father. This Moira didn't want.

She wanted to do things she thought he could never really
understand, so she would never need his approval. Father, an only
child from the country, shy in school and not knowing how to
handle girls, has tried to protect her from her earliest days. She,
fierce, has always felt this as the big pillow of a smothering movie
fiend. They have now made a certain floating peace, though if
Father approaches Moira her eyes dilate and she breathes
apprehensively: fight or flight.

She's often said, *I was made to lie on couches, smoking
cigarettes and reading Russian novels.*

I saw her one day sitting on top of the back seat of someone's
MG, a very un-Californian scarf whipping in the wind. He was
driving fast, and Moira was laughing. Aside from the danger (I
have always feared for her life), this picture seemed *outré* for our
town. Who did she think she was?

An open patio door day in early summer when Grandfather
was still alive. He was beaming at a Tiffany carafe in the
china closet which caught the light, and was humming to
himself, as he would do at lunch. I remember his gaze turning
slowly to goggle at the arrival of Moira and Babette, her fellow
bohemian. Babette was a Bad Girl, the other rider on the MG
trunk. Her black hair had flapped, raven-like, a death-warning in
the breeze.

Moira and Babette arrived with suddenly thrusting prows: the
first brassière-less day of a life in which they finally had something
to be bra-less about. Grandfather giggling. Smiling, but only as he
smiled at any member of the family. We made him so happy.
Father choking really and turning red and giving up any pretence
at smiling, staring sidewise at the mobile and insistent breasts of

Babette. It was interesting to watch him try to formulate a Question for the Girls, while gagging and levering out of his mouth the large bite of pickle that had almost killed him.

Well hello, girls—where'd you get the sweaters?

This a genius bit of Fatherdom: the way he used his basso on *sweaters* maddened Moira because of course they weren't *sweaters* at all but blinding, breast-clinging leotards of turquoise and canary. Father's growl and bulging eyes told her she was living the last seconds of her unbra'd idyll. Moira and Babette to Moira's room. Grandfather smiling at me as we sat, briefly by ourselves, at the table. Insistences and fiats of undisguised rage and anguish, Father to Mother in the kitchen.

Moira decided to be a dancer—for the second time. By dancing, you can really die. Die for art and look like a pre-Raphaelite corpse at your suburban funeral, which will mock you. It's the beauty of consumptives. Death so near. Dancing, you whittle yourself down into something painful and fragile and then you smash it into a million pieces. On each shard is written a lot of things: Diaghilev, iced coffee, lower back pain.

TB is really the look—use kohl on your eyes and stop consuming everything but Diet Coke, Bubble Yum and Marlboro Lights. Stop feeding your brain. Rebel and rebel, against anything you might have learned while dramatically dying along with the Rossettis in that stifling high school.

A slow death may be exotic. It depends on the amount of eye make-up used. The whole idea of tragedy and art angers fathers.

Moira decided to defy Father in the things he stood for. She rocketed off from the reason and order accepted as the Way in our peacefully paranoid family. Spun away into bunkum, became the beautiful prey of the insights of the supermarket and men and women who have to invent and fib up everything in the world, so alone and left behind are they.

George Washington made bedspreads out of marijuana, she told me once.

Idly one day I opened a plastic Easter egg I found on her bureau. Inside was a suspect-looking pill. Mother was there. Doubt, denial, amphetamine followed; involvement of a blamed friend and then the blamed friend's parents. Mother and Father had looked into the abyss now. That a rogue pill was to be found in our house!

At sixteen she had an involved and highly secret affair with a defrocked minister and frocked kook with long blond hair and one of the original water-beds.

Moira I knew had gone her own way entirely. I knew there would be unimaginable men and locales, cars hinted at in crime dramas. No matter how sunny Moira would sometimes be, she had already left me and I knew I wouldn't be having her back.

Just yesterday I passed by the church where Moira married for the first time. It was not 'our' church, nor of our ostensible denomination, but in California anyone with a collar and an altar will marry you. A small pine hexagon on a quarter acre, it reeked of computer-land liberalism.

Moira's wedding was memorable in that I, as usher, seated everyone wrongly. They were pretty mad about it too. Though I had never had to calculate how to seat people in a hexagon.

Before the ceremony I wandered through the hall, which wrapped round the chapel like a ring box. Unexpectedly (all things were already out of my control), I came upon Ricky, the husband-to-be, and his best man Pierce. They were smoking Luckies (American courage?), and Pierce sheepishly pocketed a flask of something as I came up. They had used something else too. I tried to look into them, to see what it was that allowed people to experience fully moments like this.

I said something silly, like, *Ready gentlemen?* and went out into the chapel to face the sore clumps of guests I'd mismanaged.

No one believed in this, even the minister. The whole thing had an air of *shotgun* about it. Though who was aiming at whom?

Live together? With her friendly, naïve little lover, both of them a month out of high school?

You must think I'm crazy, Father had said.

If they had simply lived together, they would have parted friends. Instead, thanks to Moira's stubbornness, they built a Hell in Heaven's despite, and foundered.

Moira suspected Father of forcing them to marry in order to keep them apart. Very well—she would get married and keep house (expensive in our little town). By accepting Father's dare, she would win. It would be as sweet as living in sin. She knew it would bother him immeasurably, constantly, that she had married at an inappropriate age, clouding her future with short-sighted decisions.

Moira and Ricky sighed romantically over their collection of Rudy Vallee records. Ricky took a job in a furniture store. Moira began working for a sullen pharmacist. They paid their rent and acted a little smug towards Father, who seethed but, thwarted, could do nothing. They wondered what had happened to Art, ambition. Wondered if they'd ever had any. Moira crammed her personality into a kind of 1930s exoticism. She bought old lamps with fringes on the shades and took up *Sobranies*.

Los Angeles began to loom over them. Los Angeles, which sounds like Heaven until you say it out loud. Los Angeles, where people daily burn out like so many cigarettes smoked on *Dragnet*. Los Angeles, which loomed over Ricky who dreamt of acting and singing. Loomed over Moira, the exotic, the *danseuse*, the rebel. Los Angeles of the thirties, the bungalows, the palm trees. Life there would be what they enjoyed on their records. *Down there*.

Invent for yourself a map of *Duarte*, or some equally hapless Southland place: make half-dark plots under the off-ramps of freeways. See if you could live there.

Of these places and Moira's life there I have no understanding. Of these places and Moira's life there I have no pictures. I did not want to know the reasons Moira and Ricky had gone to Los Angeles. I assumed they thought the exotic would be found there.

Once I visited her; it was like viewing a diorama. It was a visit more with her apartment than with herself. Their Rudy Vallee furniture was there, but the fun, the play was gone. I could see Ricky's heart had gone out of everything. I could see there was nothing there.

I began to get severe, typed letters from Mother (she changed now from carefree script ball to lawyerly Courier) about Difficult Times and desperate little money-making schemes (Amway and worse) and how Moira and Ricky Still Loved Each Other Though. Which couldn't have been true: they were friends and young, and hadn't wanted, or expected, love. Or got it.

Moira's letters dried up entirely. Now when I do not hear from her I am fearful, fearful as can be. She goes from voluminous correspondence to silence, by decade it seems, or according to whom she is leaning on.

That year another bureau egg was opened and another grim little secret came out, or a few secrets, parts of an LA puzzle no one wanted to put together: I had a letter from Father. He had been to visit Moira. She was dancing, yes, in a nowhere-going studio with no connections to the larger, the real. To the *financial* world of dance, as he might have put it. Small studio under an off-ramp. And there was a man about, an older South American man no one liked the sound of.

Being South American was charming to Father, who fell down at the exact moment he should have been bringing his savage judgement to bear. On Los Angeles, on Moira, on the studio under the off-ramp, on South America. But if he must confront something he feels to be bad, he often shrugs and thinks the best of it. Of this older, not-good-seeming man. Who eventually backed my sister into a corner in her kitchen and did something very wrong. Hospital, phone calls, regrets, drinks, promises. We weren't capable of helping her.

In the spring I was told in a very roundabout way that Ricky had left. And that Moira was bound for New York! A *Footlight Parade* montage: train, telegraph wires, newspapers and calendars riffled by the unseen hand of fate. I could feel her being swept along by her unhappiness. Even though she had accomplished nothing, she would be elevated by the *act* of going to New York, she'd be a Star. But it wasn't as if they had invited her.

It seems hard to believe now, seems cruel and wrong that I was in New York when Moira was there, and almost never saw her. Seems like school, where we used to pass each other as if we were strangers; once in a while Moira would sing out my name, if she were in high spirits, but that was seldom. For my part I was secretive, pimpled, made speechless by the beauty and vivacity of her gang.

Some days in New York it seems there are friends in every

street, but I never ran into Moira. Sundays I would walk from Riverside Drive down Broadway to the Battery—a strange walk of which I never tired. Often around 14th Street, or sometimes at City Hall, I felt myself in a kind of tunnel. Tunnel through the city which felt empty of her. I would wonder where in the world she was and then remember, with a pang, that she was here. Somewhere.

I wondered what romance out of New York's many romances Moira was finding. On my walks, which I could have taken with her, I found romance in funny places; she and I are quite the same. The dark elevator banks in the RCA Building; outside the Wilke sisters' pipe shop on a rainy Madison Avenue Sunday; Fulton Street around two in the afternoon.

But what of exoticism? New York hasn't much to offer—except for money.

With her anti-heroine Babette, Moira shared a studio on the East Side, above a would-be jaunty nautical bar. The Old Rum Dog, filled most nights with the ordinary people of the commercial East Side of cake shops, expensive dry-cleaners and tiny hardware outlets. Moira and Babette had a sofa, a plant and a cat, Babette's from California. The few times I was in their apartment, the cat and I studied each other. She looked Californian: I wondered if we all did. She obviously felt ill at ease in the city, but she was *handling* it.

Moira's and Babette's was an apartment where it always seemed to be summer. Night noise from the Old Rum Dog and the permanently skewed bamboo blind which flapped in the open window, in the noisy breezes of August or the mad heat of the February radiator. Babette and Moira must have walked through the winter streets in stunned silence.

The exotic? Their apartment smacked more of 'That Girl' than Paris in the twenties.

Sitting with their cat, I used to think to myself, this is an apartment where men come. What men? For Babette, lanky Jewish actors and medical students. Babette meant to study acting. She had been to a studio under an off-ramp. For Moira? I didn't know —urban hippies perhaps, or cute disco guys with dog-shaped heads. Maybe Moira and Babette only socialized in the Old Rum Dog and never brought anyone up. The place was small and Moira always got ready to go out as soon as I arrived.

Moira danced. Moira was dancing and she was in New York: these were the facts with which she decorated her proscenium. Externally true, it was something she could say to people she might meet (in the Old Rum Dog?) or to Mother and Father or to irritating people from our town whom she encountered in her imagination. But she was not a professional dancer. Every morning she filled her dance bag with socks and cigarettes and got on the subway along with a thousand others and *took class.*

It was by the Ed Sullivan Theater; I met her there sometimes. I would have a sandwich or a frigid coffee-shop salad; Moira would have only coffee—she was eating nothing. And in these little coffee shops around Times Square, she would talk and talk, talk hugely, and I never learned a thing. She never revealed herself, her thoughts, her plans. I never heard her say what she thought was going to happen to her, or what she was doing there.

Ballet was really out of the question. When she began dance for the second time it was already so late that not even the most noxious, acaloric diet would put her in the ballerina's body. But this she refused to discuss; it was going to happen. Meanwhile the studio had connections enough—probably due to its location more than anything else; there was television work and the odd Broadway audition. Moira was in New York and Moira was dancing. Babette was in New York and Babette was an actress. Moira and Babette were each spending hundreds of dollars a week of their families' money and claiming to practise their professions.

Sometimes to our coffee-shop meetings I brought friends, guys I knew from college. Brought them along as tokens—or as evidence that there were people who didn't live on nicotine and chicle alone. Whereas they looked on Moira with admiration and interest, I was worried she could sniff them out as establishmentarians, no matter what they were wearing. I felt she looked painted and undernourished. Drawn. Pained. I like to think that meeting these men, if only for coffee and gum, kept Moira on some kind of track. At least reminded her there was a world that did not demand a pose.

Mitch, the painter, entertained her. *I really like that guy*, she said.

Now he always asks about her in a way which brings back the sharp chlorine taste of the icy glasses of water we'd have in those coffee shops.

Jay, the actor, took her out once. They went all over town visiting tourist spots until Jay, suddenly tired of Moira's perpetual mystery, announced, *The wallet is closed.* Moira liked him but has quoted me this ever after. She was used to depending on her looks so that she never had to spend any money: modest doors, and wallets, opened for her.

Jules, a doctor, took her out to dinner. After kidding her for a while in his usual way, he fell silent and meditated on how different life must be in California. All the while gazing at Moira, her coffee and dance gossip and gum. What she wanted after dinner was gum.

I could go for that guy in a big way, said Moira in her Goils Together, *Stage Door* voice. She was always so sunny, so much the game girl when she was with my friends—well, perhaps I did fail: Moira views us all as shallow and straight, and saves her darker passions for men who are a bit dangerous.

Before the hormones came she enchanted Father. Or perhaps charm is a better word: she wouldn't put enough effort into really beguiling anyone. But what, as JC asked me recently, will happen when that no longer works? Simply—ends? She'll be just another person, perhaps not Moira at all. A person on whom exoticism hangs awkwardly and whose romanticizing will sound shrill.

I went away from New York, transferred to a rain and snow location because I had once been romantic enough to say I liked such weather. Moira was rescued by a policeman: rescued from the tedium of her behaviour, to which she was blind, and from the tedium of New York, of which she was beginning to tire.

Did they meet in the Old Rum Dog? It must have been there. A young policeman whose mind often wandered in the directions of more money, showbiz and girls. But also a handsome and affable policeman, and therefore an unusual policeman. Moira was writing to me then, in the 'designer' hand she had perfected on her ubiquitous graph paper. The grid she plans her whole life on. I began to get letters about 'Hubby'. These lacked the hints I had come to look for, hints of a darker side to Moira's life. She sounded quite bubbly. She must be awfully bored, I thought. Where's the exoticism in someone who is cheerful and affable?

In high school Moira once spat on a policeman.

Mother participated without shame in the romance of this romance. A suburban newspaper reader, she was filled with joy that her little girl in New York had a personal policeman to walk her to her door.

In my far posting I would come in from the rain and find letters from Mother and Moira. Moira stating in a frankly unbelievable way how life was good (Moira is ever unconvincing expatiating on outward things). Mother chirped about Moira's *beau* and reminisced in a frankly unbelievable way about Father. I would read these letters sitting by the fire, my only source of heat, and after pondering them, I would slowly push them into the grate. It all seemed remote, insincere. Reaganomic. Irritating, compared with the lush green field I could see from my window.

Moira wrote of a romantic weekend she spent with Hubby in the Poconos. Hubby's idea of romance (now Moira's?): the heart-shaped bath. Under my rain-clouds, I wondered what Moira looked like. I wondered if in-room adult movies and komplimentary champagne were now to her taste, if these would fill her metabolic need for the exotic.

I grieved that none of my family could tramp with me down my muddy road, that they had to write me of such things, that I found in them no joy of the news of home.

The second time I didn't go. Mother's and Moira's letters, bubbling over with wedding plans. In my rainy place I felt I could not bear to watch college town meet Flatbush. Such an American confrontation I couldn't bear to face.

I experienced the wedding at my fireside. According to the letters, Moira and Hubby laughed all the way across town, from wedding to reception, laughed all the way in their horse-drawn cab. Laughed at the drizzle, the traffic. Moira blew kisses to people. My sister charmed the whole of Second Avenue that day.

At the reception everybody covered their ears against the

Texas swing band. Father recited an 'Encomium' he had written.
It united love and genetic theory in a way which perplexed pretty
much everyone. It brought tears to the eyes of the old family
friend who was blind drunk and died soon after.

According to the pictures—group shots at table, chasms of
incomprehension—there was a submerged battle here: between
those who knew how to act at parties and those who thought
parties a little bit low. Hubby's bruddas clapping him on the
back. Insinuatingly handsome boys with eyes as if mascara'd.
Their dates in all the finery of Thompson Street; fingernails to
scratch the eye of God.

The old family friend's eyes rolled up into his head. Moira
smiling with the tension of the ranks before her, with relief, with
joy. This was to be a real marriage: she was having a real
wedding. The tuxedos that were owned were confident and garish,
the rented tuxedos sober and a little too earnest.

Hubby's family ran a little old restaurant on Bleecker
Street. There were always soft lamps lit. Moira and
Hubby went to live in the neighbourhood.

Hubby's eyes were green as Italian cypresses. Moira had
found the exotic again. She had been looking for it on the East
Side but it was not to be found among stewardesses.

What were the exoticisms of the West Village? Was Moira
happily breathing in and out antique bohemianism? She and
Hubby lived upstairs from a man who sold curious books. These
weren't pornographic: their high prices coupled with their utter
uselessness was what disturbed you. A pamphlet: *Use of the Killing
Jar*. A catalogue of costumes *and* manacles used by Odd Fellows
and Rebekahs. A mouldy album of photographs, all close-ups of
the ankle straps on girls' shoes. But he was a very pleasant man.

On their street was a *frisson* of Mob; perhaps many 'love'
this about the West Village. Perhaps Hubby's whispered talk was
that, to Moira, of George Raft.

Moira had once told Hubby about South America and what
he had done to her in the kitchen. Had weeping told him after
one of their earliest tender moments. Not long after they moved
to the Village, Hubby whispered to her one night that South

116

America *had been taken care of*. Moira immediately made love to Hubby in a dark chill. It was exotic that Hubby could *say* that.

Hubby's trenchant sexuality she must have found exotic as well. Green eyes glowed on the Staten Island Ferry and they made their way to the rest room.

Poconos or no, marriage itself was exotic to Moira for a time; love lived and freely given and taken. Was the future really to become old? Moira never believed that. The old white-haired woman, who had married an Italian and lived out her life in the West Village?

Moira began to become Italian. Now was not the world of nightclub, now was learning street savvy. Now was learning to spend most of her time with other women, at vegetable stand and beauty parlour. Women you were now bound to; women you had bound yourself to be.

Everyone said she looked Italian (they meant she acted Italian).

I saw her briefly one Christmas. The Moira I recalled fondly as a pleasing, earthy girl was changed, thinner even than dancing thin (she was making excuses not to take class every day). Her voice had sailed high up her nose. She seemed to delight in low talk, recounting, as the other women did, the boasts and exploits of their men.

Did she know, as she parodied the lives of these people, that she was building a wall against them and not becoming one of them? That she must eventually offend them? Moira hadn't been absorbed; she hadn't adopted anything; it was the fun of being in a TV movie. She *thought* she loved them.

Take a boy born and raised in dazzle but not cold towards it like others of the city. Dazzled, off-kilter. Take the first, the tallest, the friendliest, the handsomest, the most loved by Ma. Start pushing him this way and that. Let him do well in school but remind him that it takes money to go on in school. Tell him how much the girls will like him; remind him that Catholics get married. But that Europeans fool around. Tell him he can do anything, anywhere, what do you want with this stupid showbiz anyway? Keep him tied so close to the house, the neighbourhood, that going to 14th Street for a guilty beer seems like going away to college. Take Hubby and his mother—please.

Sleaze puts everything in perspective. Hey, guys fool around, right? Sure. Everybody knows that. It's exciting. It's uptown. Sure, I meet plenty of girls like that on the job. The things they've done to me in the truck heading for the station. Let one or two slip away, you go around see 'em later. Hey.

Especially liked leggy ones with tight skirts and wet red lips. Liked them under the bridges, disarrayed against his bold cop car. Guys fool around, right?

What were the beginnings of Moira's suspicions? Hubby's clothes or Hubby's talk?

To better control the bruddas and to save money for their loose moonlighting enterprises, Hubby suddenly moved himself and Moira into Ma's house. Exoticism was at a low ebb surely. It was impossible to make love there without being judged by the furniture, the attentive walls. Recreation became a few lines, for them both.

Now Ma had everyone within reach and she was happy that they were so miserable. Especially Moira, who may *pass* for Italian but I don't trust that girl—she's not like us, why did you marry a girl like that, Hubby?

Moira completely gave up saying she was going to dance. She would fill her bag and take the subway uptown, but only to meet some dancers in one of the coffee shops near the studio. She dropped her ballet classes—claiming or admitting what to herself I don't know—and took only jazz. This was something she could do, and with Broadway and the television studios around the corner . . . She smoked more and starved herself —difficult at Ma's—to keep her figure. Being a dancer became looking like a dancer on the subway: gum, Diet Coke, bag—dancer. She began to take class twice a month. Hubby complained of the cost. Shades of Ricky.

This was sprained, that torn, another thing bruised. Finally Moira broke her toe and had to wear an ugly wrapping on it, like a Soviet summer shoe. Hubby complained about this too. A sick wife isn't glamourous. A sick wife is a drag on the family. Could

he already see her limping around the neighbourhood at fifty
with a cane and a few vegetables in her gnarled hands, Italian
peasant death already upon her? Hubby had his own nightmares.

On her trips uptown Moira took to looking at jobs posted in
windows, the windows of Times Square so often loved and hated.
The zoo needed someone for the penguins. She got the job, even
with the Soviet shoe. *Aw, hell, that's how penguins walk anyway,*
the man said.

Here for Moira was freshness in the city. Times Square and the
dirty jumble of the West Fifties had rejected her, had *broken her
foot.* Here, if not romance or nostalgia, was a new, clean ethic.
Perhaps she thought back on the beauties of California, on the
kook and the water-bed big as Marin County. Sun and green hills,
the stroking Pacific instead of John Calvin's Atlantic. Maybe Moira
romanticized the whole ecosystem, revived the chubbette's love of
animals, began to use it all as a weapon against Hubby and Ma and
the lacquered wives of the bruddas. Against the cold, dirty, heaped-
up slush which looked dirtier now without imaginary chase-lights.

I saw Moira at the zoo during a trip to New York. I got out
of the taxi and soon found myself in a pen with a female walrus
named Sitka. The walrus came at me with, it seemed, great
difficulty. Huge thing, a moving, silting hill, with a breath that
would wake the dead. That *was* waking them. Sitka rolled to a
halt two feet from me and wobbled. She held her head up,
regarding me sidelong, as a dog might.

She wants to shake hands, said Moira.

Stunned by Sitka's breath (which in fairness would be the
breath of anyone who ate raw fish only and had two-foot-long
teeth), I held out my hand, stiffly and high, as if it were a flipper.
Sitka teetered and for a moment I thought she was going to fall on
me; issued a huge blast of her mackerelly wind and there: she was
touching her flipper to mine. She seemed happy.

In the taxi I worried whether Sitka had really been pleased
to meet me. I thought, this is how Moira thinks.

Moira also got on very well with the penguins. One penguin,
Moe, always stood high above the others, on top of their artificial
ice cake. He would see Moira coming in the gate in the morning
and bray like a donkey. The others would straighten up,

organizing themselves, looking expectant. They loved Moira. Moira who one day made an awful mistake.

Under pressure, doing someone else's job, she became irritated at the penguins, who were taking a long time eating. She threw them some fish, and instead of eating it, they were goddamn *playing* with it. All over the place. It was the first day of spring and they were excited and happy. They threw the fishes, one to another, and hiccuped and brayed and laughed. They stumbled crazily around, the fish under their feet, giggling old ladies in a fun house. All the animals had to be fed at precise times, and Moira was running late.

I'm not going to give youse any more, she announced, *even though there's still some left. Your time's up. I can't fart around wit youse guys all day.* She always spoke to them in Brooklynese.

The penguins reeled back, surprised at being addressed so sharply, but they were careful to pay attention when Moira spoke to them. They loved her and tried hard to understand what she said: you could see it in their eyes.

Moira turned to go. Some of the penguins which lived with more gusto began to bray for fish. Moira spun round and put her pail on the ground, straddling it. The penguins grew quiet and gathered round her. Coach and team; reporters and the Mayor.

Listen youse guys, she said. *All gone!*

As if to the family dog. And suddenly clapped her hands with a bang.

Penguins vomit when frightened, to lighten themselves for escape. And vomit they did to a man. At Moira's deafening handclap, echoing off the smooth walls of their enclosure, they opened up and let fly. All over their fake iceberg and Moira.

She had to burn her clothes, not an easy thing in a house on Bleecker Street. Ma and the lacquered ones complained for weeks that the building smelled. Hubby acted as though he thought Moira had done this, *worked with animals*, to get at Ma. Bleecker Street was not a place where you could discuss marine ecology, even casually.

I saw Moira again the next winter—a sad little weekend when she visited me at my hotel. Hubby was on duty. We hit the coffee shops and took each other to some favourite places: the McAnn's where you go way downstairs, the lobby of the Woolworth Building. I showed her the outside of the Wilke sisters' place. She was drawn and adult. We talked in a dry way; I did not pitch my conversation at the level of concern I felt for her.

At one point she said, *This is a good marriage.* So insistent, yet so soft, so Moira looking out the window, that I was filled with pity.

Hubby had Ma to deal with, but the hardest thing he was up against was Moira's otherness. That is the rock upon which all men have founded their rebellion against her. Moira the poet, Moira the hugely silent, the more intelligent than thou. Moira who refuses to be told what to do or to be pinned down.

She was more and more alone as Hubby stayed out doing God knows what. I worried about drugs, alcohol. Moira was imprisoned in Ma's house with no one she could talk to; with several females intent on grinding Moira out of herself or—a more attractive prospect—on getting rid of her altogether.

Hubby took her to the Poconos, drank too much and abused her, in an even lower-rent heart-shaped bath than before.

Babette utterly fecklessly married an utterly feckless Jewish–Irish car salesman who really liked drugs. It seemed the four of them were to go on holiday together.

The idea of ordure at Key West. A tropical island paved from shore to shore, coral and pines dying daily; no beach to speak of but a dump of sand imported from Miami; the idea that *everything is available*: what do you want, man, what do you want? I got everything. Drug dealers, dipsomaniacs and dorks all crowded into the same heaving bars; music so loud it can't be heard. Dark looks from the island's underclass, hived off to shoot and stab each other in side-streets over who's first to please the tourists with deals, boys, girls. Unfamiliar yet temporarily pleasing drinks. Moira and Babette, the Goils, in new and tantalizing frocks and sudden tans: corners of their breasts unseen in New York. Buy straw hats and sponges and, half-smashed, make love under the midday air-

121

conditioner, head back to the bar to meet up and score a few lines—what bad-kid bliss. Life is a breeze in the Florida Keys.

Moira had found a new moon to think about. A real tropic moon, framed by palms. Sultry nights in hut-like bars, rooms with ceiling fans. What was she communing with? Perhaps the whole place was becoming Havana. She liked the crowd she met in between fights with Hubby—who spent the whole time bombed— and watching Babette fight with her madman.

Were Moira and Babette, in the fortress of their togetherness, the cause of so much seeking of black holes by Hubby and the screwball? Wasn't Hubby reminded that Moira wasn't like him, the whole time he bought hats and drinks and drugs? Moira wasn't having a good time like she should. Like the girls in the neighbourhood would. Like the girls under the bridge against his steering-wheel.

Everyone agreed it was tremendous fun. Moira agreed tiredly, Babette sceptically, the nut madly, Hubby, depleted, angrily. His holiday stung him in the middle of La Guardia Airport: Moira was not playing along. She wasn't playing along with Ma and the other girls. He felt lonely with Moira. She isn't like us and she's driving me fucking crazy and so is Ma and everyone else.

Back through streets which were complicated with nostalgia and half-thoughts. Back to the house and the silences of Ma. Back to restraining themselves in every way in a place which was stifling, whatever the month.

Stifled: Moira's strange exuberances which were never about subjects that Ma and the girls understood. Stifled: dancing—far away now on some X-ray in a midtown file drawer. Stifled: Hubby's idea of himself, powerful at something, instead of being saddled with Ma and the bruddas and a growing *iconoclast* for a wife.

Hubby began to envy the dullest of his brothers, Paul, paid only enough for beer and cigarettes and a line or two, in cash, at the end of every day. Who gruntingly wolfed down Ma's pasta and was petted by her. Whose face was the simple one at the base of any totem-pole.

Moira's letters to me stopped completely.

A few weeks after fun in the sun, Hubby was more off his head than on, more under the bridges than ever before. He even picked up girls from outside the Tunnel. He spent his money on vodka and drugs.

Moira wasn't working. She seemed to need most of her time now just to be Moira, as if by spending time alone in her room, away from the others, she could somehow grow strong again.

All came to nought: a broken mirror, food all over the walls, Ma shrieking but in secret delight, Hubby drunk and more—standing frightened over Moira, crumpled and bleeding in the kitchen corner.

She moved out immediately—went uptown to a dancing friend. She didn't speak to Hubby and didn't go back. He arrived four or five times, soulfully addressing his side of the door, claiming to love her, claiming to have flowers. Moira never opened it. She never said a word. He would return, hours later, loud and abusive and raging, pounding the door with his fists and once attacking the hinges with a crowbar. The last time he said he had a gun.

He was a sick policeman with a mother who had killed the life in him, and he was going to learn about Moira's determination, that quality she had been putting in her storehouse for years—choosing not to use it in school, not being able to see it bear fruit in dance. She would go away from Hubby and never see him again. He had *interrupted* her.

The phone rang, next to the window on my rainy field. Nothing had happened to my field but rain successive to sun; it didn't seem as if enough time had passed in the field for these things to have happened to Moira.

Can't you come here and help me? she said. *I'm moving to Florida. Hubby's been hitting me. I'm sick now.*

The whole family had left the building on Bleecker Street. The restaurant was closed for the afternoon. I could see that the street, the halls and this room were echoing for Moira. I taped boxes together and she filled them.

You might think you would somehow recognize the *things* of someone of your own blood; I found myself unbelieving in the face of her kitchenware. *These* plates? The witnesses of Hubby's cruelty. Moira divided their material life down the middle: six tumblers each, six sets of flatware; she got the antique mirror and he got the sofa.

I watched her pack her clothes, clothes that were not Moira: vivid blouses, restrictive skirts, bright stuff with shoulder pads like Fallingwater. What sort of places had these evening gowns been worn to? Had they ever got above 14th Street? Was Moira happy when she stepped out in them? Or did the ends of evenings have scripts already?

These clothes were what they were trying to make her. What use would they be in Florida? She wasn't going to be that person now.

We waited for the movers. I dragged a heavy trunk across the floor, gouging the wood. From that point on, Hubby only talked about money: did she have to wreck the joint? Moira sat and smoked and kept cleaning up after herself until the last minute, the way she'd learned from the Women with Nothing Else To Do: picking up the tiniest flecks of ash with a licked fingertip. Life in this house, I thought.

The movers took away Moira's junk. The building was still silent, but I knew someone would be watching from across the street. In a drawer she found an unfamiliar lipstick and cried. It was startlingly red.

A dull day had turned a brilliant, warm blue. We drove uptown with a wacky cabbie who flirted with Moira. He wore his dark glasses on a string and had a tropical shirt. She enjoyed it. Was she in Florida already?

Life is a breeze in the Florida Keys. Life is a breeze in the Florida Keys. Life is a breeze in the Florida Keys. Moira's mantra: she had begun saying it because she thought it was corny and funny; now she was clinging to it.

The day after moving Moira out, we took an awful series of short flights in the interest of economy. We were punch-drunk with the events of the week by the time we got on the plane. Moira sat in the back, near the tail, where she always feels safe. Wants to be *the last to go*. Sat in the back near the tail smoking and having bottled cocktails and even eating a little.

I couldn't bear to look at Moira so damaged and thin and hurt. She had that hopeful, hangy look children put on in times of great pain. They don't know everything can always get worse.

At Memphis, we stumbled off the plane and rambled along unfamiliar hallways and ramps. Moira chided me for buying a local paper. We sat down, stunned, in a coffee shop and decided to eat. We were together now (having been apart on the plane) and Moira took up her slow, quiet diatribe: what had happened to her and Hubby, her *epic*. Full of it already, but listening, I got up for mustard. Moira's shocked face told me it wasn't a moment to leave the table. I registered this but felt caught in the act. *Well, goodbye!* I said, waving jauntily and hurrying away. She laughed loudly, and I thought, why, this *is* Moira that I have with me.

We laughed again at Miami. We laughed at a big red suitcase which was making the rounds of all the baggage carousels, like a dog looking for its forgetful mistress. Where are you a-headin', Big Red? How long will you wander?

Life is a breeze in the—

I hated Florida on sight. As soon as we stepped out of the plane at Key West I felt I had never washed my clothes. I felt as if I were zitted, I felt the way you do when you wear too much clothing to the theatre.

By taxi to Cap'n Spinney's Motel, agreeably crummy, with old-fashioned matchbooks of which we both approved. It was late but Moira was going to call her gang. She needed to walk in somewhere, surprisingly, beautifully, remarkably, upon these people where she'd determined she'd found a home.

At a big table heaped with Japanese food I took a step into Moira's life such as I had never done. Midnight: we were both loopy from the flight and the strain of the past week. Moira didn't seem relieved. Indeed, she was overwrought: she was still poised on New York's threshold, not Florida's. But after the airplane drinks and mixed nuts and things that blow dry air in your face, the food was restoring and the beer refreshing. Who was paying?

Moira was ignoring me now—that was fine. She needed to take her shoes off and sink, away, alone. I tried not to be

125

sceptical of the ooze.

She has always assumed that anyone with a drink is *fine* anyway.

I found myself talking to some people from everywhere. People who had been kicked out, or had kicked themselves out, of every state, job, marriage and idea there is. These were people who had daily quelled their gorges, day after day battling unknowing as Moira had done, in some other place, off-island, off-key and had vacationed here—stunned by the brilliance, the availability, the *pleasing drinks* of life once they had walked out of their offices, coffee shops, off-ramp studios and on to the plane and Key West. A riot of availabilities. These are people you read about but would never want to know, people who after two weeks of pleasing drinks and erections decide to *move* to the place where they've had their holiday.

They had all run away and forgotten, easily or with help, everything about life. Each decided to build a little network of crimes and guilty pleasures and take that for the world. They do not know that pleasure does not have to be paid for. They do not know that there are people in the world who need them.

Words rot in Key West: the news is controlled by knobs next to the air-conditioner; it's something to be turned down, then off by the bartender when you shamble, blissful, in.

Moira was pale and intense and trembling a little. Japanese food was not for her. The beer seemed only to have magnified her needy state. She was talking ardently, worried, to a curly man named Willy. He had arrived at the restaurant half an hour after we did. Moira had been on the phone to him, and a few others, from Cap'n Spinney's. I remembered Willy's name; he had seemed expectant, hopeful, happy when he arrived. He looked a little sombre now that Moira had been talking to him for half an hour.

Here, she had brought him a whole planeful of New York, of the mad thoughts you have in limbo. The longings you feel, the loves, in airports and airplanes. Willy was going to find out what it was to be the particular focus of Moira. She was explaining it, if he but knew, through a miasma of hiding places, cigarettes, Diet Coke, bubble gum, her first marriage, Xanax, sushi and beer. Explaining, tragic, quite beautiful. Pale and nervous side by side with the chubby complacency of all these people who had given up.

I figured I knew the score, now that I knew Moira had selected someone, that there was a partner with whom she'd dream up moon and palm. I supposed Moira would disappear into what trailer or boat or rotting apartment Willy had, and that I would have several humid days to myself with no one to talk with, and Moira speaking to me already from inside the Romance of the Tropics. But it wasn't like that: around one in the morning I saw Moira and Willy holding hands, at arm's length, looking at each other. He made to go and she pulled him closer, intent on kissing him, which he manoeuvred into lightly, on the cheek. She seemed happy enough with that and watched him leave. He seemed to know that something large and troubling had arrived for him.

Moira and I went back to Cap'n Spinney's, back to our refrigerated room. I got in bed and slept; Moira smoked for several hours and toyed with a bottled cocktail she'd been too preoccupied to drink on the Memphis–Miami flight. She sat by the air-conditioner and looked out at Cap'n Spinney's pool, which glowed murkily and suggested *organism*.

She began looking for a place the next day. Father had sent her some money but it wasn't a lot: not like the life's savings you saw people blowing on every corner. The humidity appalled me. Just in walking from Cap'n Spinney's to the T-shirt shops, Cuban cafés and bars that constituted everyone's complete errands, I was oppressed, depressed and drenched. After three hours I felt *I* had lived the lives you saw oozing away and softening in the faces on Duval Street.

We began visiting realtors, New York women in severe, air-conditioned offices who hadn't any idea why someone would come to Key West, except that people were renting. Moira wanted a more tropical realtor. We found several—lounging at wickerwork desks in clean cut-offs and tropical shirts, and studying Moira. Eyes offered lower rents than mouths. I feared for her, but knew I had to let go of this. I would soon be back in my rainy place. Perhaps Willy was a good man and would look out for her. He didn't look ready to. Moira was phoning him rather more often than he'd anticipated. Willy kept the tropical boulevardier's extended night, but she wasn't sleeping at all.

Moira didn't want to share a house. There were two kinds of apartments: strange buildings from the 1930s, lino'd and fluorescent lighted in the 1950s into horror-movie sets, where echoes never quite stopped; and over-detailed efficiencies in poorly remodelled houses—inept tilework and cheap, ornate ceiling fans.

There is nowhere for normal people to live, I remarked to Moira on the street. She glanced at me, rueful and chastened by the rents.

She looked longingly at these overdone boxes while the hungry realtors watched her. Her money would not last long, especially as she was acting as though she were on holiday. Which is how everybody acts in Key West—until they run out of money. Then Key West loses interest in you. You become something tourists turn away from.

I have never had such a difficult parting. I had to go back to my rain. I felt I might expire in the shallows of Key West. For the first time I felt I was abandoning her, crabbed and mean. I felt resentful that Moira hadn't, couldn't have visited me in the rainy place. I wanted her to see that people can live with themselves. That they can love each other. That life can be believed.

We drank a bit, Moira and I, the night before I left. I was rocked in the taxi and knocked side to side in the little plane. When I got to Miami I ordered two Pepsis and two beers, and left the beers on the bar as if they had suddenly become giant combination breakfasts, greasy, steaming and odious.

Moira bloomed. This was one of her bloomings. Moira, whose body, speech and self change to suit the drama and the romance of the day. And the danger. Moira, who as I have grown to love her has gone from chubbette to feisty earth mother to strange, spooky, rickety dancer to a loud, over-toiletted, tough, scrawny Carmine Street cackler. To abused divorcee, drawn and introspective. To tropical flower: her wavy hair lustrous with coconut oil, vibrant colours on her eyes and lips. In the snapshots she has sent me from time to time, she and

Willy in front of their motel room, I have seen her silky brown legs. Moira lovely, piquant and raw, shackled to something.

Along with everyone on Key West, Moira now worships the wrecked people: Isadora, Patsy Cline, Elvis, Judy Garland. We're wrecked too and we hear you singing.

Drugs. A hole down which I do not want to lose her. But what could I do from the rainy place? Really, drugs are the *jewel* of the Republican economy, not at all its nemesis. Drugs are the business of the place, not straw hats or pleasing drinks or sponges. Drugs. Perhaps: she is there and so are they and that is all there is to say.

She sank. About waist-deep, ran aground on the reef of the waiters, bartenders, hangers-on. Life is a breeze in the Florida Keys: this is what Moira now believes. The people she follows are as damaged and unworldly as a bunch of actors, and as theatrical in their comings and goings and weepings. Their little tragedies, seasonal matings, scenes of anger and regret.

So it was Moira on the phone this morning, alone again.

He's gone. Moving out. I feel sad.

I told her I would go to see her. I pictured being rocked in the little plane, the air-conditioner at Cap'n Spinney's and the pleasing drinks and the dangers there.

I remembered Moira staring out all night at the murky pool, loved her, and did not say so.

IF YOU CARE ABOUT

FREEDOM OF EXPRESSION

IF YOU'RE WONDERING WHAT YOU CAN DO ABOUT

CENSORSHIP IN THE ARTS

IF YOU'RE CONCERNED ABOUT THE FUTURE OF THE

NATIONAL ENDOWMENT for the **ARTS**

THEN YOU SHOULD JOIN

THE LITERARY NETWORK.

The Literary Network is a new project, jointly administered by Poets & Writers and The Council of Literary Magazines & Presses (CLMP). LITNET will coordinate public education and advocacy efforts around issues pertaining to freedom of expression. If you're a writer, editor, librarian or bookseller (or someone else who cares about these issues), you need LITNET (and LITNET needs you). To be added to our mailing list and receive our free newsletter, please write:

THE LITERARY NETWORK

COUNCIL OF LITERARY MAGAZINES & PRESSES
154 CHRISTOPHER STREET #3C
NEW YORK NEW YORK 10014

LOUISE ERDRICH
THE NAMES OF
WOMEN

Louise Erdrich

*I*kwe is the word for woman in the language of the Anishinabe, my mother's people, whose descendants, mixed with and married to French trappers and farmers, are the Michifs of the Turtle Mountain reservation in North Dakota. Every Anishinabe *Ikwe*, every mixed-blood descendant like me, who can trace her way back a generation or two, is the daughter of a mystery. The history of the woodland Anishinabe—decimated by disease, fighting Plains Indian tribes to the west and squeezed by European settlers to the east—is much like most other Native American stories, a confusion of loss, a tale of absences, of a culture that was blown apart and changed so radically in such a short time that only the names survive.

And yet, those names.

The names of the first women whose existence is recorded on the rolls of the Turtle Mountain Reservation, in 1892, reveal as much as we can ever recapture of their personalities, complex natures and relationships. These names tell stories, or half stories, if only we listen closely.

There once were women named *Standing Strong*, *Fish Bones*, *Different Thunder*. There once was a girl called *Yellow Straps*. Imagine what it was like to pick berries with *Sky Coming Down*, to walk through a storm with *Lightning Proof*. Surely, she was struck and lived, but what about the person next to her? People always avoided *Steps Over Truth*, when they wanted a straight answer, and *I Hear*, when they wanted to keep a secret. *Glittering* put coal on her face and watched for enemies at night. The woman named *Standing Across* could see things moving far across the lake. The old ladies gossiped about *Playing Around*, but no one dared say anything to her face. *Ice* was good at gambling. *Shining One Side* loved to sit and talk to *Opposite the Sky*. They both knew *Sounding Feather*, *Exhausted Wind* and *Green Cloud*, daughter of *Seeing Iron*. *Center of the Sky* was a widow. *Rabbit*, *Prairie Chicken* and *Daylight* were all little girls. *She Tramp* could make great distance in a day of walking. *Cross Lightning* had a powerful smile. When *Setting Wind* and *Gentle Woman Standing* sang together the whole tribe listened. *Stop the Day* got her name when at her shout the afternoon went still. *Log* was strong, *Cloud Touching Bottom* weak and consumptive. *Mirage* married *Wind*.

Elise Eliza McCloud with her husband, standing in front of their new house (1940).

Everyone loved *Musical Cloud*, but children hid from *Dressed in Stone*. *Lying Down Grass* had such a gentle voice and touch, but no one dared to cross *She Black of Heart*.

We can imagine something of these women from their names. Anishinabe historian Basil Johnston notes that 'such was the mystique and force of a name that it was considered presumptuous and unbecoming, even vain, for a person to utter his own name. It was the custom for a third person, if present, to utter the name of the person to be identified. Seldom, if ever, did either husband or wife speak the name of the other in public.'

Shortly after the first tribal roll, the practice of renaming became an ecclesiastical exercise, and, as a result, most women in the next two generations bear the names of saints particularly beloved by the French. *She Knows the Bear* became Marie. *Sloping Cloud* was christened Jeanne. *Taking Care of the Day* and *Yellow Day Woman* turned into Catherines. Identities are altogether lost. The daughters of my own ancestors, *Kwayzancheewin—Acts Like a Boy* and *Striped Earth Woman*—go unrecorded, and no hint or reflection of their individual natures comes to light through the scattershot records of those times, although they must have been genetically tough in order to survive: there were epidemics of typhoid, flu, measles and other diseases that winnowed the tribe each winter. They had to have grown up sensible, hard-working, undeviating in their attention to their tasks. They had to have been lucky. And if very lucky, they acquired carts.

I t is no small thing that both of my great-grandmothers were known as women with carts.

The first was Elise Eliza McCloud, the great-granddaughter of *Striped Earth Woman*. The buggy she owned was somewhat grander than a cart. In her photograph, Elise Eliza gazes straight ahead, intent, elevated in her pride. Perhaps she and her daughter Justine, both wearing reshaped felt fedoras, were on their way to the train that would take them from Rugby, North Dakota, to Grand Forks, and back again. Back and forth across the upper tier of the plains, they peddled their hand-worked tourist items— dangling moccasin brooches and little beaded hats, or, in the summer, the wild berries, plums and nuts that they had gathered from the wooded hills. Of Elise Eliza's industry there remains in the family only an intricately beaded pair of buffalo horns and a piece of real furniture, a 'highboy', an object once regarded with some awe, a prize she won for selling the most merchandise from a manufacturer's catalogue.

The owner of the other cart, Virginia Grandbois, died when I was nine years old: she was a fearsome and fascinating presence, an old woman seated like an icon behind the door of my grandparents' house. Forty years before I was born, she was photographed on her way to fetch drinking water at the reservation well. In the picture she is seated high, the reins in her fingers connected to a couple of shaggy fetlocked draft ponies. The barrel she will fill stands behind her. She wears a man's sweater and an expression of vast self-pleasure. She might have been saying *Kaygoh*, a warning, to calm the horses. She might have been speaking to whomever it was who held the camera, still a novel luxury.

Virginia Grandbois was known to smell of flowers. In spite of the potato picking, water hauling, field and housework, she found

Elise Eliza McCloud and Justine Gourneau (1927).

the time and will to dust her face with pale powder, in order to look more French. She was the great-great-granddaughter of the daughter of the principal leader of the *A-waus-e*, the Bullhead clan, a woman whose real name was never recorded but who, on marrying a Frenchman, was 'recreated' as Madame Cadotte. It was Madame Cadotte who acted as a liaison between her Ojibway relatives and her husband so that, even when French influence waned in the region, Jean-Baptiste Cadotte stayed on as the only trader of importance, the last governor of the fort at Sault St Marie.

By the time I knew Virginia Grandbois, however, her mind had darkened, and her body deepened, shrunk, turned to bones and leather. She did not live in the present or in any known time at all. Periodically, she would awaken from dim and unknown dreams to find herself seated behind the door in her daughter's house. She then cried out for her cart and her horses. When they did not materialize, Virginia Grandbois rose with great energy and purpose. Then she walked towards her house, taking the straightest line.

That house, long sold and gone, lay over one hundred miles due east and still Virginia Grandbois charged ahead, no matter what lay in her path—fences, sloughs, woods, the yards of other families. She wanted home, to get home, to be home. She wanted her own place back, the place she had made, not her daughter's, not anyone else's. Hers. There was no substitute, no kindness, no reality that would change her mind. She had to be tied to the chair, and the chair to the wall, and still there was no reasoning with Virginia Grandbois. Her entire life, her hard-won personality, boiled down in the end to one stubborn, fixed, desperate idea.

I started with the same idea—this urge to get home, even if I must walk straight across the world. Only, for me, the urge to walk is the urge to write. Like my great-grandmother's house, there is no home for me to get to. A mixed-blood, raised in the Sugarbeet Capital, educated on the Eastern seaboard, married in a tiny New England village, living now on a ridge directly across from the Swan Range in the Rocky Mountains, my home is a collection of homes, of wells in which the quiet of experience shales away into sweet bedrock.

Elise Eliza pieced the quilt my mother slept under, a patchwork of shirts, pants, other worn-out scraps, bordered with small rinsed and pressed Bull Durham sacks. As if in another time and place, although it is only the dim barrel of a four-year-old's memory, I see myself lying wrapped under smoky quilts and dank green army blankets in the house in which my mother was born. In the fragrance of tobacco, some smoked in home-rolled cigarettes, some offered to the Manitous whose presence still was honoured, I dream myself home. Beneath the rafters, shadowed with bunches of plants and torn calendars, in the nest of a sagging bed, I listen to mice rustle and the scratch of an owl's claws as it paces the shingles.

Elise Eliza's daughter-in-law, my grandmother Mary LeFavor, kept that house of hand-hewed and stacked beams, mudded between. She managed to shore it up and keep it standing by

Virginia Grandbois LeFavor on her way to fetch drinking water (1932).

stuffing every new crack with disposable diapers. Having used and reused cloth to diaper her own children, my grandmother washed and hung to dry the paper and plastic diapers that her granddaughters bought for her great-grandchildren. When their plastic-paper shredded, she gathered them carefully together and one day, on a summer visit, I woke early to find her tamping the rolled stuff carefully into the cracked walls of that old house.

It is autumn in the Plains, and in the little sloughs ducks land, and mudhens, whose flesh always tastes greasy and charred. Snow is coming soon, and after its first fall there will be a short, false warmth that brings out the sweet–sour odour of highbush cranberries. As a descendant of the women who skinned buffalo and tanned and smoked the hides, of women who pounded berries with the dried meat to make winter food,

137

who made tea from willow bark and rosehips, who gathered snakeroot, I am affected by the change of seasons. Here is a time when plants consolidate their tonic and drop seed, when animals store energy and grow thick fur. As for me, I start keeping longer hours, writing more, working harder, though I am obviously not a creature of a traditional Anishinabe culture. I was not raised speaking the old language, or adhering to the cycle of religious ceremonies that govern the Anishinabe spiritual relationship to the land and the moral order within human configurations. As the wedding of many backgrounds, I am free to do what simply feels right.

My mother knits, sews, cans, dries food and preserves it. She knows how to gather tea, berries, snare rabbits, milk cows and churn butter. She can grow squash and melons from seeds she gathered the fall before. She is, as were the women who came before me, a repository of all of the homely virtues, and I am the first in a long line who has not saved the autumn's harvest in birch bark *makuks* and skin bags and in a cellar dry and cold with dust. I am the first who scratches the ground for pleasure, not survival, and grows flowers instead of potatoes. I record rather than practise the arts that filled the hands and days of my mother and her mother, and all the mothers going back into the shadows, when women wore names that told us who they were.

LUC SANTE
THE CONTENTS
OF POCKETS

Time in its passing casts off particles of itself in the form of images, documents, relics, junk. These forms repose in cardboard boxes and closets, in old houses and attics, in filing cabinets and mini-storage warehouses, in museums and libraries. In a great city such as New York there are collections of artefacts and bone-yards of information everywhere. One such collection is the Municipal Archives, which occupies a lower corner of the old Beaux-Arts Surrogate's Court building at Chambers and Centre Streets, and which contains birth and death and marriage records, the files of former mayors and district attorneys, the leavings of city commissions and departments. It is cool and well-lit, not musty, and every day researchers and genealogists sit at the microfilm readers dowsing their way through copies of, say, the 1895 Police Census, looking for a faint footprint that may have been left there by someone who cannot be recalled in any other fashion.

I worked there as well and on my third visit, I was approached by the director, Kenneth Cobb, who wondered if I'd be interested in seeing the Police Department photo collection. A library cart was wheeled out from a back room, laden with fifteen fat ring-binders in archival boxes. As soon as I pulled out the first volume and began leafing through the pages of prints, my eyes widened. Nothing in the reams of photographic documentation I'd sorted through—countless inert pictures of buildings, posed ranks of functionaries, fuzzy views of empty streets—had prepared me for this. Here was a true record of the texture and grain of a lost New York, laid bare by the circumstances of murder. Lives stopped by razor or bullet were frozen by a flash of powder, the lens according these lives their properties—their petticoats and button shoes and calendars and cuspidors and beer bottles and wallpaper. The pictures were not just detailed documents, either, but astonishing works in their medium. I thought I had come across the traces of a forgotten master, who seemed to prefigure the pitiless flashlit realism of Weegee while having affinities to Eugène Atget's passionate documentary lyricism. A style announced itself, deliberate and inimitable.

Confusingly, the photographs in the albums were organized by no principle that I could detect. Although there were 1,400 images in the collection, considerably fewer were actually represented by prints: the negatives were glass plates, many cracked, ruinously chipped, or their emulsion stuck to the envelopes in which they had been stored. The captions were erratic. A truly enigmatic image might yield up no more information than 'homicide victim male interior'. The most I was able to ascertain was that the pictures dated from between 1914 and 1918, a slice of the New York Police Department's documentation that had been extracted, shaken up and then dropped.

The pictures would not leave me alone and I returned a number of times to look at them, until finally plunging into the task of investigating their context and the circumstances of their making.

The collection, I eventually learned, was the only one to survive a 1983 clean-out of the old police headquarters on Centre Street, when workers removed roomfuls of files and dumped them into the East River. The city's archivists were informed too late, but, according to John R. Podracky, now curator of the Police Academy Museum, they got there in time to find a small room under a staircase that had been overlooked. It contained filing cabinets that held those 1,400 plates, housed in manila envelopes, neglected for nearly three-quarters of a century and allowed to deteriorate.

The Panther Boys three men shot (no homicide). Injured were John Russell, Jerome Geigerman, and George Cisneros.

The location might be a political club, but the size of the room suggests a meeting hall for one of the many fraternal organizations (Odd Fellows, Knights of Pythias, Ancient Order of Foresters). The scuff marks suggest the aftermath of a function, which may have been held not by the regular tenants of the hall, but by one of the gangster-connected associations which specialized in 'rackets', balls organized for the purpose of making profits on ticket sales and the rake-off from the bar. It is probably not by design that the photographer focused on the floor-boards and the chair and piano-stool to the right to the exclusion of the rest of the room, which gives the photograph an unwarranted air of mystery. In fact, the case in question here is probably a very simple one, an intra-gang brawl. The men seated on the left are the presumed gang members (a few of them trying to conceal their identities), while the standing figures and possibly the men on the right are police. Those seated forms all the way at the rear might be the injured parties. Of these, John Russell and George Cisneros dissolve into history, but the name of Jerome Geiger would turn up later in the *New York Times*: once in 1918, when he was picked up as a member of an auto theft ring (shifting more than five hundred cars a year, not a small number for the time), and again in 1925, when he was held as part of a gang of rum-runners. From the file number, the case can be dated approximately as early December 1915.

Double homicide #708 6/17/15.

Two bodies, no weapon and the clear indication (a bloodied pillowcase) that one party died in bed: a crime of passion or an anachronistic gangland-style execution? The missing weapon proves a red herring, however, as the date points the way to newspaper accounts, among which the following, in the *New York American*, seems definitive:

WIFE SLAIN BY A SUITOR NONE KNEW
MAN WHO KILLED MRS. CORNELIUS AND HIMSELF NOT BURGLAR, AS AT FIRST THOUGHT, BUT ADMIRER IDENTIFIED AS GEORGE F. MCAGHON, OF THE PENNSYLVANIA RAILROAD. HE LEAVES FOUR YOUNG CHILDREN. CLIMBS INTO BROOKLYN HOME OF HIS VICTIM THROUGH A WINDOW. MYSTERY IS STILL DEEP IN CASE.

George McAghon, an assistant yardmaster of the Pennsylvania Railroad, was the man who killed Mrs. Barbara Cornelius, a 24-year-old bride, in the bedroom of her apartment at No. 90 Hopkinson Avenue, Brooklyn.

The husband, Carman Cornelius, rushed from the room calling for help when he was awakened by McAghon, whom he thought a burglar.

Evidence of Mrs. Cornelius's love affair was found in love notes on the backs of picture postcards hidden among feminine keepsakes in a trunk. They were signed only 'G.' They carried no postmark, but had been mailed in an envelope addressed to 'Bessie.'

Coroner Frank Senior and Coroner's Physician Dr. Charles Wuest determined that there were two pistol wounds in Mrs. Cornelius's temple and one in McAghon's head. McAghon's hand bore a powder smudge.

One shot, aimed at the fleeing husband, was found buried in the wall opposite the window through which McAghon entered.

Carman Cornelius is connected with a produce house in one of the Brooklyn markets. He usually leaves for work at one o'clock A.M., but was home on account of his health. McAghon entered about 1:30 A.M.

It was his second marriage. The dead woman, née Barbara Seilein, was named as co-respondent in his divorce case. McAghon was never seen in the neighborhood, but Mrs. Cornelius had often used the pay telephone in a drugstore two blocks away at Decatur and Hopkinson Streets.

McAghon was required to carry a gun at his job. He was 35 years old and lived at No. 160 Erie Street, Jersey City. He had been an assistant foreman at the Harsimus Cove yard of the Pennsylvania Railroad for two years, at $120 monthly.

He was said to have had temperate habits, and attended St. Mary's Catholic Church. His wife had been dead two years, and his home was kept by his sister, Jennie McAghon. He leaves four children: Elizabeth, 12 years old, Margaret, 10 years, Mary, 7 years, and Jimmie, 5 years.

Identification of McAghon was made fourteen hours after the arrival of the police by William J. Morris of the Pennsylvania Railroad. Captain Duane of the Seventh Branch Bureau had traced the place where the dead man's clothing had been purchased to a store in Jersey City.

The window was only five feet from the pavement, and was open except for a wire screen. While climbing in McAghon was in full glare of several street lamps.

In the centre of the picture, bright with the glare of the magnesium powder, is the reflection of the door through which Cornelius fled. We seem to be in possession of most of the facts, but have no idea why the murder-suicide took place. Was it premeditated or a reaction to the husband's presence? Was Barbara Cornelius as treacherous as the allusion to her co-respondence is meant to suggest? Was the husband as weak and as unknowing as the husbands in farces? We can wonder, too, about the scheduling of the trysts, which for McAghon must have involved a very long journey that included two ferry crossings and a lengthy streetcar ride all the way to Bedford-Stuyvesant.

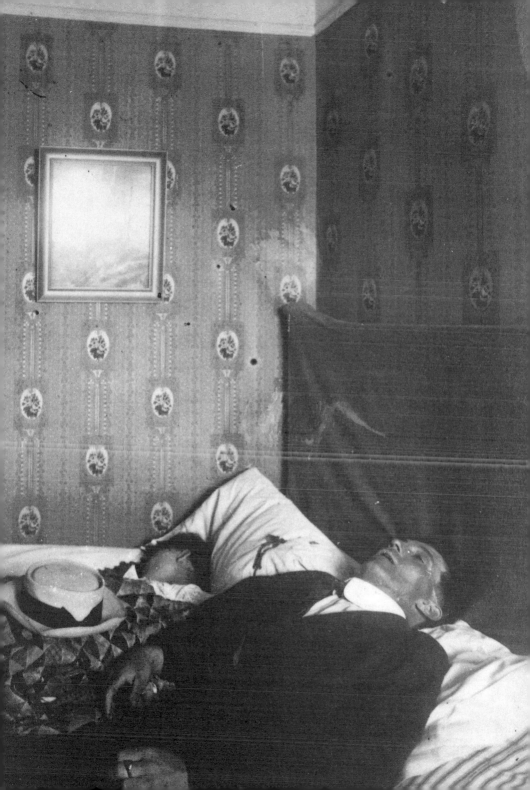

Homicide (female) 1917 (undersize) #1724 6/24/17. [Undersize refers to the size of the plate—smaller than the normal eight by ten.]

This mysterious picture, in its wet light, looks like a still from an early movie serial. The date suggests that it may represent the aftermath of the following incident that was reported in the *New York American*, 25 June 1917:

GIRL SLAIN, MAN SHOT IN JOY RIDE
CABARET SINGER IS KILLED WHEN THREE 'FRIENDLY' STRANGERS ATTACK HER SWEETHEART

They were out for a good time in a big limousine—three young men and two girls. After a laughing tour of three cabarets it seemed perfectly natural to invite three other men for a ride vaguely remembered by Allan Thompson of No. 503 West 105th Street, the driver of the car, as acquaintances.

Under the joyous white lights they piled in—Helen Wheelan, 17 years old, of No. 165 East 127th Street; Kitty Naughton, 23 years old, of No. 309 West 141st Street; Frank Devlin, of No. 140 West 103rd Street; Walter J. Brennan, of No. 309 West 141st Street; Thompson and the newcomers—and were off for the cool night roads of early yesterday morning.

The three strangers, one of whom, police say, is an ex-convict, waited for a lonely spot in the Bronx. Then one made an insulting remark to Miss Wheelan. Devlin, her sweetheart, demanded an explanation.

'We'll have this out right here,' retorted the stranger. The automobile stopped at 134th Street and Willow Avenue and the party got out.

Suddenly, according to police accounts, all three of the strange men attacked Devlin. Devlin went down; a revolver flashed and two shots went through the struggling man's spine; three more shots struck Miss Wheelan, killing her instantly.

Devlin was rushed to Lincoln Hospital, where he is said to be in danger of death. He told Coroner Healy he would not die before avenging his sweetheart's death. The other two men are held on $5000 bail as witnesses.

Four more arrests followed the discovery of the bullet-marked machine in a nearby garage last night. Harold Butler, of No. 165 West 128th Street; Julia Touhey, Miss Naughton's 18-year-old cousin, of No. 161 West 66th Street; and Theodore Kialy, of No. 56 West 100th Street, were locked up as witnesses.

Miss Wheelan, the murdered girl, was employed in a Broadway cabaret. Devlin, a private detective, had been attentive to her for several months.

The *New York Times* reported the story the previous day, but its account is flatter. In a follow-up the *Times* reveals that Thompson was the chauffeur for one Harry Bergman, a real estate dealer of West 94th Street—it was Bergman's car—and that Wheelan was killed shielding Devlin with her body and that the shots were thought to have been fired by Harold Butler. Eventually Michael J. Negliano of East 118th Street, a process server by trade, owned up to the shooting, claiming that Devlin had attacked Butler and then himself. 'Negliano thought he was firing in self-defense, because Devlin had been telling Miss Wheelan to "show him the gun."' Although the location in the photograph accords with contemporary map features for the vicinity of 134th and Willow in the Bronx (there is still a railroad overpass there and at the time there was also a ground-level trunk line), it may be difficult to accept the supine figure as having been a seventeen-year-old cabaret singer, and this can only be countered by pointing to changes in fashions as well as possible bloating.

Photo of dead body of Marion Hart who was murdered in shanty at Old Stone Rd & Bullshead Golden 1915.

The newspapers next to her body supply the date of her demise. Although she was a *New York Times* reader, that paper did not carry the story of her murder. It did, however, appear on 14 October in the *New York American.*

Woman Miser Slain; Two Boarders Held

With her throat cut from ear to ear, and a carving knife by her side, Marion Hart, 39 years old, was found dead in her lonely cottage, No. 1093 Old Stone Road, Bull's Head, Staten Island, last night.

Calvin Decker, 39 years old, an oysterman, who boarded with her, found the body.

Decker and Julia Watson, 29 years old, who also boarded with the dead woman, were locked up.

Before she took Decker and Miss Watson as boarders the dead woman lived alone for some years and was regarded by the villagers as a hermit and a miser.

The *New York Evening Mail* states that the house was Decker's, that Hart, thirty-eight years old, had been his housekeeper and had been slain with an axe. No weapon is seen in the picture. 'Housekeeper' may be a euphemism for common-law wife. The papers had been fascinated by misers ever since the days of Hetty Green, the 'witch of Wall Street', who was reputed to possess a fortune but saved tiny pieces of soap in an old stocking. Hart may have been thought a miser simply because she was educated enough to be a *Times* reader and yet lived in a shack. The *New York American* refers to the epithet in the past tense in the body of the story, yet it uses it in its headline, which might make the reader believe that the killing had been over money. Such a motive is certainly not implausible, and if the killer had been an acquaintance there might not be any reason for the room to have been ransacked, but the question hangs. The dog (in the second picture) is frightened or docile, no more perturbed by the presence of police than, presumably, by the murder.

No caption. This wasn't the 1915 case of the man who was killed in a pool hall by being pelted with billiard balls, but the redness of the man's face does point to possible haemorrhaging. The smear on the floor in the foreground might be a patch of blood. The object dangling from a string suspended from the ceiling in the centre is the cue-stick chalk, and the ominous object that also depends from the ceiling to the left is, of course, the gas jet.

No caption. The licence plate is of 1918 issue. The story is almost certainly related to the following story in the *New York Times*, 9 November 1918:

FIND BODY IN A BARREL
MURDERED MAN HAD THROAT CUT AND 24 STAB
WOUNDS

Three small children playing in a vacant lot in 45th Street, between Eighth and Ninth Streets [sic], in Brooklyn, at dusk yesterday came across a wine barrel the head of which had been covered by burlap nailed to the sides. They tore this off and saw a pair of feet sticking out. They ran away frightened and told a man, who notified the police of the Fourth Avenue Station. Captain Arthur Carey, Chief of the Homicide Bureau, took fingerprints and ordered the body removed to the Fourth Avenue Station.

There it was found the man had been murdered. His throat was cut, his face and forehead gashed, and there were 24 stab wounds on the upper part of his body. Identity was established by means of a draft card found in a pocket of the coat. This showed he was Gaspare Candella, with a police record here, in Boston, and in Washington, D.C.

Candella lived at 1,529 East 54th Street, Brooklyn. The police say the man was killed as a result of a feud.

The practice of stuffing bodies into barrels, usually with their tongues slit, is an old Mafia way of taking care of snitches. It was a habit associated with the New York City Mafia's first great capo, Ignacio Lupo, and was probably not ignored by the Brooklyn Camorra, either. In 1918 Lupo was in jail and many other old leaders were in the process of being forcibly retired, while the young bloods of the *Unione Siciliane* were waging a city-wide leadership war. Candella may well have been a victim of this fray. The only other conceivable explanation would be a particularly demented crime of passion.

#1104 3/5/16 Pasquale Caruso shot and killed.

This exceedingly odd photograph belongs to a case that was well-covered in the press. This is what the *New York American* wrote (6 March 1916):

VETERAN, 80, KILLS MAN, 64, WITH WAR GUN
AGED BROOKLYN RESIDENT SLAYS NEIGHBOR AFTER BEING SLASHED IN FIGHT

With an army blunderbuss that he had carried in Italy's wars Pasquale Caruso, 80 years old, last night shot and killed Giuseppe Certona, 64 years old. Caruso is a portrait painter and lives at No. 1402 66th Street, Brooklyn. He was walking near his home when three sons of Certona threw snowballs at him. He walked in to their home, No. 1409 66th Street, to protest to their father. A bitter quarrel with Certona followed, and Certona is alleged to have slashed the aged man across the face with a knife.

Caruso hurried across the street to his own home, Certona following. Just inside the door was a blunderbuss. Caruso discharged it in Certona's face, killing him instantly. Then he fell fainting over the form of his victim.

The *New York Times* the same day headlined its story HIS CHAPLIN WALK CAUSE OF A MURDER. Apparently Caruso's rheumatism affected his gait, so that Certona's sons did not merely throw snowballs, they yelled, 'Charlie Chaplin, Charlie Chaplin,' and there was a whole mob of boys, not just Certona's. In any event, Caruso, described by the *Times* as a plasterer, blew off most of Certona's head with the gun with which he had fought under Garibaldi. Thus this photograph, apparently so mysterious as a portrait of an erect corpse, must be a portrait of Caruso, the murderer. His eyes, on close inspection, prove to be open. The setting now reveals itself as a police station, with its institutional bi-colour paint job, its big desk, its fat electrical cord (the newspapers are being held up to concentrate the light). Caruso was old and hard-pressed. One hopes the court was lenient with him.

This selection, like the remaining cases I came upon in the Municipal Archives, is steeped in obscurity. It includes a murder-suicide (George McAghon and Barbara Cornelius) and two fights that led to deaths (Helen Wheelan and Giuseppe Certona). The details of other cases are unknown; many were dropped unsolved.

What went on in the tenements was a long way from the world stage. The record of such murders as the *New York Times* found room for speaks of desperation, brutality and randomness. A father threw his two children out of the window; a woman smothered her sister's baby in a fit of jealousy; 'in the last six weeks,' fourteen infants' bodies were recovered from the East River. People were shot at card games, dances, after being put out of dances, tossed from taxi-cabs, beaten to death on Broadway. A hospital orderly was killed by a patient; a patient was slain on his sickbed. A man was killed for refusing a cigarette; a boy was killed in a feud over a baseball game. A policeman was beaten to death by a mob. People were killed by: razors, revolvers and axes; a cheek bite, a fountain pen driven into the brain, acid poured into the mouth by a maniac.

At the least, it can be said that the pictures here represent a cross-section of what murder and its locales looked like at the time. Nearly all the male victims are dressed in collar and tie and, before being killed, would have worn a hat. Dark three-piece suits predominate. The women endured assemblages of underwear that would have required hours of laborious laundering; and their hair, uncut and pinned, demanded constant care. Their rooms, often tiny, are comparably adorned with highly decorative wallpaper (cheaper, in those days, than having the walls painted) and often threadbare but ornate carpets, sometimes laid over complexly patterned linoleum floors. There are curtains, flounces, runners, doilies, ancestral portraits, pennants and framed prints. Those who lived in the tenements had to fit their beds around a stove and a table. Those who lived in hall bedrooms had space only for a twin mattress and the smallest chest of drawers. These rooms are lit by gas, nearly four decades after the incandescent bulb. Few would have had toilets, which were located in the hall, and virtually no one had a bath. The rooms may be tidy but most, in a time of overdressed furnishings and before the vacuum cleaner, are not clean—just as the streets are not. Garbage has accumulated nearly everywhere.

The occupations we find among the recorded cases are: assistant railroad yardmaster, oysterman, lodging-house keeper, cabaret singer, private detective, chauffeur, process server, plasterer, contractor, undertaker, wine seller, 'railroad man' and something in connection with a produce house at a market. Many of the unidentified may have had positions in factories—or on the docks or in stables. The faces are mostly beyond our reckoning: try to put an age to any of them.

But the faces also say, '*Et in Arcadia ego.*' We cannot know what led them to the bedrooms, vacant lots and bar-room floors where they met death. Had one of the young women begun life in a pleasant rustic monotony and then followed her ambitions to the metropolis? Was Marion Hart a runaway wife from a brutal Moravian settlement in western Pennsylvania who had found peace and anonymity in a squatter's shack in the obscure middle of Staten Island? Was she killed for love or money or in a mindless drunken frenzy? Was the youth, dead at the end of the pool table, a ladies' man with a smooth line of patter who finally got his from one of a series of enraged husbands? How many were born on farms? Which of them could swim, or play music, or divine the age of a horse at a glance, or do fast mental arithmetic, or tell good jokes? How many were in love?

Outside a crowd gathered as the body was carried to the Black Maria, people craning their necks to get a view, small children excited, a few acquaintances crying softly, others cornering the landlady to make a deal for the furniture or unbloodied bedding. People would have been stunned for a few hours or a few days, but before long would have forgotten about the incident except as a place-marker in their historical memory and come to refer to 'the winter that Willie Murphy across the street was killed.' The bodies eventually would be removed to an ethnic graveyard in the vast cemetery tracts of central Queens, or, perhaps, to the mass trench on Hart's Island in Long Island Sound.

In the streets of New York, meanwhile, the police would carry on, finding, tagging, photographing and covering an unending parade of supine figures in hallways and bars and salt marshes and parked cars. The pictures will be filed somewhere, in the backs of the drawers, in a pile, in a basement, until finally a flood or decay or time removes the names and incidents from all memory. Before long it would be as if they had never existed at all.

ANDREW MOTION
BREAKING IN

In September 1946, when he was twenty-four, Philip Larkin went to work as sub-librarian at University College, Leicester. Within three weeks he had met Monica Jones, a lecturer in the English Department. After three years they had become lovers. After another six months Larkin left Leicester for the library at Queen's University, Belfast, where he stayed for five years, seeing Monica regularly but at widely-spaced intervals. In 1955 he was appointed Librarian at the University of Hull, and remained there for the last thirty years of his life. During this time he and Monica took annual holidays together, met at least once a month, wrote to each other and/or spoke on the telephone nearly every day. The relationship was in certain respects deeply troubled (by jealousies, by distance), and in others very happy. Monica was Larkin's steadfast companion and his soul-mate. He dedicated *The Less Deceived* to her: it was the only collection of poems he dedicated to anyone.

In September 1961 Monica bought a small house in Haydon Bridge in Northumberland, on the main Newcastle–Carlisle road. (Her family had originally come from that part of the world.) She meant it to be a bolt-hole—somewhere she might escape the various worries of her private life and her university work. Larkin was initially suspicious of the house but soon admiring. He took holidays there, hunkered down in it for weekends, always visited at New Year. When he wouldn't or couldn't leave Hull, Monica was often in Haydon Bridge alone—writing Larkin letters, waiting for him to ring. The house was their special place, their burrow.

In June 1983, when she was sixty-one, recently retired from Leicester, and living in Haydon Bridge more or less full-time, Monica developed shingles. Larkin, who was staying, took charge. He ferried her south to Hull and put her in hospital, where she lay half-blinded and in great pain for several days. Then he brought her back to his own house in Hull. She stayed ten months—until the following April—before returning to

Monica Jones and Philip Larkin, c. 1955. This photograph was taken by Philip Larkin with his delayed action camera.

Photos: © Estate of Philip Larkin

Haydon Bridge, meaning to re-start her independent life. But she was still unwell, and anyway Larkin missed her. Within a few days he had decided to collect her again. He helped her pack, then sat in the car while she checked for last things, drew the curtains, switched off the electricity at the meter, and locked the front door. Anxiously, he drove her back to Hull.

Larkin thought Monica was fatally ill. In fact, he was. Within a year he was in hospital for tests; on 2 December 1985 he died of cancer. Monica stayed in Hull—depressed, sick and exhausted. She wanted her own life back but couldn't reach it. She worried about her house in Haydon Bridge but was too ill to get herself there.

Early in 1986 Monica asked me to write Larkin's biography, and over the next few years we saw a great deal of each other. She sat in what had once been Larkin's chair, his tweed coat still slung over the arm. I sat on the sofa, his Rowlandson watercolour on the dark green wall behind me. Sometimes I formally interviewed her; sometimes we just chatted. Sometimes we looked at photographs of him or by him; sometimes we read his books. There was no hurry. She had known Larkin better than anyone. I had to ransack her memory.

Monica said nothing about the letters Larkin had written her. If I asked where they were she would shrug—lighting another cigarette, pouring another drink. Did this mean she didn't want me to see them? Or had they, like his diaries, been destroyed? She wasn't telling.

One day out of the blue she said most of the letters were in Haydon Bridge. Why didn't we drive up together to get them? It was a forlorn hope—she was too ill—yet she didn't want me to go without her. The house was theirs: a secret place, where she and Larkin had lived to the exclusion of all others. Dark-curtained and unvisited, it held their continuing, unbroken life together. Once the door had been opened, that life would be over.

Months passed. Monica grew more frail. Eventually she decided I would have to go alone. I drove up with a friend from Hull, Marion Shaw, in the autumn of 1989. As far as I knew, no one had been into the house for five years.

We roller-coastered the wet road towards Hexham, then on. Rain was swirling in from the North Sea behind us. So much had fallen in recent weeks, the moors were yellow and sour-looking. As we ducked down into Haydon Bridge, streams bulged in the ditches beside us.

The house was even smaller than I'd expected, and uglier. Packed into a tight row near the Old Bridge, on the main road, it had a jaded white front, a slate roof, plain modern windows and a front door which opened straight off the street. I got the key from a neighbour and opened up—but the door was stuck. Peering through the letter-box, the rain falling on my neck and back, I could see why. There was a mound of junk mail on the mat: offers of free film, estate agents' bumf, cards from taxi companies and window cleaners.

I shoved the door violently and we were in. A tiny box of a hall; the sitting-room to the left; stairs rising straight ahead. The stairs looked crazy. There was no carpet (just the pale section where a carpet had once been) and at the sides of each step—cans of food. One of those had leaked, oozing blood-coloured treacle into a puddle at my feet, I tried to wipe it up, scrape it up, somehow get rid of it, with a piece of junk mail. It was impossible. In the end I hid it beneath a few bright envelopes.

The smell was worse when I turned on the electricity. Sweet open-air dampness like a rotten log—but also fusty. And there was noise too, noise I couldn't recognize. A roaring, but somehow subdued. When I turned into the sitting-room I understood. Outside the window at the back, beyond a cramped cement yard and a tow-path, there flowed a gigantic river. The Tyne; invisible from the road. Within the first few seconds of looking, I saw a full-grown tree sweep past, then heard the trunk grinding against the bridge away to my left, out of sight.

The window was broken—a hole like a star-burst and slivers of glass on the purple carpet.

We weren't the first people here for years, we were the

second and third—at least the second and third. The drawers in a sideboard lolled open, empty; in the grate, jagged pieces of crockery poked out of a sootfall; there was a dark circle in the dust on a table where a vase had stood. And there were books all over the floor—books flung about for the hell of it—and a deep scar on the window-seat where something heavy had been manhandled into the yard then away along the towpath.

We tiptoed through the shambles, closing up, straightening, tidying, our hands immediately grey with dust. It was wet dust, sticking to us and clinging in our noses and lungs. Monica hadn't told me where I might find the letters, but it didn't matter. They were everywhere. In books, down the side of a chair, under a rug, on the window-seat. A few lay flat and saturated in the yard, scrabbled out when the last burglar left.

It was the same upstairs, though the dust seemed lighter there, maybe because the rain had eased off outside and the sun was starting to break through. The river sounded quieter, too, and I could see a family on the opposite bank—a man, a woman and two children, walking a dog.

I went into the lumber room, into a jungle of clothes and hangers which had a small box at its heart, stuffed with letters.

Nothing in the bathroom.

In the smaller bedroom: under the window overlooking the river, a bed with letters both inside and underneath it, and a cupboard crowded with damp dresses which tore when I touched them.

In the larger bedroom: more letters in books, an empty case of wine, an ironing board with a half-ironed dress draped across it.

When I got downstairs I realized I was breathing in gulps, as if I were swimming.

We counted the letters into plastic bags. There were nearly two hundred of them. Then we went through the house again, found the last handful, turned off the electricity, locked up, returned the key to the neighbour,

Opposite: Monica Jones, c.1955, photographed by Larkin.

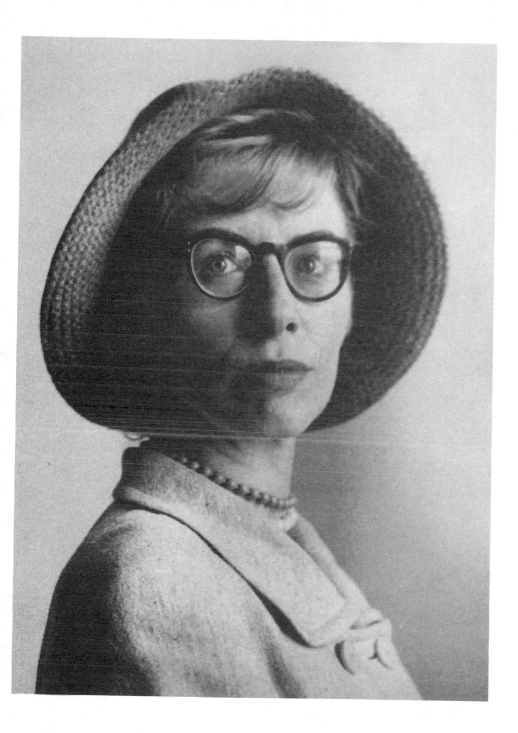

arranged for the window to be repaired and climbed into the car.
The sun had gone in; it was starting to rain again. Larkin had sat
in the same place, squinnying at the little house, feeling anxious. I
felt exhilarated and ashamed.

I wasn't the last. A week or so after I'd taken the letters back
to Monica, a van drew up outside the house in Haydon
Bridge and two people got out, kicked open the front door
and stole nearly everything inside. If the letters had still been
there, they would have gone too. By the time this happened, I'd
read them—and two hundred or so more, that Monica revealed
Larkin had written to her in Leicester.

ALL BOOKS GREAT AND SMALL
The Reader's Catalog

The Reader's Catalog is the ultimate bookstore. We can deliver any US-published book to any location in the world. Call our operators at 1-800-733-BOOK, 8 AM to 8 PM EST, for information on titles, authors, or shipping (or FAX us, 24 hours a day, at (212) 307-1973).

Whether you want to stay on the cutting edge of fiction or you want to know who's saying what about philosophy, religion, or science—our quarterly bulletin, a magazine of each season's finest books, will challenge, amuse, and inform you. Fill out the coupon below to receive our latest and forthcoming issues—**FREE**, and with no obligation to do anything, ever again.
By the way—we do videos, too.

The Reader's Catalog, a 1,382-page volume, contains an annotated listing of the best 40,000 books in 208 categories. Priced at $27.95, it's not only an indispensable reference, but a remarkable tool for locating (and obtaining) your favorite titles.

✂ -

Return this coupon in an envelope to:

The Reader's Catalog
250 West 57th Street, Room 1330, New York, NY 10107

❏ Please send me a *free* bulletin.
❏ Please send me The Reader's Catalog at $27.95 plus $4.95 for shipping.

❏ $32.90 enclosed. Make check or money order payable to The Reader's Catalog.
Please charge my ❏ American Express ❏ Visa ❏ MasterCard.

Name

Address

City/State/Zip

RICHARD HOLMES
AMONG THE TULIPS

When young James Boswell arrived in Holland in August 1763 at the age of twenty-two, his first impulse was to commit suicide. When he departed ten months later something much more alarming had occurred: he had fallen in love—or half in love—with a Dutch girl more intelligent than he.

After a respectable education at Edinburgh University, studying under David Hume, Boswell had run riot for a year in London, fathering an illegitimate child and flirting with deism, gambling and dreams of military glory. His redoubtable father, Lord Auchinleck, had called an abrupt halt to this dangerous libertinage and, recalling his own youthful sojourn at Utrecht (the Boswells had distinguished Dutch relatives in their Scottish ancestry), he despatched his prodigal son for a period of moral improvement among the Calvinist worthies, burghers and professors of the United Provinces. He was to acquire tone and intellectual rigour at the famous Law School in the cloisters of the huge, shadowy cathedral of Utrecht.

Arriving in the Hague from Harwich, Boswell embarked alone on a sluggish canal boat drawn by lumbering cart-horses for the nine-hour journey to Utrecht, suddenly overcome by his 'own dismal imaginations'. His whole life seemed to grind to a gloomy halt amid these intolerable, green, empty flatlands. In Utrecht, at the Castle of Antwerp Inn, he was given an attic bedroom packed with ancient, dark wood furniture. There he was served a dry meal on a polished tray.

> At every hour the bells of the great [cathedral] tower played a dreary psalm tune. A deep melancholy seized upon me. I groaned with the idea of living all winter in so shocking a place. I thought myself old and wretched and forlorn . . . All the horrid ideas you can imagine, recurred upon me. I was quite unemployed and had not a soul to speak to but the clerk of the English [Presbyterian] meeting . . . I thought that I should go mad . . . I went out into the streets, and even in public could not refrain from groaning and weeping bitterly . . . I took general speculative views of things; all seemed full of darkness and woe.

Opposite: James Boswell, 1764.

National Gallery of Scotland

Such was Boswell's introduction to the improving delights of Holland.

He thought desperately of going to Berlin, Geneva or Paris, 'but above all of returning to London and my dear calm retreat in the Inner Temple.' Escape seemed the only alternative to madness. He seized upon an American doctor he found in the doorway of the inn and accompanied him on a rapid tour of Gouda, Amsterdam and Haarlem. On returning to Utrecht he was again overcome by horror and fled to Rotterdam half-determined to re-embark for home. He wrote to his old friend George Dempster (a Scots lawyer and Member of Parliament eight years his senior) who was in Paris, and, 'irresolute and fickle every hour,' begged him to rendezvous immediately at Brussels. Answering this *cri-de-coeur*, Dempster flung himself into the next mail coach and covered the 186 miles from Paris in thirty hours, only to find that Boswell, overcome by guilt, had returned to Rotterdam, having finally resolved 'to go up to Utrecht for a week, and force myself to study six hours a day during that time.' If that failed to steady his nerve—well, he would try Leiden.

Dempster sent him a gentle letter of advice, based on his own superior experiences. To start with, he must accept that the glooms of British academia would be as 'a joke to Utrecht.' He must crack the conundrum of Dutch money and Dutch language. He must resign himself to the inspiring company of 'Dutch professors in tartan nightgowns with long pipes.' Like a good Christian, he must consider Utrecht as a vale of tears which would lead eventually 'to a better life in another country.' He must regard Holland as 'the dark watery passage which leads to an enchanted and brilliant grotto. For such is a French academy . . . ' Meanwhile, to ward off Calvinistic gloom: 'I should think you might amuse yourself in acquiring the French, keeping a journal and writing to your friends, and debauching a Dutch girl.' He must grow immune to silence, smoking, dullness and stinking cheese, and 'try to Dutchify your immortal soul.'

Boswell duly survived his first week in Utrecht, taking lodgings in the north-east corner of the cathedral square in Keizershof buildings, and hiring a Swiss manservant, François Mazarac, who was a paragon of punctuality—'I am quite ready to lay a bet on him against all the clocks in the country.' By the end of September he had established a proper Dutch routine of severest virtue, combining classical, French and legal studies with a little billiards and fencing by way of recreation. He was up at six-thirty a.m., read Ovid until nine, Tacitus till eleven and attended Professor Trotz's lectures on Civil Law at midday. In the afternoons he walked briskly round the tree-lined boulevard of the Utrecht Mall, bowing to the academical worthies, did a two-hour French conversation class and dined with the Reverend Robert Brown, an English pastor, and his family, practising Dutch. In the evenings he wrote a one-page essay in French or Dutch, a ten-line verse stanza, and composed entries in his daily journal and letters to his friends, who were properly amazed at this transformation.

There were one or two suspicious anomalies in this spartan perfection: he slipped out to a Dutch tailor and ordered two dazzling suits, 'of sea-green and lace, and scarlet with gold' for future parties; and his fencing-master turned out to be ninety-four years old. His early rising also produced curious effects:

> As soon as I am awake, I remember my duty, and like a brisk mariner I give the lash to indolence and bounce up with as much vivacity as if a pretty girl, amorous and willing, were waiting for me.

(Early rising was always a delicate subject with Boswell, and he once considered patenting a device for tilting his bed into a vertical position, so that he slid out painlessly from under the blankets on to the floor.)

Lord Auchinleck wrote to congratulate his son on his resolutions and advised him to study the management of cattle and the Dutch 'contrivance for making their dung in no way offensive to them,' and also to cultivate the society of Count Nassau, a prime mover in the Utrecht beau monde.

By October, Boswell was so spiritually well-regulated that he drew up at immense length a philosophical resolution about his future life, grandly entitled 'The Inviolable Plan', in which he determined to foreswear all excesses and mould himself into a 'Christian gentleman', distinguished lawyer and Scottish paterfamilias. He promised himself to consult this document frequently and stick faithfully to all its commandments. Dempster now recommended the exemplum of Dutch society: 'Examine their industry, their commerce, the effects of frugality, freedom, and good laws.'

Boswell had studied the English travel literature about Holland, notably the *Observations on the United Provinces* by the seventeenth-century British ambassador to the Hague, Sir William Temple; and the popular volume on the Netherlands in Thomas Nugent's *The Grand Tour* (1749). A vivid stereotype of Dutch virtues emerges from these works: stolid, hard-working, earthbound, egalitarian, commercially-minded, hygienic and irremediably dull. Temple summed it all up in a diplomat's measured and crafty formula, carefully dispensing praise with one hand and withdrawing it with the other.

> Holland is a country, where the earth is better than the air, and profit more in request than honour; where there is more sense than wit; more good nature than good humour; and more wealth than pleasure: where a man would choose rather to travel than to live; shall find more things to observe than desire; and more persons to esteem than to love.

But it was Thomas Nugent's comments on Dutch domestic life which particularly intrigued Boswell, whose Inviolable Plan included the search for a virtuous wife:

> The women have the whole care and management of their domestic affairs, and generally live in good fame; a certain sort of chastity being hereditary and habitual to them. They are more valued for their beauty, than their genteel carriage. A great many of them understand trafick [trade] as well as the men; and it may be said, that most of them wear the breeches.

They were, in short, the opposite of French women (who haunted Boswell's wilder dreams), and, allowing for the breeches clause, were tantalizingly marriageable. This solemn thought gradually came to occupy Boswell, the reformed rake and earnest student, a good deal.

In mid-October the Utrecht social season opened, and Count Nassau held the first of his grand soirées. A certain shift in moral priorities now emerged in Boswell's outlook.

> Dress in scarlet and gold, fine swiss, white silk stockings, handsome pumps, and have silver-and-silk sword-knot, Barcelona handkerchief, and elegant toothpick-case which you had in present from a lady. Be quite the man of fashion and keep up your dignity.

But he still urged himself to be sober and serious. 'Don't think it idle time, for while abroad being in good company is your great scheme and is really improving.' These exhortations now become a regular chorus in his memoranda for the journal, summarized by the repeated word *retenue*—prudence and restraint.

> Always try to attain tranquillity . . . Learn *retenue*. Pray do. Don't forget in Plan . . . The more and oftener restraints, the better. Be steady.

It was in this mood that James Boswell met the first of his Tulips, the colourful Dutch ladies who would hover entrancingly before him, blooms to be plucked—as he thought—for the greater improvement and decoration of the Boswellian pasture. Here, as he hoped, was the true meaning of his Dutch cultivation. Here the traveller would become a truly European gentleman.

She was the Count's young sister-in-law, la Comtesse Nassau, a glamorous and elegant lady married to a septuagenarian husband and renowned for her charm, her boredom and her love affairs. The inflammation greatly improved Boswell's French and his self-esteem. He was soon crowing in his letters:

> Our noblesse are come to town and all is alive. We have card-assemblies twice a week, which I do assure you, are very brilliant, and private parties almost every evening. Madame la Comtesse de Nassau Beverweerd has taken me under her protection. She is a lady that, with all your serenity, would make you fall on your knees and

utter love speeches in the style of Lord Shaftesbury's *Philosophical Rhapsody*, and that would please her exceedingly, for she delights in Shaftesbury's benevolent system. I really trembled at the transition which I made last week. But I have stood firm . . .

During the next few weeks Boswell danced attendance on the thirty-year-old Comtesse, his dry academic days alternating with glittering candle-lit evenings. He encouraged himself with ethical instructions: 'La Comtesse is charming, delicate, and sentimental. Adore her with easy affability, yet with polite distance, and acquire real habits of composure.' But he began to suspect that Thomas Nugent had not entirely understood the intriguing charms of Dutch women. He steadied himself by writing essays on the 'horrible fogs and excessive cold' of the climate; he tested himself by refusing to have a fire in his rooms until November, 'studying three or four hours on end shivering like an Italian greyhound;' and he sobered himself writing notes on the eccentricities of Professor Trotz—his fund of historical anecdotes and his memories of Friesland that made Utrecht sound like the centre of world civilization and 'the seat of felicity'.

The airy gallantry of the Comtesse did not however solidify into a flirtation. Unknown to Boswell she was involved elsewhere and duly produced an illegitimate child the following year. Though he upbraided himself—'no love; you are to marry'—he also admitted that he was 'sorry somehow' that his virtue was 'not to be put to the trial.' The Comtesse did on the other hand rapidly introduce him to Utrecht society and even drew up a list of eligible ladies for Boswell's edification. From November onwards the names of two other Tulips began to sprout regularly in Boswell's memoranda: Madame Geelvinck and Mademoiselle de Zuylen. One of his earliest memories of the latter was of her playing an expert game of shuttlecock.

Catherina Elisabeth Geelvinck was a Dutch merry widow. The charming, spoilt daughter of an exceedingly rich local family of merchants, she married at eighteen, produced a child at nineteen and was fortuitously widowed at twenty. Now twenty-four, exceedingly beautiful and with a large private income, she laid waste the drawing-rooms of Utrecht with broken-hearted suitors. Students sang about her, and foreign visitors (especially the minor German nobility) got drunk in her honour. She was known universally and somewhat breathlessly as *la Veuve*. Low-voiced, cool and coquettish, she spent vast sums on the latest Paris fashions to show off her splendid, milky charms. Her large brown eyes had a slight cast, and transfixed Boswell with their hint of sexual naughtiness. In reality Madame Geelvinck had a calculating heart, poured all her emotions into her only son and comported herself with enough care to achieve two more marriages and an even larger income. But for Boswell she was an immediate challenge.

Isabelle van Tuyl van Serooskerken, the expert shuttlecock player, was the eldest daughter of the aristocratic family of van Tuyl, with their ancestral castle at Zuylen, just outside Utrecht. Very different from the languid Madame Geelvinck, she was a young woman of the new age: essentially restless, enquiring, forever dissatisfied with the world about her. She was the same age as Boswell and the very opposite of all his assumptions about Dutch women. Tall, fun-loving, brilliantly quick and clever, she had a fine open face with a high intellectual forehead and carelessly brushed back auburn hair which seemed to flame above her head. From the start she both fascinated and frightened Boswell; she was capable of wrong-footing him at every turn. His very first entry about her says he had put on 'foolish airs of passion for Miss de Zuylen'; his second that he had been deeply shocked by her 'unlimited vivacity'.

Isabelle was highly educated: encouraged as a child to read and write by a clever Swiss governess, she had pursued her studies in classics, mathematics and philosophy, not always regarded as the most ladylike of subjects. While her younger sister married, Isabelle obtained her own apartment at Zuylen (overlooking the gatehouse where she could observe the comings and goings of the world) and read Plutarch, Newton and Voltaire late into the night. In her late teens she began to write a stream of stories, essays, poems and letters in French, and patronized the Utrecht bookseller for the latest titles. She became expert in algebra and conic sections, the harpsichord, shuttlecock and witty repartee. She grew mocking about decorous behaviour, dull marriages, Calvinist religion, even money and the weather.

At twenty, Isabelle met a Swiss army officer at the Hague named Constant d'Hermenches, an aristocratic rake twice her age. They began a clandestine correspondence (via the Utrecht bookseller) which was to last over a decade. The correspondence sealed Isabelle's reputation in Utrecht for eccentricity and unladylike behaviour. In fact the letters are exercises in style and self-analysis, rather than romance; they give a matchless picture of daily life at Zuylen and Utrecht and contrast Isabelle's freethinking views on marriage with d'Hermenches's worldly cynicism.

At the time of Boswell's arrival in Holland, Isabelle had completed a satirical short story, 'Le Noble', telling of a romantic elopement from an ancestral Dutch castle surrounded by a moat, with an unmistakable resemblance to Zuylen. In a scene that shocked Utrecht society, the heroine, Julie, hurls down from her bedroom window a series of oil-paintings of her illustrious forebears, in order to form a bridge by which she can escape over the moat into her lover's arms. The story was signed 'Zélide', and it was by this literary pseudonym that Boswell came to refer to her.

While Boswell's social life began to flourish, his private existence in his solitary lodgings at the Keizershof was less easy. He was dogged by depressions and the old longing for dissipation. He admonished himself: 'Fight out the winter here, and learn as much as you can. Pray, pray be *retenue*.' Cheerful and amusing in company, he relapsed into deepest gloom in his lodgings, where the huge cathedral tower cast its shadow over his windows, always standing between himself and the watery winter sunlight. He worried about his future and mused on Calvinist questions of predestination and damnation. He was a young man discovering a contradiction in his own nature—his own national characteristic, perhaps—and slowly finding that the only palliative was what had begun as a light-hearted hobby: his obsessive, self-analytical journal-keeping. Boswell was discovering the controlling element of his literary genius: the impulse towards an astonishingly candid autobiographical form. Describing himself through others, he would end by describing others through himself, with unparalleled intimacy, sensitivity and wit. It was a pleasure that grew out of pain; a sociable form that grew out of extreme solitude; a strategy of survival learned by a traveller in a foreign land.

At the same time as his launch into the drawing-rooms of Utrecht, Boswell almost committed an unpardonable *faux pas* in the streets by getting involved with a drunken group of students, rashly revealing his rakish propensities. He entered this memorandum for the night of 23 November.

> At night you had truly an adventure. You saw an entertainment of Dutch students; a concert; all keen on meat and drink; then marching like schoolboys with *Kapitein* and frightening the street. Then home; then saw the masks, and one like a woman; then house again, conditionless, drank roaring—songs. King George [the toast Boswell proposed amidst the mêlée]. Compliments paid you etc. Mark all in Journal.

The following day, in penitential sobriety, he anxiously recorded this close shave with his private, uncivilized self, and issued a stern warning.

> Yesterday you recovered well after your riot with the Dutch students. But remember how near you was to getting drunk and exposing yourself, for if you had gone on a little longer, you could not have stopped. You have important secrets to keep . . . always shun drinking, and guard lips . . .

Boswell's public reputation survived this lapse, and in December he set off for the Hague to celebrate Christmas, look up his distant Dutch relatives, make contact with the British ambassador and take stock of his position. For there was now a delicate question forming in his mind, as he later explained to his friend Temple in the bluffest manner he could command.

> There are two ladies here, a young, handsome, amiable widow (Madame Geelvinck) with £4,000 a year; and

185

> Mademoiselle de Zuylen, who has only a fortune of
> £20,000. She is a charming creature. But she is a *savante*
> and a *bel esprit*, and has published some things. She is
> much my superior. One does not like that. One does not
> like a widow, neither. You won't allow me to yoke myself
> here? You *will* have me married to an English woman?

Boswell found out a good deal about his Tulips at the
Hague, much of it through dinner-party gossip. He found the
Dutch habit of intimate gossip fascinating—everyone seemed to
know everyone else's secrets, rather on the same principle that
Dutch parlours never had their curtains drawn against the
onlookers' gaze. He learned to provoke the gossip with innocent
questions, and practised recording the dialogue in his journal.

He passed 'three weeks in the most brilliant gaity' at the
Hague, pleasantly surprised by a style of living that was 'much in
the manner of Paris.' He was presented to the Prince of Orange
and all the foreign ambassadors and cut a fine figure in his
alternating suits of scarlet and Leyden green. He noted 'formerely
such a change of life used to unhinge me quite;' but he felt in
control of himself and returned calmly to Utrecht—now 'the seat
of the Dutch muses'—in mid-January 1764 to resume his studious
regularity 'with much satisfaction'. But the real reason for his
equanimity was less the philosophic pleasure of Professor Trotz's
lectures than the tantalizing delights of the Utrecht salons, where
his Tulips were now blooming again before his eyes.

By the end of January he was engaged in an intricate social
minuet with the three ladies. The Comtesse tended to be jealous,
the widow to be flirtatious, the *bel esprit* to be satirical. It was all
very good for his education. A typical evening of this amorous
dance occurred on 28 January, which Boswell recorded with the
greatest satisfaction.

> At Assembly you was easy with *la Comtesse*, but saw her
> piqued. You must make up this by easy complaisance, as
> she can do you more service than Zélide. You played
> cards with Madame Geelvinck—charming indeed. You
> said to Zélide 'I love Sue' etc. But the contrary is true
> with you and me.

The 'I love Sue' was a mocking reference to a popular song about falling in love with a girl before the lover had even met her. Boswell was implying that he felt like that about Madame Geelvinck, but not about Mademoiselle de Zuylen, alas. Zélide was quite up to this teasing, and replied with ironic regret: 'Oh, *I* was prepossessed in *your* favour.' This hit its mark, and afterwards Boswell feared he had been 'too severe' with Zélide.

By February it was clear that Madame Geelvinck, with her huge brown eyes and generous inviting figure, was winning ascendancy in Boswell's heart. The Comtesse began to concentrate on beating Boswell at cards, but Zélide—who was less flattered than amused by Boswell—adopted a more subtle strategy to hold his attention. Alone among the ladies at Utrecht, Zélide had penetrated the introspective side of Boswell's character; she already suspected that he kept an intimate journal (this was one of the 'secrets' that Boswell always feared he would let slip) and guessed at his literary leanings. She saw that he played and experimented with human nature—his own and everyone else's. She saw that he loved drama, complication, self-revelation: the comedy of human identity and exchange. Indeed in this, as in his depressions and solitude, he was much like herself. She therefore teasingly announced that she had written 'Character Portraits' of many of her friends—including the Comtesse and Madame Geelvinck—and also of herself, and that if he continued to amuse her Boswell might eventually see them. This was to prove an intellectual seduction quite as powerful, in the long run, as Madame Geelvinck's promising *décolletage*.

As Boswell plunged towards that delicious object, Zélide's subtler influence continued to make itself felt, although not enough to spoil the would-be lover's self-importance.

At Assembly you appeared in sea-green and silver and was really brilliant—much taken notice of and like an ambassador. You begin to be much at your ease and to take a true foreign polish. Madame Geelvinck was charming. You told her you expected to see her 'Character' by Zélide. She said, 'It is not interesting.' You

187

> said, 'Oh, do not say that to me' . . . You played whist
> well. After it you felt, for the first time in Holland,
> delicious love. O *la belle Veuve!* She talked low to you and
> close, perhaps to feel breath. All the *Heeren* looked blue.
> You took her to the coach, and your frame thrilled . . .

Throughout February this tantalizing courtship among the cards
and candles continued, with Madame Geelvinck whispering in
her low voice, 'looking all elegance and sweetness,' patting
Boswell's hand and 'correcting his French delightfully.' 'You are
much in love,' he wrote. 'She perhaps wishes to marry rationally.
But have a care.'

Meanwhile a very different sort of friendship was developing
with Zélide. Boswell was introduced to her family at their Utrecht
house and became a particular favourite with her father. He was
also much liked by her brothers, sharing tales of field sports and
the army. Zélide could speak fluent French and English, and also
helped him with Dutch. She could still sometimes be 'nervish' and
too boisterous for his taste, making fun of anything conventional
—even religion or marriage—but on the whole she played gently
with Boswell, and talked seriously about his studies.

> You drank tea at Monsieur de Zuylen's. He shook you
> cordially by the hand. All was *en famille* and fine. You
> talked of your [plan for a] Dutch Dictionary.

Just occasionally she played the *bel esprit* and delivered one of her
shafts of ironic knowledge, so that he winced.

> You supped elegant at Mademoiselle de Zuylen's with [her
> uncle] the General etc. She said, 'You write everything
> down.' Have a care. Never speak on that subject.

But now, almost without Boswell being aware of it, Zélide had
set up an emotional triangle in which the lines of power and
affection played continually against each other in his heart. While
he was officially 'in love' with Madame Geelvinck, he was 'in
confidence' with Zélide: he courted one woman, but confided in
the other.

This pattern is steadily revealed in his memoranda.

Opposite: Isabelle van Tuyl van Serooskerken.

From a private collection

Yesterday you sent note to Madame Geelvinck, quite
young man of fashion . . . At Assembly you was quite at
ease. You begin really to have the foreign usage. You
said to Zélide, 'Come, I will make a pact of frankness
with you for the whole winter, and you with me.' You
talked freely to her of prudence. But you talked too
much. They all stared.

Madame Geelvinck perhaps understood what was happening
better than Boswell. When he declared his love for her openly on
19 February, she responded with the greatest tranquillity. Boswell
was a little put out, as he records.

Boswell: But did you not know that I was in love with
you?
Mme Geelvinck: No, really. I thought it was with
Mademoiselle de Zuylen; and I said nothing about it.

In other conversations (Boswell was now revelling in his dialogue-
writing) Zélide's name keeps cropping up at the very point where
Boswell is trying to be most intimate with his glamorous widow;
she is summoned up at the exact moment that should be most
private. It must have been very tiresome for Madame Geelvinck
to be flirting through the invisible presence of this third party:

Boswell: Madame, I am discreet. I would that my heart
were plucked out for you to see.
Mme Geelvinck: Are you good natured?
Boswell: On my honour. I am a very honest man with a
very generous heart. But I am a little capricious, though
I shall cure that. It was only a year ago that I was the
slave of imagination and talked like Mademoiselle de
Zuylen. But I am making great advances in prudence.
Mme Geelvinck: Have you good principles?
Boswell: Yes. When I say, 'That is a duty,' then I do it.
Mademoiselle de Zuylen says that I am never bored, but
I do get bored, though I never show it.

The widow had many other admirers, but Boswell joyfully
kept up his siege, reporting back to Zélide on his manoeuvres: he

cornered *la Veuve* at card parties, whispered to her behind the potted plants at the Assembly and even got himself invited to her little son's birthday party—a notable *coup*—tactfully informing her that the boy was like 'a spark from the sun in heaven.' However at the end of the month Madame Geelvinck announced that she was leaving for the Hague, and though she promised to write, Boswell knew he was now doomed to play the much less satisfactory role of abandoned suitor. On the day of her departure, after a restless night, he rose before dawn, slipped a flask of gin in his pocket and hurried over to the St Catherine's Gate to watch her coach leave Utrecht. It was freezing, but deploying his new-found Dutch he talked his way into the sentry's guard-post and, huddled in the doorway, he watched her pass. 'She looked angelic, and that glimpse was ravishing. You then treated the sentinel with Geneva [gin]. You stood on the ramparts and saw her disappear. You was quite torn with love.'

Boswell then marched manfully off to his fencing lesson, but was miserable—'very bad all day'—and had an awful premonition that his depression was about to return. He managed to keep up a good front at the Comtesse's evening reception, but fell into gloomiest reflections back at his lodgings. He now had only one Tulip left, and the next morning he tried to take comfort from that.

> Love has now fairly left you, and behold in how dreary a state you was in. At night you was listless and distressed and obliged to go drawling to bed. This day study hard; get firm tone; go on. Mademoiselle [de Zuylen] will be your friend.

He had need of her. In March the dreaded Utrecht depression returned. The weather became damp and foggy—although not cold enough for skating—and he caught a severe head-cold which lasted for nearly six weeks. He then received news from friends that his illegitimate son Charles had died. The regular Assemblies closed down for the season. He felt horribly marooned. There was only one source of light.

> You was fine with Mademoiselle de Zuylen. She was amiable. She said you might see her at home at least

once a week . . . She said *la Veuve* had no passion, and often ill humour. This girl trusts you; like her . . . Shun marriage. Today, honey for cold.'

Boswell's battle with gloom, ill-health and homesickness was to last until April, and Zélide gradually became his main ally in the fight.

She gave him her 'Character Portraits' to read and also probably her satirical story 'Le Noble'. She began to share confidences with him, describing her claustrophobic situation at the castle at Zuylen and hinting at her clandestine correspondence with Constant d'Hermenches. But Boswell was never quite sure how to respond, how far to trust her; she was so changeable, so clever. He never quite admitted his guilty secret about Charles to her.

You told her you was distressed for the death of a friend, and begged to see if she could be company to the distressed. She said yes, but she soon showed her eternal laughing . . . You told her she never had a better friend. She said, 'I believe it.' This day *retenue*; be firm and only silent. What a world is this!

When he was impatient with her, he considered writing a comedy about the absurdities of her life, her bluestocking intrigues and her stolid Dutch family (of which, in reality, he was very fond). It was to be entitled *The Female Scribbler*, with a good range of character parts, and himself as the 'sensible' foreign hero. It would contain 'old, surly squire; weak, ignorant mother; light, trifling lover whom she does not care for; foolish maid; heavy, covetous bookseller; generous, sensible lover etc.' In this mood he also vented his spleen on the Comtesse, by the more direct method of trouncing her at cards.

La Comtesse was truly chagrined. But you knocked a pair of ducats out of her pocket at cards. This turned up her Dutch nose . . . After dinner you said imprudently you had so bad a view of life that you could do almost anything.

By now Boswell was again swinging through terrible extremes. On one day he rose 'dreary as a dromedary'; on the next he was valiantly determined to 'sustain the character of a country gentleman.' He received a 'sweet and elegant letter' from Madame Geelvinck in the Hague, and momentarily thought her 'the finest prize in the Provinces'; but then found—'alas! it did not elevate your gloomy soul.' He tried eating at a raffish hotel in the Oudkerkhof, but then came home in misery.

> You dined at Koster's—blackguards. You was direfully melancholy and had the last and most dreadful thoughts. You came home and prayed. You read Greek, and Voltaire on the English.

He tried to drown himself in study: Xenophon, Plato, Civil Law, his idea for a Dutch dictionary; but ended up discussing predestination with the Reverend Brown.

Assailed by thoughts of suicide, Boswell turned his mind to his warlike Scottish ancestors and went out one winter's dawn into the deserted meadows beyond Utrecht Cathedral where he performed a curious ritual with a dress sword.

> You went out to the fields, and in view of the [cathedral] tower, drew your sword glittering in the sun, and on your knees swore that if there is a Fatality, then that was also ordained; but if you had free will, as you believed, you swore and called the Great God to witness that, although you're melancholy, you'll stand it, and for the time before you go to Hague, now own it.

Then he went grimly off to Professor Trotz's lecture.

Later in the day he returned to the cathedral, climbed the narrow stone steps to the top of the tower, over 350 feet high, and stood silently looking down on Utrecht, and far out across the stretching misty expanse of Holland, pierced with innumerable spires, towards his homeland far in the north. Then he hurried off and took tea with Zélide.

Zélide's highly iconoclastic views on marriage gradually came to fascinate Boswell, providing not merely a diversion to his melancholy, but something of a solace. He found a new role: no longer the desperate, lovelorn traveller, he became the wise, amusing, philosophic friend.

Her autobiographical 'Character', which he kept among his papers with a series of sheets headed 'Portrait of Zélide', provided him with much material for reflection. In many ways she seemed strikingly like himself (though he would never admit this), and her situation was one that he instinctively understood. Certain passages went straight to his heart. Zélide had written of herself:

> Realising that she is too sensitive to be happy, she has almost ceased to hope for happiness. She flees from remorse and pursues diversion. Her pleasures are rare, but they are lively. She snatches them, she relishes them eagerly. Aware of the futility of planning and the uncertainty of the future, she seeks above all to make the passing moment happy. Can you not guess her secret? Zélide is something of a sensualist. Too lively and too powerful feelings; too much inner activity with no satisfactory outlet: there is the source of all her misfortunes.

Boswell could identify with that restlessness, that secret 'sensuality', that excessive 'inner activity', only too well. It was exactly these things that he was trying to curb in himself. So he set out to curb them in Zélide instead. He would not so much court this Tulip as cultivate her, guide her and if necessary defend her in the little daily duels of Dutch gossip. He would become her advisor and her champion. It was understood that she was wittier, cleverer perhaps, than he; but in exchange it was also to be understood that he was wiser, more morally sound, than she. That is the role that Boswell now assigned to himself, and which, with touching vanity, he assumed that Zélide (not to mention her parents) would gratefully accept from a young Scottish gentleman of parts. It was one way, after all, of avoiding suicide. And psychologically it also represented a subtle shift from the autobiographical to the biographical mode.

Boswell was determined to stay on in Utrecht—to 'stick to his post'—until the end of the academic year in June. But it was Zélide, not Madame Geelvinck, who now held him. He wrote long letters to his friends Dempster and Temple, and even to his father, explaining his depression and also his determination.

> It is certain that I am subject to melancholy. It is the
> distemper of our family. I am equally subject to excessive
> high spirits. Such is my constitution. Let me study it, and
> let me maintain an equality of mind.

They all wrote back encouragingly, Lord Auchinleck with the
greatest feelings of sympathy, having experienced similar
emotions in youth. He bracingly quoted Virgil:

> You are not therefore to despond or despair; on the
> contrary, you must arm yourself doubly against them, as
> the poet directs: '*Tu ne cede malis, sed contra audentior
> ito.*' ['Thou shalt not give way to misfortune but strive
> against it with greater daring.']

And he warned gently against his son's amatory flights: 'Your
Dutch wit and Dutch widow are not so easily caught as our Scots
lasses.'

As part of his philosophic strategy, Boswell now told Zélide
that he was busy finding her an ideal husband in England who
would greatly improve her moral outlook. This was an ingenious
form of displaced courtship. Temple was chosen for this
delightful task, and he responded enthusiastically to this new
double intrigue of his wayward friend.

> So the Countess turns out to be a jilt. I am already in
> love with Mademoiselle de Zuylen. Charming creature!
> young and handsome, *une savante et bel esprit.* Tell her
> an Englishman adores her and would think it the greatest
> happiness of his life to have it in his power to prostrate
> himself at her feet. You shall have the widow. Don't be
> angry.

Boswell might have been angry, or at the least a little put
out, had he known in what spirit of mischievous fun Zélide
received these confidences and observed all his grand, philosophic
manoeuvrings. Her own side of the story can be traced through
the letters she was sending almost daily to Constant
d'Hermenches. She first mentioned Boswell in March. 'When I go

to the Assembly, I chat and play with a young Scotsman, full of good sense, wit, and *naïveté*.' The emphasis was undoubtedly, for Zélide, on that *naïveté*. By May, she was relishing his plan to make her 'more rational, more prudent, and more reserved' through the curious mechanism of marriage to a Scotsman: 'I am greatly amused.' She was running rings round him; it was this fact which gave her such a genuine pleasure in his company.

Boswell was now in the liveliest state of confusion about his own feelings. While speaking to Zélide of reason and prudence, he was secretly planning a thoroughly imprudent visit to the red-light district in Amsterdam, as a way of treating his depression and completing his Dutch education. While singing Zélide's praises to Temple, he was simultaneously writing in extreme exasperation in his journal.

> Yesterday you continued in a kind of delerium. You wrote all day. At night you was at Monsieur de Zuylen's . . . Zélide was *nervish*. You saw she would make a sad wife and propagate wretches. You reflected when you came home that you have not made enough use of your time. You have not been active enough, learned enough Dutch, enough of manners.

Yet when Zélide was criticized by a Dutch naval captain, Peter Reynst, he again leapt faithfully to her defence. Reynst had remarked cuttingly that Zélide had been brought up in Geneva, where there was 'unlimited wit among the ladies' but a total lack of 'good principles'. She sacrificed 'probity to wit', like a typical bluestocking.

Boswell answered with a gallant broadside. 'I fought like her champion. I said, "That young lady makes me feel very humble, when I find her so much above me in wit, in knowledge, in good sense."'

Reynst politely demurred. 'She lacks good sense and consequently she goes wrong; and a man who has not half her wit and knowledge may still be above her.'

Boswell pretended to disagree, but did not know exactly what to reply, for it was secretly just what he thought himself. Boswell believed that it was the male sex who must always command, out of a natural God-given superiority. Zélide directly challenged this notion. It was a profound clash of cultural assumptions, in its own way a clash between Enlightenment and the advance shock wave of Romanticism. If Boswell aspired to be an Enlightenment *philosophe*, Zélide was already acting like a Romantic rebel. Boswell added a comment that is one of the most acute things ever observed about Isabelle de Zuylen.

> I thought [Reynst's criticism] very true, and I thought it a good thing. For were it not for that lack [of good sense], Zélide would have an absolute power. She would have unlimited dominion over men, and would overthrow the dignity of the male sex.

At the end of May, Boswell took the canal boat to Amsterdam, in an ecstasy of nerves and expectation, to assert the God-given superiority of man in a Dutch bawdy-house. At the same time he had accepted an invitation from 'dear Zélide' to visit her for the first time at her family castle. The two expeditions, which took place within twenty-four hours of each other, reveal his divided self with a comedy worthy of Diderot.

Boswell chose a Saturday night for his Amsterdam expedition. Having spent all Friday night awake on the canal boat 'among ragamuffins', he arrived 'restless and fretful', put up at Grubb's English Hotel and spent the morning paying courtesy calls on a series of Scottish clergymen. He then dined with an English merchant, drinking a good deal. These psychological preparations were somewhat marred by his realization that he had no condom to protect himself against venereal disease, and he did not know where to purchase one in Amsterdam. (The eighteenth-century condom was usually made of animal-bladder, and referred to as a 'sheath' or 'armour'; it was expensive and therefore considered to be reusable in an emergency.)

Trusting to luck, Boswell blundered off to a bawdy-house at five o'clock. 'I was shown upstairs, and had a bottle of claret and a *juffrouw*.' But on closer inspection Boswell concluded that the girl had more need of a doctor than a customer and excused himself. 'I had no armour, so did not fight. It was truly ludicrous to talk in Dutch to a whore. This scene was to me a rarity as great as peas in February.' He suddenly felt ashamed of himself, wondering what he was doing in 'the sinks of gross debauchery', and he fled in deepest gloom. Back in the streets he then upbraided himself for moral cowardice: 'so sickly was my brain that I had the low scruples of an Edinburgh divine.'

But the comedy was not over. Boswell rushed off to another Scottish clergyman, James Blinshall (there seemed to be an endless supply of these hospitable reverends in Amsterdam), and sat talking of 'religious melancholy like a good sound fellow' until nine in the evening. This revived his spirits, and he then went drinking at a Scottish tavern called Farquhar's 'among blackguards', and supped with an Irish peruke-maker. It was, he thought hazily, turning into 'a queer evening' altogether. By eleven he was back on the streets looking for a *speelhuis*, the Dutch equivalent of a dance-hall. But he had no guide (and still no 'armour').

> I therefore very madly sought for one myself and strolled up and down the Amsterdam streets, which by all accounts are very dangerous at night. I began to be frightened and to think of Belgic *knives*.

But weaving through the narrow alleys, he persisted until he heard music, found the *speelhuis* and 'entered boldly.'

One can just about reconstruct the scene from his by now rather confused notes. A band was playing in one corner; the place was packed with sailors and whores; everyone was dancing and drunk. Boswell lurched to the bar, obtained a drink and a pipe and launched himself into the mêlée, talking wildly in Dutch to anyone he bumped into. 'I had near quarrelled with one of the musicians. But I was told to take care, which I wisely did.' He was transfixed by the extraordinary fancy dress worn by all the girls. Finally he found one got up in 'riding-clothes', with a mass of lace frou-frou, and cheerfully danced with her 'a true blackguard minuet'. For a little while he forgot everything in this strange, erotic *pas de deux*. 'I had my pipe in my mouth and performed like any common sailor.' Then he was suddenly tired and drunk and hopeless. 'I spoke plenty of Dutch but could find no girl that elicited my inclinations. I was disgusted with this low confusion.' Boswell staggered out, miraculously found his way back to Grubb's Hotel, and 'slept sound.'

He played out the final act of his great Amsterdam expedition, which he realized had turned into low farce, on Sunday morning. He went meekly off to the English Ambassador's chapel, heard a 'good sermon', dined and then returned to hear James Blinshall preach. He was overwhelmed by 'all the old Scots gloomy ideas', and determined on one last sortie before the return to Utrecht.

> I then strolled through mean brothels in dirty lanes. I was quite splenetic. I still wanted armour. I drank tea with Blinshall. At eight I got into the *roef* of the Utrecht boat. I had with me an Italian fiddler, a German officer, his wife and child.

So his wild weekend finished penitently, on a subdued domestic note. Boswell did not know whether to be more ashamed by what he had attempted to do in Amsterdam, or by what he had failed to do. Back at Utrecht he was 'changeful and uneasy' all day. There was nothing for the philosopher to be proud of, either way.

His expedition to Zuylen was such an absolute contrast that even Boswell was somewhat bewildered by his own capacity for extremes. In response to Zélide's invitation, he and the Reverend Brown walked the five miles to the ancestral castle on the Vecht, and were instantly captivated by the old moated building with its four pointed turrets reflected in the still waters. Gazing round at the ancient brick gatehouse, the cobbled paths, the formal gardens and the stretching vistas of beech trees opening out on to placid water meadows dotted with windmills, Boswell had a new vision of Zélide's existence. She became for him the daughter of a magic domain, a princess in an enchanted tower, imprisoned perhaps by her own brilliant perversities, which the wandering young philosopher must waken with a kiss. Or the spiritual equivalent of a kiss. This image of Zélide, like a figure out of a Dutch fairy tale, would never quite leave Boswell. And her enigmatic quality, her refusal ever wholly to yield her mysterious independence of soul, became for him a symbol of Holland itself.

They returned that evening to Utrecht, and dined with the assembled van Tuyl clan. Boswell at once set about charming Zélide, summoning up all his Scottish sagacity, teasing, reasoning, playing his philosophic part to the full. She was highly responsive, and together in that elegant company, they danced a very different kind of minuet, each wondering who was in love with whom.

> Zélide was too vivacious, abused system, and laughed at reason, saying that she was guided by a *sentiment intérieur*. I was lively in defence of wisdom and showed her how wrong she was, for if she had no settled system one could never count on her. One could not say what she would do. I said to her also, 'You must show a little decorum. You are among rational beings, who boast of their reason, and who do not like to hear it flouted.' Old De Zuylen and all fifteen friends were delighted with me.

After dinner Boswell and Zélide slipped away and walked together outside in the fine spring evening, wandering into 'a sweet pretty wood'. It was the moment for romantic declarations, but Boswell carefully changed tack, and deployed his double intrigue.

> I delivered to Zélide the fine compliments which my friend Temple had charged me to deliver; that is to say, the warm sentiments of adoration. She was much pleased. I talked to her seriously and bid her marry a *bon baron* of good sense and amiable manners who would be her superior in common life, while he admired her fine genius and all that.

Zélide gazed at Boswell with amusement. 'She said she would marry such a man if she ever saw him. But still she would fain have something finer.' They turned to go back into the house, and Boswell risked a final shift of direction.

'I said she should never have a man of much sensibility. For instance, "I would not marry you if you would make me King of the Seven Provinces."'

Zélide burst out laughing, and later reported the whole conversation to d'Hermenches. 'He told me the other day that although I was a charming creature, he would not marry me if I

had the Seven United Provinces for my dowry; I agreed heartily.'
So the princess and the philosopher dallied, and in 'fine, gay, free
conversation did the minutes fly.'

There was not enough time left for Boswell to resolve his
own paradoxes, or those of Zélide. His Dutch sojourn was
drawing to its close. In early June, Lord Marischal, an old
friend of Lord Auchinleck's, arrived at the Hague and announced
that he had come to take Boswell on the next stage of his
European journey. He promised to take him into Germany on a
visit to the Prussian Court of Frederick the Great. Boswell's
thoughts swung rapidly from love to glory, and he began to pack
his law books, while ordering 'a genteel flowered-silk suit'.

Boswell's last days were spent in a flurry of visits to Zélide in
her enchanted castle and a series of extended farewells. He swung
between passion and relief. Peter Reynst informed him that
Zélide was 'really in love' with Boswell. 'I believe it. But I was
mild and *retenu*.' On 10 June, he rushed up to Zuylen in a
splendid hired chaise and his mood was very different.

> I was in solid spirits in the old château, but rather too
> odd was I; for I talked of my pride, and wishing to be
> king. Zélide and I were left alone. She owned that she
> was hypochondriac [melancholy], and that she had no
> religion other than that of the adoration of one God. In
> short, she discovered an unhinged mind; yet I loved her.

He saw her again on the eleventh, when she was in 'a fever
of spirits', as was he. On the twelfth he met her at her music
master's, where she played delightfully and then took him for a
walk. 'I was touched with regret at the thought of parting with
her. Yet she rattled on so much that she really vexed me.' It was
all very confusing to Boswell.

On 14 June, he again leapt into his chaise to take his final
farewell at Zuylen. Once more the talk was of husbands: of
Boswell's ideals of deference and Zélide's notions of freedom.
Their conversation was inconclusive. 'I owned to her that I was
very sorry to leave her. She gave me many a tender look. We
took a kind farewell, as did all the family.' They had agreed to

write secretly to each other, and that evening Zélide began a long letter to pursue him into Germany. 'I find you odd and lovable,' she wrote succinctly. Meanwhile back at Utrecht the Scottish chaplain observed: 'It is lucky that you are no longer together; for you would learn her nonsense, and she would learn yours.' Boswell manfully agreed.

On the eve of Boswell's departure from Utrecht, old Lord Marischal, who had evidently heard a great deal of Zélide, mischievously announced that he would be fascinated to visit Zuylen himself. Accordingly Boswell found himself one last time at the castle. With curious Dutch formality, they all sat round drinking tea in the open air, while the swallows spun round the moat and along the darkening colonnades of beech. Boswell drew Zélide aside, and she whispered, 'Are you back again? We made a touching adieu.' Then she gave him the letter, which he was told not to read until he was actually and really going.

> Zélide seemed much agitated, said she had never been in love, but said that *one* might meet with *un homme amiable*, etc. etc. etc. for whom *one* might feel a strong affection, which would probably be lasting, *but* this amiable man might not have the same affection for *one*. In short she spoke too plain to leave me in doubt that she *really* loved me. But then she went with her wild fancy, saying she thought only of the present moment.

All was confusion and Boswell told himself she was 'a frantic libertine'. In the circumstances, it was a conclusion of the most perfect irony.

It was dusk when they rose to leave. Zélide gave Boswell her hand, and in the half-light of that Dutch still life, he thought he could glimpse a painterly luminescence: 'The tender tear stood crystal in her eye. Poor Zélide!' Or rather, poor Boswell.

The next day he left for Germany.

Boswell and Zélide never met again, although they corresponded in a desultory fashion over the subsequent four years. Boswell did finally propose marriage, and Zélide, inevitably, turned him down.

IAN HAMILTON
A COLOSSAL HOARD

For James Boswell, admiration was a busy, intimate affair. Although he was enormously vain, he was a stranger to embarrassment, and this unusual mix often seems to have been his greatest strength. Boswell wanted to be more than a mere biographer: he wanted to imprint his own personality on the life he planned to write, even as that life was being lived.

Boswell had the highest reverence for Johnson. He spent three years fishing for an introduction and when they finally met he was gratified to be treated with a proper brusqueness. Boswell felt 'no little elation at having now so happily established an acquaintance of which I had been so long ambitious,' and—when it began to seem that Johnson liked him—'a pleasing elevation of mind beyond what I had ever before experienced.' This is the stock language of the seasoned hero-hunter. Boswell was addicted to the famous: Rousseau and Voltaire were two of his prize scalps, and he was forever writing letters to celebrities in order to connect their names with his. Like many another hero-worshipper, Boswell believed that his own gifts and temperament were nearer to the heroic than to those of the mediocre mass: he *deserved* to be close to Johnson—more than an incompetent sycophant like Oliver Goldsmith did, for instance. By keeping Johnson's flame he would also be attending to his own. And from this point of view, he has been thoroughly triumphant. The Dr Johnson of the popular imagination is indeed Johnson as first imagined by James Boswell. Ursa Major, the Great Cham, the auld dominie and all the rest of it have been drawn directly from the *Life*. The verb 'to Boswellize' now has a meaning in the language.

Every so often, efforts are made to liberate Johnson from the ardent custody of his disciple, to insist that Johnson was a *writer*, not a chop-house aphorist, that he had an inner life to which Boswell had no access and would not have understood. And, it is also pointed out, the *Life of Johnson* is not really a full Life at all. Boswell came late upon the scene and his attachment lasted for just over twenty of his subject's seventy-five years. The book runs to about fourteen hundred pages: of these, under three hundred cover life-before-Boswell.

It is this focus on Johnson the mature celebrity, and more particularly on Johnson as he functioned in the hearing of James

Boswell, that can stir professional Johnsonians to indignation: such as these wish us to read the master's books, not listen to his chat. Boswell was not so abjectly worshipful that he held back from itemizing much Johnsoniana that was hard (even for him) to take: the 'uncouth' dress, the 'slovenly particularities' of his apartments, the 'disgusting eating habits', the prejudices and the inconsistencies (Johnson's 'varying of himself in talk'). But even here the biographer could plead that he was acting on orders issued from on high: 'If a man is to write a Panegyrick, he may keep vices out of sight, but if he professes to write a life, he must represent it really as it was.' This is the drift of all Johnson's pronouncements on the subject of biography. He destroyed a mass of his own papers before he died and he knew pretty well what he had bequeathed to Boswell. And Johnson was 'well apprised of the circumstances.' Whether fond or irritated—and with Boswell he could easily be both—he would not have wished to disappoint one so transparently susceptible to disappointment; and he had seen enough of Boswell's journals to know the kind of *Life* that he would write. He also knew what Boswell's verdict, conscious or unconscious, would turn out to be: that Johnson 'great and good as he was, must not be supposed to be entirely perfect.' The burden of the *Life* is not, at any level, inconsistent with this verdict, and the verdict itself is one for which Johnson himself would happily have settled.

Boswell too, we suspect, would have wished to be remembered in this way, as great and good though not entirely perfect —and indeed this is how most of us now think of him. But he had to wait a long time for his just verdict. The nineteenth century deplored him and it was not until the 1930s that his reputation was substantially restructured. Thanks to some strange scholarly discoveries in Ireland and in Scotland, a new Boswell was presented to the world; the *Life of Johnson* was revealed to be not so much a marvel of eighteenth century stenography as a work crafted with considerable literary cunning, and Boswell himself was found to be darker, funnier and more troublingly complicated than the buffoon figure that had seemingly been set in marble by Thomas Macaulay's notorious 1831 review:

A man of the meanest and feeblest intellect . . . He was

the laughing stock of the whole of that brilliant society which has owed to him the greater part of his fame. He was always laying himself at the feet of some eminent man, and begging to be spit upon and trampled upon . . . Servile and impertinent, shallow and pedantic, a bigot and a sot, bloated with family pride, and eternally blustering about the dignity of a born gentleman, yet stooping to be a talebearer, an eavesdropper, a common butt in the taverns of London.

The story of the hoard of papers begins with Boswell's death in 1795. His will named three literary executors: Edmund Malone, who had helped him with the *Life*, and two other trusted friends, William Temple and Sir William Forbes. Their instructions regarding the papers were 'to publish more or less' as they saw fit, and—although they derived 'rich entertainment' from the Journal—their conclusion was that dear old Boz had in it 'put down many things both of himself and others that should not appear.' It was agreed that any decision about the selection and possible publication of excerpts should be left until Boswell's seventeen-year-old second son had come of age. This son, James, had been Boswell's favourite: 'An extraordinary boy . . . He is much of his father.'

The new Laird of Auchinleck, and Boswell's heir, was Alexander, and he seems to have shared the family's general touchiness on the subject of his father's literary fame. Alexander was a proud young laird and, twenty years old at his father's death, he hated to see Boswell ridiculed in satires and cartoons as Johnson's whipping boy. Walter Scott probably summed up the Auchinleck view most accurately when he wrote that Boswell's book, 'though one of the most entertaining in the world, is not just what one would wish a near relation to have written.' This was indeed the attitude of Alexander's wife: she was the one who sent Joshua Reynolds' portrait of Johnson to the saleroom. Boswell had bequeathed a few financial problems.

Altogether, there was a feeling that the Boswell name had suffered sufficient exposure to the public gaze. Consequently, the great cache of manuscripts was set to one side: some of it was at

Auchinleck, some still in the hands of the executors and some with James, who lived in London. Alexander perhaps did not even open the boxes stored at Auchinleck; James showed an interest but never followed through in any systematic way. And then, in 1822, both he and Alexander died: James of a sudden illness and Alexander in a duel. Each was in his forties. And by this time, the three executors were also dead. Their original idea had been to collect the papers together in one place but Forbes, the chief executor, died ten years after Boswell and one lot of manuscripts still languished at his Scottish home. Nobody at Auchinleck had ever shown any great interest in retrieving them and now, with James and Alexander dead, perhaps nobody knew that they were there. The new laird was another James, aged fifteen in 1822. He, with his mother's guidance, was also disposed to keep the lid on his ancestor's private writings.

The performance of Boswell's immediate heirs and executors is strangely unimpressive, considering their credentials and their tastes. Boswell's two sons were, in their different ways, both literary men. Alexander was a bibliophile and ran his own private press at Auchinleck, specializing in reprints of rare books, and he was active in Edinburgh literary circles (hyperactive, on occasions) where he tended to remind people of his father: according to John Gibson Lockhart, Alexander had all of 'Bozzy's cleverness, good humour, and joviality, without one touch of his meaner qualities' (which nicely encapsulates the then-current view of Bozzy). Maybe Alexander was too gregarious and impulsive to have taken on the job of sorting through a mountain of old papers: whatever the reason, he was busier in the service of Burns's posterity than of his father's. With Burns, it was anyway merely a matter of putting up a statue.

James—as Boswell anticipated—was a much likelier bet. He was a lawyer and a literary scholar and he was close to Malone: indeed such was his closeness that Malone chose him as *his* literary executor. James worked with Malone on his great edition of Shakespeare, and, after Malone's death, it was James who inherited the task of completing the twenty-one volumes, adding prefaces, notes and even a glossarial index.

The first test of what, by default, had gradually become the Auchinleck position took place in 1829, when John Wilson Croker was preparing his edition of the *Life of Johnson* (an edition which would provoke Macaulay's wrathful words on Boswell, not to mention his even more wrathful words on Croker, whom he loathed). Croker wrote to Auchinleck, asking about any surviving Boswell papers, but got no reply. A prominent politician, he was greatly piqued and at once enlisted Walter Scott to act as go-between. Scott did his best but in spite of all 'importunities and influence' Croker continued to be shunned. In the preface to his edition, he complains about his treatment and not altogether face-savingly concludes that 'the original journals do not exist at Auchinleck: perhaps to this fact the silence of Sir James Boswell can be attributed.'

At the back of Croker's mind, the suspicion probably was that the Boswell heirs had had a bonfire and were reluctant to admit it; and he believed he had some other grounds for thinking so. Malone, in a footnote to the fifth edition of Boswell's *Life*, made reference to a letter having been 'burned in a mass of papers in Scotland.' The theory now is that 'burned' was a misprint for 'buried' and that it was this misprint, coupled with Croker's official-sounding statement in his preface, that started the myth which prevailed throughout the century: the myth that Boswell's papers were destroyed.

Nearly thirty years later, in 1857, a certain Major Stone, late of the East India Company, was out shopping in Boulogne and noticed that some of his purchases had been wrapped in a letter signed 'James Boswell'. The major asked where the wrapping had come from and was told that a bundle of paper had been bought from a hawker. Stone managed to get hold of what was left: ninety-seven letters by Boswell to William Temple, his friend and literary executor. The story of how the letters got to France is complicated (to do with Temple's eldest daughter marrying a debt-ridden clergyman who had been forced to flee across the Channel), but it is probably just as well that the material surfaced where it did: an English-reading shopkeeper might have thought twice about subjecting her customers to Boswell's true confessions. When the Temple letters were published, they were heavily expurgated—not heavily enough, though, to disguise their predominating flavour: the boozy, libidinous Boswell who wrote without inhibition to his chum was close enough to the Macaulay caricature for the family to feel thoroughly justified in its policy of silence. And in the England of 1857 no outsider was going to lament that material similar to this had been destroyed.

The Boswell family had in any case undergone a change. The James who had rebuffed Croker died in the year of the Temple letters' publication and his death marked the end of the direct male line: the Boswell papers were now controlled by women. There was the dowager, Alexander's widow (who lived on until 1864), there was James's widow (who died in 1884) and there were two daughters, Julia and Emily. Emily eventually married an Irish peer, Lord Talbot de Malahide, and it was after her death in 1898 that the contents of Auchinleck were gradually removed to Malahide Castle, near Dublin. The Talbots had one son, yet another James.

Between the death of James in 1857 and the removal to Malahide (which was probably completed in 1915), there were three significant events in the great Boswell papers' saga. In 1874, the Reverend Charles Rogers edited a collection of Boswelliana (based on papers which had once belonged to James, the biographer's second son). Rogers, having in mind the Malone footnote and Croker's preface, freshly underscored what was now the generally accepted view: 'Boswell's manuscripts were left to the immediate disposal of his family; and it is believed that the whole were immediately destroyed.' No contradiction was issued by the family and the myth was thus revitalized.

When the Auchinleck collection was transferred to Malahide Castle, most of it was stored in an ebony cabinet of which Boswell himself had been particularly fond. In the process, some superficial sorting seems to have been done: enough, anyway, for Lord Talbot and his second wife (he had remarried in 1901) to begin speculating on the possible cash value of the hoard. Like all Boswells and sub-Boswells, the Talbots were seriously short of cash. At some point, Lord Talbot's brother, a distinguished colonel in the Royal Engineers, even went so far as to begin *reading* Boswell's Journals. For this alone, Milo Talbot earns his niche in literary history. It was by now more than a hundred years since Boswell's death and, so far as we know, not a single page of the Journals had been read by anyone since the original executors' examination.

Milo's verdict was that some sort of publication should be countenanced and that handsome profits might well be afoot. In 1911, he sent a censored typescript of the Journals to John Murray. The firm of Murray had long been sensitive on the matter of private papers and had recently been re-embroiled in a controversy over Byron's estate. Even so, it seems remarkable that the publisher should have reacted to Boswell as he did. Acknowledging receipt of what we now think of as one of the century's great literary *coups*, Murray reported to Lord Talbot that both he and his reader had, on reading the material, experienced both 'disappointment' and 'dismay'. Presumably, he said, Lord Talbot was familiar with Macaulay's 'poor opinion' of Boswell (an opinion now eighty years of age):

> But Macaulay had not seen these journals: had he done so he would have added that [Boswell] was an incurable sot and libertine: conscious of his own iniquities: sometimes palliating them as 'Asiatic satisfactions quite consistent with devotion and with a fervent attachment to my valuable spouse': sometimes making resolutions of amendment which were not carried into effect, but always lapsing into the slough of drunkenness and debauchery and indolence.
>
> The occasions on which he records that he was intoxicated, and even blind drunk are innumerable, and over and over again he notes that 'he ranged the streets and followed whores' or words to that effect.
>
> Many passages have been cut out, I presume on account of their immorality, but if they were worse than many which remain they must have been very bad indeed.

Murray could see that the Journals might conceivably be of interest to a Boswell biographer but believed that publication would be to nobody's advantage: 'If we eliminate the passages which have already been published'—by which he meant any bits that had gone into the *Life of Johnson*—'those which are unpublishable: and those which are too trivial for permanence, the residuum is I fear very small.'

After this, the Talbots decided to sit on their typescript for a while; more than likely, they accepted Murray's view. But the secret of the Journals' existence was now out, at least locally: dinner guests at Malahide Castle were shown the ebony cabinet and told what it contained. There were even occasional readings from the Journals.

None of these goings-on was reported in the English Department of Yale University where Professor Chauncy B. Tinker was working on a book about the young James Boswell, and preparing what he believed would be a definitive edition of Boswell's correspondence. In July 1920, nine years after the Talbots' overtures to Murray, Tinker placed an advertisement in the *Times Literary Supplement* requesting owners of any Boswell letters to get in touch with him. He got two replies, both directing him to Malahide. Tinker at once wrote to Talbot and received this answer from the son: 'I am very sorry I am unable to give you any letters of James Boswell for publication. I regret I cannot meet your views in this respect.'

Astonishingly, Tinker accepted the brush-off and quietly proceeded with his work. His edition of the letters was by this stage well advanced and would be his *magnum opus*: according to one of his distinguished colleagues, 'he was in fact consciously or unconsciously inhibited from vigorous and persistent enquiry by not really wanting to turn up a large new mass of Boswell letters.' Tinker's edition appeared in 1924 to the applause of academe. Only then did he brace himself for a second crack at Malahide.

By this date the Talbot personnel had somewhat changed. Lord Talbot had died in 1921 and his son succeeded to the title at the age of forty-seven. Three years later, he married an actress half his age, one Joyce Gunning Kerr. This new Lady Talbot was untouched by any lingering traces of Boswell family pride, and she had literary pretensions. Her husband, a racing man, had none. Thus, when Tinker made his second approach, it was Joyce Gunning Kerr who invited him to tea at Malahide and who chastized him for not having sought Talbot permission before issuing his 1924 edition of the *Letters*.

Tinker was then allowed to peek inside the ebony cabinet.

What he saw there both amazed and sickened him. He wrote to a friend:

> I was led into an adjoining room, where I found myself standing in front of the famous 'ebony cabinet'—a sort of highboy with many drawers. The drawers which I was permitted to pull open were crammed with papers in the wildest confusion. I felt like Sinbad in the valley of rubies. I glanced—panting the while—at a few sheets. One was a letter from Boswell to Alexander, then a schoolboy. At once I realized that a new day had dawned for Boswellians, and that for C. B. Tinker there was a dreadful crisis, the resolution of which would alter the whole of his future life. (I did not sleep that night.)

Tinker was not allowed to take anything away, nor to copy any of the papers. He left Malahide feeling that his life's work lay in ruins.

Perhaps the kindest way of explaining Lady Talbot's conduct here is to remember that she was more of an actress than a scholar. Less charitably, it might be conjectured that she knew Tinker would soon spread the word; in Boswell matters, his authentication carried weight.

In a July 1925 postcard to A. Edward Newton, the eminent American book collector, Tinker cried: 'Everything here and nothing to be touched. I have been on the rack.' Within days, the rare book trade was alerted. Cables were fired off to Malahide. The Talbots, though, stood firm: the collection was not for sale.

The same American book collector seems to have been the only person to divine that the owners might need subtler handling. 'I'll bet a hat someone works this invaluable mine.' The someone did not take long to appear. Newton reported the Tinker mission and its aftermath to Lieutenant Colonel Ralph Hayward Isham, an amateur collector and part-time Boswellian, telling what he knew of the ebony cabinet, of Tinker's anguish and of the Talbots' opposition to a sale. He may even have mentioned that the youthful Lady Talbot could be susceptible to Isham's legendary charm. For Tinker, the Malahide treasure trove spelled ruin. And so it did for Isham, although he did not

Photo: Peter North

JOYCE, LADY TALBOT DE MALAHIDE

recognize this at the time. As soon as Newton planted the idea, there was engendered in Isham an obsession which over the next quarter of a century would dominate his life, soaking up all his money, spoiling his marriages and even from time to time imperilling his sanity.

Isham had a curious background. A thirty-five-year-old American of considerable wealth, educated at Cornell and Yale, he had served in the British Army during World War One and had by this means acquired an English accent and a range of upper-bracket British friends to go with his 'strikingly handsome physical appearance, [his] great charm of manner and formidable powers of persuasion.' A 'fascinating devil' was the common designation, supported now and then by rumours to do with his volatile temperament and his wicked way with women. Thus armed, Isham laid siege to Malahide Castle and after two years of silver-tongued negotiation, the million-word Boswell hoard belonged to him—at a price of around thirty-five thousand pounds, which was low but a good deal more than he could actually afford. Page by page, with deletions *passim* in the Talbot hand, the collection was shipped to the United States. Isham at once appointed an editor, Geoffrey Scott, and set about constructing a monument to the 'new' Boswell, and to his own sterling conduct in the field: a de luxe eighteen-volume limited edition, on antique paper and with eighteenth-century typography. The idea was to finance the five-year project by advance subscriptions and by the sale of subsidiary rights.

From the start, Isham's scheme was plagued by irritations and setbacks: Geoffrey Scott died and had to be replaced; Lady Talbot was intent on censoring the Journal and was not pleased to learn that Isham's lieutenants were deciphering the words she had inked over; the money was forever running low. Isham's personal funds had been exhausted by the purchase and after a time he was having to borrow from friends and even to sell off the odd manuscript. A further irritant, although one not wholly unwelcome in its substance, was Lady Talbot's habit of suddenly discovering new bundles of Boswelliana: for instance, an old croquet box was found to be stuffed with Boswell papers, including the manuscript of his Hebridean Journal. A hayloft would eventually yield further gems. Now and again, Isham found himself experiencing spasms of the Tinker syndrome; how much *more* would turn up after his edition was 'complete'? There were, after all, some gaps in the Malahide Castle haul: letters from several of Boswell's known correspondents (including Johnson), the complete manuscript of the *Life* and, most serious of all, the section of the Journal which recorded Boswell's arrival in London and his first encounters with Johnson. Isham assumed—and maybe even hoped—that such items had been lost.

What Isham did not know, as he rushed his 'definitive' edition towards a 1934 completion date, was that most of these items had already been discovered, not at Malahide, which might not have surprised him, but at Fettercairn House in Aberdeenshire. In 1930, an Aberdeen University lecturer, Claude Colleer Abbott, was researching the life of the eighteenth-century poet and philosopher

James Beattie. Beattie's biographer had been Sir William Forbes, Boswell's chief literary executor. Searching for Beattie material at Fettercairn, Abbott started coming across odd items of Boswelliana: a fair copy of the London Journal (1762–63), letters from Boswell to Forbes, and to Boswell from several well-known figures of his day. There was a packet marked by Boswell 'Concerning Ladies' which contained notes to the biographer from his admirers and a lock of hair. Abbott did not at once know the significance of what he had found: for example, he believed that the London Journal had already been turned up at Malahide. It was evident, though, that 'the house must be systematically searched.' There were cupboards stuffed with papers and a large double attic 'tremendous with lumber of all kinds, the accumulation of generations. Boxes, small and great, abounded.'

With exemplary self-control, Abbott did keep to a system in his search so that, needless to say, the best find of all came last. On the fourth day, he finally reached 'the farther end of the right hand attic':

> Nothing had been touched there for years, and of papers there was no sign. A great wooden box, extricated with difficulty, held nothing but rolls of wall-paper. But when I moved the next up-sided table I saw, wedged in between other furniture, a small sack, rather like a small mail-bag, with rents here and there from which letters were ready to drop. Quickly I dragged it out. A loose letter fell. It was written to Boswell. Down the winding stairs I hurried the sack, wondering whether all the contents could possibly concern Boswell. Before emptying the papers I drew out another loose letter. The omen was favourable. Soon I knew the truth. The sack was stuffed tight with Boswell's papers, most of them arranged in stout wads, torn here and there, and dirty, but for the most part in excellent order. Neither damp nor worm or mouse had gnawed at them. My luck held. Almost to the last corner I have tracked the main find.

The Fettercairn haul ran to some sixteen hundred items: two-thirds of these were letters written to Boswell. There were also over three hundred drafts or copies of letters in Boswell's own hand, seven 'major manuscripts', and over two hundred letters by Johnson—collected by Boswell for his *Life*. In addition to all this, there were many miscellaneous notes, lists and registers and a bundle of contemporary newspaper articles and cuttings.

Lacking this treasure, the glorious Isham edition of *The Private Papers* could hardly fail to seem somewhat diminished, although its editor—Frederick A. Pottle—had always been careful to point out that there were gaps. Isham and Pottle had good reason to feel annoyed that for five years, between 1931 and 1936, neither Abbott nor his prospective publisher, the Clarendon Press, had thought it correct to tip them off. The *sangfroid* of the Press seemed particularly impressive since—during this time —it had been negotiating with the Isham camp about an English edition of the *Private Papers'* Index. The head of the Clarendon Press was R. W. Chapman who, since the 1920s, had been engaged on his own edition of Johnson's letters. Solidarity among scholars was not for him a rigid principle. Lord Clinton, the owner of Fettercairn, had asked for a policy of secrecy and Chapman was afraid that if he did not go along with this, he would lose access to the papers; both as a publisher and as a Johnsonian, he was unable to countenance a deprivation of this magnitude. Johnson letters were in short supply. Isham possessed but one; Abbott had scored an unbelievable two hundred.

Behind all this mild skulduggery was the fear that the Fettercairn haul might actually *belong* to Isham. He had bought from the Talbots the whole of their collection of Boswelliana, and this included any papers that had not yet, at the time of purchase, come to light. Since the Talbots were the heirs of the Boswell estate, the Fettercairn booty must, in law, be theirs and thus, by contract, Isham's. Between 1936 and 1938, Isham fought in the Scottish courts for recognition of his claim, and won. A combination of legal technicalities, disputes over costs, and— during the war—a nervousness about exposing priceless Boswelliana to a hazardous Atlantic crossing, postponed Isham's second, rather battered, Boswell triumph until 1948. Then, at last, the great collector's photograph appeared on the front page of the *New York Times*: 'The Boswell Papers discovered at

Fettercairn House in 1931 and for twelve years in the custody of the Court of Session are now released and have reached these shores,' he said. A year later, Isham sold his entire collection, both Malahide and Fettercairn, to Yale for nearly half a million dollars.

Isham died in 1955, aged sixty-four, and Frederick A. Pottle, who worked with him almost from the start and was often exasperated by his 'histrionic' ways, wrote of him that 'he accomplished what was essentially desirable for Boswell's papers':

> he brought them together and then turned them over to a great institutional library where they could be expertly handled and made available to scholars and the general public. In a period of little over twenty years, working deliberately, adroitly, and with great courage, he reassembled Boswell's archives in the face of a complication of difficulties which no ordinary collector would or could have surmounted . . . He deserves the unstinted gratitude of posterity.

And so he does. And so, too, do several of the saga's supporting personnel. And yet, surveying the story from a distance, it is hard not to wonder why the whole thing took so long. The attitude of the Boswell family at the outset can readily be understood, and we can see too how the Malone misprint, the Croker preface and the Macaulay review helped to perpetuate a bonfire myth. But with the entry of the scholars, we might have expected a speedier dénouement. It is particularly hard to fathom why, for nearly 150 years, nobody thought to take a look into the estate of Sir William Forbes. It was Forbes, after all, to whom Boswell first entrusted his great archive, and every Boswell scholar knew this. Even after Malahide, neither Tinker, Isham or Pottle thought to ask the most obvious of questions: what did Sir William *do* about the papers during the ten years between his appointment as executor and his death in 1806? And after that, what did his family do? If any investigation on these lines had been begun, it would have led swiftly to Fettercairn, and Isham for one might have been spared—or denied—his twenty years of biblio-heroics.

JOHN BANVILLE
LIFE AND ART

He arrived in Paris for the first time huddled on a hay cart. That was a morning in the May of 1702, blustery and wet, with silk in the air and Dutch clouds piled up and a dull pewter shine on the river. He was on the run: something to do with a woman. The authorities in Utrecht were looking for him. His mother had wept; his father the roofer, that rude man, had swung a punch at him. He was eighteen and already had a cough—Gillot, his first teacher, told him he sounded like a crow. What was his name then? Faubelin, Vanhoblin, Van Hobellijn: take your pick. He changed his name, his nationality, everything, covering his tracks. He never lost those Dutch gutturals though, at which his fancy friends laughed behind their hands.

For a week he lay on a pallet wrapped in his cloak in a dirty little room above Gérin's print shop on the Pont Notre Dame, shaking with fever and grumbled at by the *maître*. Below him the other student hacks copied holy pictures all day long, lugubrious madonnas, St Jeromes with book and lion, ill-proportioned depositions from the cross. The stink of turpentine and pigments seeped up through the floorboards, and he would say that forever afterwards all studios smelled to him faintly of sickness. There was a war going on and the streets were thronged with beggars showing off their stumps.

He worked at the Opéra, painting sets, and even acted in the drama on occasion. Acting did not suit him, though: too much like life for him, who did not know how else to live except by playing parts. He went to the Comédie and stood in the pit amid the ceaseless noise and bustle and the stench of bodies, lost in contemplation of that glowing world above him on the stage. He never followed the plots, those ridiculous farragos, but watched the actors, studying their movements, their stylized, outlandish gestures. Afterwards he sat alone for hours in the Café Procope, sketching from memory. One of his first submissions to the Academy was a harlequinade in oils, very prettily done, he thought, with just the right balance of gaiety and menace. Second prize. Well.

Le grand hiver

It is the winter of 1709, after the disaster of Malplacquet. There was famine in Paris: mothers would not let their children out alone for fear they would be taken and eaten by the poor. Ice on the Seine, and that strange, thin, sour smell in the air for months that everyone said was the smell of the dead on the battlefield, blowing on the wind all the way down from Valenciennes. In the Tuileries one black night a tree exploded in the frost. Vaublin had been studying with Gillot for four years and was sick of it, the nagging and the sneers, the petty jealousies. Gillot was another like himself, watchful and secretive, a misanthrope. In the end they quarrelled, unforgivable things were shouted and Vaublin left and went to work with his friend Claude Audran at the Luxembourg Palace. Audran was the curator of the palace gallery. Vaublin sat every afternoon for hours, until the light faded and his fingers seized up from the cold, copying Rubens's series on the life of Marie de' Medici, plundering all that old master's secrets. Such silence around him there in those vast, gilded rooms, as if the entire city were dead. He stood at the windows and watched the winter twilight coming on, the icy mist turning the same shade of pink as the big-bummed figures on the canvasses behind him.

He was living in the rue Dauphine then, with an excitingly sluttish girl he had picked up one night at the Veuve Laurent and who had stayed because she had nowhere else to go; he knew that as soon as she could find a rich protector she would leave him. Her name was Léonie: my lion, he called her, in his ironical way. He brought her to the comedies but they bored her; she was deficient in a sense of humour. She complained of having to stand in the pit and spent the time watching with envy and resentment the jewelled ladies with their gallants up in the boxes. He painted her as a court beauty, in a borrowed gown and hat.

She stood before the finished portrait for a long time, wrinkling her nose and frowning, and at last pronounced it bad: her waist was too deep (it is true, his female figures are always long-waisted), and he had got her nose all wrong. Why had he made her expression so mournful? And what was she supposed to be looking back at, with her head turned like that, in that awkward way?

The past, he said, and laughed.

That night he coughed blood for the first time, a frighteningly copious flow. Léonie surprised him with her tenderness. She swabbed the blood where it had soaked the sheet, and made a tisane for him, and sat and rocked him like a baby in her arms. Her brother, she said, had suffered from consumption. When he asked her what had become of him she was silent, which was the answer he had feared. He lay against her breast and shivered, light-headed with terror and a sort of shocked hilarity, watching the candle flame shake and sway as if it were the little palpitant flame of his own suddenly frail, enfeebled life.

His friend Antoine La Roque had lost a leg at Malplacquet. Tell me, Antoine, Vaublin asked him, did you think you were going to die? What was it like?

But Antoine only laughed and claimed he could not remember anything except lying on the field and watching a huge thick gold cloud in the zenith floating slowly out of his view. La Roque occasionally contributed art criticism to the *Nouveau Mercure*. Don't worry, Jean, he said gaily, I'll write your obituary.

Fête galante

Living people were too much for Vaublin: he preferred his figures fixed. These strange moments that he painted, so still, so silent, what did they signify for him? He has put a stop to things; here in these twilit glades the helpless tumbling of things through time comes to a halt. His people will not die, even if they have never lived. They exist in stillness; if they were to stir they would vanish.

I like in particular the faint but ever-present air of the perverse that hangs over all his work. From a certain angle these polite arcadian scenes can seem a riotous bacchanal. How lewdly his ladies look, their eager eyes shiny as marbles and their cheeks pinkly aglow, as if from a gentle smacking. Even the props have something tumescent about them, these smooth pillars and tall, thick trees, these pendulous and rounded clouds, these dense bushes where the Marquis's men are lurking, hung like stallions, waiting to be summoned into service.

The parks, the great parks, how he must have loved them, at Anet and Chantilly and Montmorency and Sceaux, above all Sceaux. One summer midnight there he came upon a girl sitting weeping on a stone bench in the park and took her hand without a word and led her through the shrubbery to a little moonlit clearing and made love to her beside a broken statue, smelling her faintly musty, mossy smell and tasting the salt of her tears. She clasped him to her flat little breast and crushed her mouth against his cheek and gasped a word he did not catch—the name of whoever it was she had been weeping for, he supposed—and in a moment it was over and she lay against him in a kind of languorous exhaustion. Over her shoulder he saw in the moonlight an enormous toad come flopping towards them over the grey grass. He never saw the girl again; she remained in his memory only as a scrap of lace, a sharply indrawn breath, the salt taste of tears. The toad he would remember always.

Another war was dragging to a close. The peace was signed at Utrecht. Vaublin was amused; he did not associate his birthplace with peacemaking. He recalled his father standing in the street one summer morning drunk, locked out of the house, in his shirt and boots and no breeches, shouting up abuse at the window of the bedroom where Vaublin's mother cowered on the bed and wept with Vaublin and his little brothers clutched about her (Lancret, Vaublin thought, would do the scene nicely, with his taste for sentiment). That was Utrecht for him.

The Swede Carl Gustaf Tessin called on him and bought a score of counterproofs and ten originals. Vaublin was living then on the quai de Conti, alone, in big, shabby rooms with a good north light. Tessin wrote of him in one of his lively letters home:

> He has promised to paint me a *Festival of the Lenten Fair*, for which I have advanced one hundred livres of the agreed three hundred. It will be his masterpiece, provided he puts the final touches to it, but if he falls

into his black humour and his mind is possessed, then away he'll go and it's goodbye masterpiece.

Vaublin went daily to the Fair and wandered among the crowds, looking, looking. He liked the marionette shows and the coarse burlesques, the clumsier the better. He had his favourite characters and painted them again and again: Mezzetin, the scheming valet; poor Gilles, who clowned on the tightrope and always got beaten; and, of course, Polichinelle, that spiteful hunchback. There was something frankly malignant in these spectacles that appealed to Vaublin. He detected the same note, much refined, in the smooth, cruel little comedies of Regnard and Dancourt. The actors from the Comédie sat for him in costume. Paul Poisson, La Thorillière, old Baron, all the leading figures. They were perfect for his purposes, all pose and surface brilliance. They would strike an attitude and hold it for an hour without stirring, in a trance of self-regard. They brought him backstage to the first-night parties, frantic affairs presided over sometimes by Dancourt himself, a plump, self-satisfied cynic. He painted Dancourt's wanton daughter Mimi in the figure of Finette, in a silver gown—how he loved the nacreous sheen and shimmer of those heavy silks! with a little hat, playing her lute and turning towards the viewer a glance at once wistful and lascivious.

You have made me seem very stout, Mimi said, and looked at him peculiarly, with shining eyes, as if she might be on the point of tears, and gathered up her things and hurried from the studio.

He thought he had offended her, but when next he encountered Dancourt at the theatre the playwright regarded him with cold merriment and said, My daughter, poor doe, is quite smitten with you, you know. Was it a joke? It came to him yet again how little he understood of people.

The double

A curious episode. It was in the summer of 1717, when the dolts in the Academy had at last accepted him as a member—he had presented his *Pélegrinage à l'île joyeuse*; even they could not find much fault with that—and he was moving in exalted company, that he first began to be aware of the presence in the city of this shadowy counterpart. At first it was amusing, when an acquaintance would meet him on the Pont Neuf and stare in surprise, saying he had seen him not five minutes ago in Saint Germain with a lady on his arm and wearing a scarlet cloak. He suspected a conspiracy among his friends to play a hoax on him. Then he began to notice the pictures. There were *Fêtes galantes* and *Amusements champêtres*, and even theatrical scenes, his speciality, the figures in which seemed to look at him with suppressed merriment, knowingly. They were done in a style uncannily like his own, but hastily, with technical lapses and scant regard for quality of surface. Yet they were good—they were alarmingly good, in their hurried, slipshod way. No Lancret or Pater would be capable of such mingled delicacy and power, such dash and daring. They looked like the rushed work of a great master, tossed off in an afternoon or two for an impatient and not very discriminating patron. At times, though, he had the feeling that they were aimed directly at him, an elaborate, monstrous gibe meant to mock his pretensions and the flaws in his technique. But who would be so lavishly gifted that he could afford to squander so much effort on a pointless joke? He tried to get a good look at them, but somehow they always eluded him: he would glimpse a *Récréation galante* being carried between two aproned porters out of a dealer's shop, or a gold and green *Île enchantée* over the fireplace of a fashionable salon just as he was being ushered from the room; when he made enquiries of the collectors that he knew, even the most expert among them could not help him, and only shrugged and said that what he was describing sounded remarkably like his own work. One night at a carnival ball in the Comtesse de Verrue's house on the rue du Cherche-Midi he elbowed his way through the crush and managed to station himself near an interesting little *Fête champêtre*, but the light was poor and the air thick with candle smoke and the fug of bodies, and he could not even make out the signature, a slanted scrawl done with a loaded brush and underscored by a broad black line; at first he thought, with a spasm of something that was almost fright, that the initial was V, but it might as easily have been a U or a W. His nose was almost touching the varnish as he searched for a familiar face among the figures, or a tell-tale quirk of the brush that might reveal the painter's identity, when Madame Verrue, the *Dame de Volupté* herself, came up to him in that languorously suggestive way that she had and took his arm and led him off to talk to some bore about money.

Everyone must have been talking money in those early days of the System. Law's bank had opened on the rue Quincampoix, and cargoes were on their way from the Indies and Africa and China, and suddenly it seemed everyone was rich in paper money. Vaublin, with his peasant's love of substance, preferred gold. He kept it under the floorboards and sewn into the lining of his cloaks. He discovered in himself a distressing inclination towards gambling, though; almost every other night he would find himself seated at cards at the house of the Loyson sisters, watching in a hot sweat, a terrible smile fixed on his face and the air whistling in his papery lungs as the pile of yellow coins at his elbow steadily dwindled. It was an escape from the studio, from the waiting canvas, from that daytime world of meticulous, mad labours. It was risk against caution, abandon against care, chance against rule. Let it go, let it all go; what did he care.

He was thirty-three that year. His health was worse than ever. Someone told him he would believe anything—that fresh air was debilitating, and for weeks he did not venture out of doors during daylight hours. He was painting pure dreams now, locked in the solitude of his studio. He did not use models, he could not bear the presence of another near him when he worked; it had always filled him with silent fury, the way they sighed and shifted and tried to make idiotic conversation. Now he no longer needed them. When he wanted a face or a gesture he went to his old sketch-books, or cannibalized his finished work from the past. He was not interested in the individual: he would have been content to give the same features to all his figures, it did not matter, a nose, eyes, mouth, all the same. What he was after was something intangible, some simple, essential thing that perhaps was not human at all. He came increasingly to recognize that the centre of a painting, that point of equilibrium from which every element of the composition flows and where at the same time all is somehow ingathered, was never where it seemed it should be. The challenge was to find it and work from there. It could be a patch of sky, the fold of a gown, a dog scratching its ear, anything. He was in a hurry all the time. He had never believed in himself, never thought of what he was doing as art; that was what the masters did, real work, while he played. Now he would leave pieces unfinished, thrust them into a corner face to the wall, disgusted with them, and rush on to new subjects, new scenes. He had a feeling constantly of being hindered; some days he had almost to fight his way to the easel, as if there really were an invisible double there before him, crowding him aside. The light dazzled him, the air rattled like stones in his chest.

He witnessed the deportation of wives for the colonists in Louisiana. Women had been rounded up from the stews and the prisons and given a cotton shift and put on board ship in hundreds at the quayside below his windows. There were riots, all night the sky was red with fires. Next day he began work on the *Embarquement pour l'île d'amour*.

That summer was hot. He went out in the pale nights, mingling with the masked, excited crowds at the public balls in the Palais Royal. He liked crowds, liked the clamour and the crush and the feeling of being in the grip of a vast, shapeless, flowing force. He even enjoyed in his bleak way the breathlessness, the sense of teetering on the very brink of panic and suffocation. He could bear it all only for a little while; often he would end up clinging to a pillar in the tree-scented darkness of the Allée d'Argenson, doubled up and coughing out his life. His friend Madame de Caylus nagged at him to have more care.

Look at you! she would cry, when he came hobbling into one of her soirées at midnight, ashen-faced and panting harshly, look at you, Jean Vaublin, you are killing yourself! And she would take his chill, trembling hands in hers and sit down with him on a divan and smile at him chidingly and peer into his face, until he too smiled despite himself and looked away from her and bit his lip like a little boy scolded by his *maman*. Her sympathy irritated him. Sometimes it frightened him, too. She had a way of turning aside from him and letting her face go hard and blank like the face of one turning aside from a deathbed. She plied him with all sorts of crazy cures; it was ice-cold baths one week and cold compresses the next. He tried them all, of course; they seemed only to make him worse. Once, when she pressed him to let her doctor bleed him—as if he were not bleeding enough already!—he flew into a rage.

There is no help for me! he shouted at her, don't you know that?

The summer ended. Autumn was damp and chill that year, with week-long fogs. His strength was failing. When he stepped to the canvas another, heavier arm seemed to lift alongside his. No help, no help on earth.

L'embarquement

He went to England at the end of 1719. Where did he sail from, where did he land? So many things I do not know about him and never will. That must have been the beginning of his final period of hectic wanderings. He had intended to spend a month in London but stayed for half a year. He saw the celebrated Doctor Mead and allowed himself to believe his lungs could be cured. Mead put him on a regimen of quinine and fresh oxblood and took him to Old Slaughter's in St Martin's Lane where he drank Dutch gin and water and ate a pig's foot boiled in brine.

We must fatten you up, sir, the doctor said, and clapped a big soft hand on his meagre shoulder and laughed in his jolly way.

Vaublin grinned uncontrollably into his glass and blushed; how childish these hearty, capable people made him feel. Will I live, doctor? he asked, direct as ever, and the doctor stared at him in consternation and laughed even louder.

Live, man? he roared. Of course you'll live! But he did not say for how long.

Mead was the author of a scholarly work, *The Influence of the Sun and the Moon on the Human Body,* and bored Vaublin with enthusiastic talk of tides and ecliptics and cosmic harmony.

The moon only reminds me of Pierrot, Vaublin said dreamily

229

—and Pierrot, of course, reminds me of myself. A silence followed and then the doctor cleared his throat and changed the subject.

He was an authority also on poisons.

One bright day in April, when Vaublin had coughed up what seemed to him must be at least a litre of blood, he asked the doctor shyly if he would prepare a fatal draught for him, in concentrated form, so that he could carry it with him for use if life at the last should become unbearable—not worth the candle, he said, smiling wryly, pleased with the English phrase. The doctor refused, of course, and grew quite indignant. Things were never the same between them after that.

In June Vaublin returned to France, sicker now than when he had left. Paris was silent, dazed with the great heat of that summer and the shock of economic collapse: the System had failed, Law's bank was closed, the speculators had been ruined. In July came news of the plague in Marseille; the city was declared officially dead. Vaublin had thought he would not live to see the decade change, yet here he was, still hanging on while others all around him died. In January his father had succumbed to the purpural fever; in his heart he was glad that man had not outlived him.

Self-portrait

Poor Vaublin at the end dragging himself all over Paris with the angel after him; that was dying, no mistaking it. He was terrified they would bury him before he was absolutely dead, since after all, as he said, he had never been absolutely alive. Wait for the green spot, he urged them, only half in jest, wait for the gangrenous green spot, as they used to do with the ancient kings. And he laughed, on the verge of tears, as he always seemed to be in those last weeks. He experienced strange periods of euphoria standing before that enormous canvas, lost in the picture surface, almost a part of the paint, his hands working faster than his brain could follow. And then the terrible, sweat-soaked nights, and the recurring dream: the figures in the picture coming dazedly to life like the survivors of some huge catastrophe. And in the mornings shivering at the window in the thin dawn-light, amazed it was all still there, large as life, the roofs, the river, the quayside wreathed in mist, all there and not caring anything for him. Paris! he cried, Paris, I'm dying! And wiped his nose on his knuckles. The figure at his back in the corner always now, watching him with quiet interest, waiting.

He had rented a little attic room on the Île in the house of an old Jew who prayed aloud in the night, keening and sighing. In the mornings a girl from the bakery next door brought him bread and apples, a flask of wine, saying nothing, standing big-eyed in the doorway while he delved for pennies in his purse. When she was there he heard his breathing, how bad it was.

What month is it? he asked her one day.

July!

It was hot. He was so tired, so tired. He left the door open and she began to come in, venturing a little farther each day. She stood by the wall with her hands behind her and watched him work. She was so quiet he could forget she was there. She came back in the night and slept with him, held him shaking in her thin, pale arms. When he woke in the mornings she was gone. He put on his smock and walked to the canvas barefoot. It was so much bigger than he. He felt as if he were afloat on some dense, brimming surface. Each brush stroke dragged with a liquid weight. He drifted amongst the figures, bumping softly against this one or that, feeling their insubstantial thereness. Once, working up close against the canvas, he coughed and stippled a patch of sky with blood. He gave Pierrot the girl's face and then painted it over with his own. A self-portrait, the only one he ever did. That night from his pallet, the girl asleep with her bum pressed against his side, he lay and looked at the great pale figure glimmering above him and grinned in the dark. My monster. Me. And then suddenly, without realizing it, died.

The author wishes to acknowledge the great catalogue on the life and works of Antoine Watteau, *Watteau: 1684–1721*, by Margaret Morgan Grasselli and Pierre Rosenberg, with the assistance of Nicole Parmantier (National Gallery of Art, Washington, 1984).

Mandatory Reading

T hat's what political insiders say about *The New Republic*. And they're not the only ones. Bill Clinton reads it. Al Gore even writes for it. And each week freshly printed copies are hand delivered to the White House.

But *The New Republic* covers more than politics. It covers the entire cultural landscape with reviews of books, films, theater and the arts that explore contemporary issues — from unexpected and unorthodox points of view! To see for yourself, return this coupon now or call 1-800-274-6350.

Name (please print)

Street

City, State, Zip

Yes, send me 48 issues for just $44.95
❏ Payment enclosed   ❏ Bill me
❏ Please charge my:
   ❏ Visa   ❏ MC   ❏ AmEx

Account #

Expiration date

Signature

Return this coupon with payment to:
The New Republic
P.O. Box 52333
Boulder, CO
80321-2333

Allow 3-5 weeks for your first issue. Offer good for U.S. addresses and new subscribers only. Foreign please add $30 for surface mail.

5RC11

LORNA SAGE

DEATH OF THE AUTHOR

There's a piece on Byron by William Hazlitt in which, as he's routinely and genially abusing the latest instalment of *Don Juan*, he learns that Byron is dead. Well, of course, Hazlitt says, he *was* the greatest writer of the age. The sudden deaths of contemporaries wrong-foot us: we have to turn too quickly into posterity's representatives. A living writer is part of the unsatisfying, provisional, myopic, linear, altogether human present, but add a full stop and you can read the work backwards, sideways, whatever, because now it's an *oeuvre*, truly finished.

Angela Carter annoyed people quite a lot when she was alive ('I certainly don't seem to get the sympathy vote,' she observed with more than a shadow of satisfaction when last year's big prizes were announced). But when she died everyone scrambled to make up for it, and perhaps there was more than a shadow of satisfaction behind some of those glowing obituaries, too: she isn't going to come up with any more surprises; that disturbing sense of someone making it up as she went along will fade; Literature can take its course. For the first time I see that there's at least one virtue in literary biography: a 'Life' can demythologize the work in the best sense, preserving its fallibility, which is also the condition for its brilliance.

This has been critical heresy for a long time. Writers' lives merely distract us from the true slipperiness and anonymity of any text worth its salt. A text is a text is a text. Angela, of course, was of the generation nourished on the Death of the Author (Barthes, 1968 vintage), as was I.

Looking back, she recaptured some of the euphoria of that time:

> Truly, it felt like Year One . . . all that was holy was in the process of being profaned . . . I can date to that time . . . and to that sense of heightened awareness of the society around me in the summer of 1968, my own questioning of the nature of my reality as a *woman*. How that social fiction of my 'femininity' was created, by means outside my control, and palmed off on me as the real thing.

Angela Carter, 1985.

Photo: Vincent Mentzel

But she went on to qualify the 'sense of limitless freedom' you get by sloughing off the myths with a sentence which ought to stand as the epigraph to any attempt at a biography of her : 'I am the pure product of an advanced, industrialized, post-imperialist country in decline.' Well, perhaps not. But it is a remark that captures her tone pretty exactly: I can just see the *moue* of amused disgust (but also *disgusted* disgust at the same time, morally and intellectually fastidious disgust) with which she'd greet the notion that you could somehow levitate out of history.

A Life doesn't have to reinvent its subject as a 'real' person. Angela Carter's life—the background of social mobility, the teenage anorexia, the education and self-education, the early marriage and divorce, the role-playing and shape-shifting, the travels, the choice of a man much younger, the baby in her forties—is the story of someone walking a tightrope. It's all happening 'on the edge', in no man's land, among the debris of past convictions. By the end, her life fitted her more or less like a glove, but that's because she'd put it together, by trial and error, *bricolage*, all in the (conventionally) wrong order. Her genius for estrangement came out of a thin-skinned extremity of response to the circumstances of her life and to the signs of the times. She was, indeed, literally thin-skinned: her skin was very fair, pink and white; she weathered quite a bit but never tanned, and you could see the veins easily. You might almost say her body *thought*. She had very good bones and was photogenic, so that it didn't matter that she'd stopped looking in mirrors and painting her face. She let her hair grow out white in wisps two or three years before she got pregnant. I could have been a grandmother by the time she was a mother, and I was younger than she. The shape a woman's life takes now is a lot less determined than once it was. Or: the determinations are more subtle, you're *sentenced* to assemble your own version.

Beginning

There's a theory, one I find persuasive, that the quest for knowledge is, at bottom, the search for the answer to the question: 'Where was I before I was born?'

In the beginning was . . . what?

Perhaps, in the beginning, there was a curious room, a room like this one, crammed with wonders . . .

> Angela Carter, 'The Curious Room', *SPELL* (*Swiss Papers in English Language and Literature*), 1990

She cultivated the role of fairy godmother and/or witch, and—in *The Bloody Chamber* (1979) rewrote the Bluebeard story with pistol-toting Mother riding to the rescue at the last minute. However, it was not her own mother, one of a family of 'great examination-passers' (a scholarship girl who'd left school at fifteen to work at Selfridges) who provided the model for this kind of figure, but her maternal grandmother, who'd come originally from South Yorkshire. Granny came to the rescue in the year of Angela's birth (1940) and evacuated herself and her grandchildren from south London back to the gritty coal-mining village of Wath-upon-Dearne, kidnapping them safely into the past for the duration of the war.

Skipping a generation took Angela back to 'Votes for Women', working-class radicalism, outside lavatories and coal-dust coughs. Granny ought, perhaps, to have surfaced in the fiction as the spirit of social realism, though actually it makes sense that she's in the magical mode, since her brand of eccentric toughness was already thoroughly archaic from the point of view of the post-war and the south of England. In Angela's last novel, *Wise Children*, the granny-figure is killed in the Blitz, but bequeaths to her adoptive grand-daughters Dora and Nora the Brixton house that offers them a safe haven when they have to retire from the stage. 'When the bombardments began, Grandma would go outside and shake her fist at the old men in the sky . . . She was our air-raid shelter; she was our entertainment; she was our breast,' says Dora.

237

Grandma figures *as* the house in this book, the matriarchal space of the Carter house of fiction—'but the whole place never looked *plausible*' (Dora again). In a *New Review* series on 'Family Life' back in 1976, Angela wrote that her grandmother 'was a woman of such physical and spiritual heaviness she seemed to have been born with a greater degree of gravity than most people.'

> Her personality had an architectonic quality; I think of her when I see some of the great London railway termini, especially Saint Pancras, with its soot and turrets, and she overshadowed her own daughters, whom she did not understand—my mother, who liked things to be nice; my dotty aunt . . .

Grandmother is a larger-than-life 'character' for her—Leninist Lizzie, the heroine's minder in *Nights at the Circus*, looks like another avatar—but mother is almost a missing person. Not unusual this, at all, particularly for daughters growing up in the 1940s and 1950s, with upwardly socially mobile mothers who'd given up work: women girlified, exiled and isolated in domesticity, who hadn't 'done anything' with their education. She wrote about her Scottish journalist father with obvious pleasure: 'very little to do with the stern, fearful face of the Father in patriarchy . . . there was no fear' ('Sugar Daddy' in *Fathers*, Virago, 1983). Whereas about her mother, who was younger but died first, she was wry, oblique, regretful, protective: 'There was to be no struggle for my mother, who married herself young to an adoring husband who indulged her, who was subject to ill-health, who spoke standard English, who continued to wear fancy clothes.' Angela was supposed to do something with her own education, so instead of course she married young herself, in reaction against what her mother wanted for her, though it didn't last long. If you look for the provenance of the feminist writer, mother is the key. The women who really nailed patriarchy weren't on the whole the ones with authoritarian fathers, but the ones with troubled, contradictory mothers: you aim your feminism less at men than at the picture of the woman you don't want to be, the enemy within. In this case, the girl–wife. Hence (again) a motive

for skipping a generation, in imagination. Back to Gran.

It wasn't a card she openly played until she got older, when she took to fairy tales and ribaldry. However, the whole *camp* quality of writing of the 1960s derives from this sense of a lost (deliberately distanced) reality: working-class, northern, matriarchal. None of this could she *be*, or speak directly for, but she could do it in pastiche —and she did, writing in ghostly quotation marks. If there was nearly nothing 'natural' about her style, this was perhaps because her kind of family background introduced her early on to the notion that the culture was a dressing-up box and to the bliss and nightmare of turning the clock back. That is what *The Magic Toyshop* (1967) is about—slipping out of your precarious middle-classness into the house of (superficial) horrors and (libidinal) mirrors. Ten years after that she said to me in an interview (I'd asked, 'Do you think your environment shaped you?'):

> Well, my brother and I speculate endlessly on this point. We often say to one another, How is it possible such camp little flowers as ourselves emanated from Balham via Wath-upon-Dearne and the places my father comes from, north Aberdeenshire, stark, bleak and apparently lugubriously Calvinistic, witch-burning country? But obviously, something in this peculiar rootless, upward, downward, sideways socially mobile family, living in twilight zones . . .

This is not about nostalgia but connects with a quite different contemporary sensation: of coming at the end, mopping up, having the freedom of anomie.

'Perhaps, in the beginning, there was a curious room . . . ' Crammed with wonders? The beginning, for Carter, is a magical lumber-room. Over the years her own south London house came rather to resemble this cabinet of curiosities. It was a toy-box long before her son Alexander arrived, though he completed its transformation so that there was hardly room to swing a cat. Indeed, the cats were eventually exiled to the garden. A letter she wrote to me just after that first 1977 interview records the beginnings of this process:

The NEW REVIEW piece is smashing. Thanks. The only snag, as far as I'm concerned, is that I only have the one script, alas, so that a number of the details of my autobiography are repeated in the 'Family Life' piece —repeated word for word, what's more. Which is a great tribute to my internal consistency, I suppose; only, my childhood, boyhood and youth is a kind of cabaret turn performed, nowadays, with such a practised style it comes out engine-turned on demand. What a creep I am.

And I always get cast down by my own pusillanimity. The notion that one day the red dawn will indeed break over Clapham is the one thing that keeps me going. Of course, I have my own private lists prepared for the purges but . . . I'm more interested in socialist reconstruction *after* the revolution than the revolution itself, which seems to mark me out from my peers. We have just had the exterior of this house painted quite a jolly red, by the way. The front steps look as if the Valentine's Day massacre had been performed on them. However, I also managed to persuade Christine downstairs to have a *black* front door so it is the jolly old red & black & VIVA LA MUERTE & sucks boo to Snoo's barley and bamboos; we're going to have a *real* Clapham front garden, the anarchist colours & pieces of motorcycle & broken bottles & used condoms lightly scattered over all . . .

PS I didn't manage to post this until today, Sunday, or rather 00.30 Monday morning, after a brisk search for the letter (in Portuguese) inviting me to this ruddy do [a Festival of Free Art], which begins to look more and more like a nightmare. Chris ['Christine downstairs'] wants me to bring home a 6 ft. ceramic cockerel. I have house-guests, just arrived, having driven from Nepal— the sister of a Korean ex-boyfriend of mine plus her bloke. Mark has strained a muscle in his back—I'd planned to have him push me around in my wheelchair in 20 years time; what if I have to push *him* around in one in 5 years time? It's like a soap opera in this house, an everyday story of alternative folk, I suppose.

You can see in the discussion of the decor here something of her inverted dandyism; also the self-consciousness which was her inheritance, for better and for worse. The whole place 'never looked *plausible*.'

Middle

> They seemed to have made the entire city into a cold hall of mirrors which continually proliferated whole galleries of constantly changing appearances, all marvellous but none tangible . . . One morning, we woke to find the house next door reduced to nothing but a heap of sticks and a pile of newspapers neatly tied with string, left out for the garbage collector.

> Angela Carter, 'A Souvenir of Japan', *Fireworks*, 1974

Japan (1969–72) had been her rite of passage in between, the place where she lost and found herself. Being young was traumatic: she'd been anorexic, her tall, big-boned body and her intransigent spirit had been at odds with the ways women were expected to be, inside or outside. Looking back to her teenage years, she always made the same joke:

> I now [1983] recall this period with intense embarrassment, because my parents' concern to protect me from predatory boys was only equalled by the enthusiasm with which the boys I did indeed occasionally meet protected themselves against me.

Her first marriage she portrayed as a more or less desperate measure, with her making the running ('Somebody who would go to Godard movies with me and on CND marches and even have sexual intercourse with me, though he insisted we should be engaged first'). And in her five 1960s novels the point of view is interestingly vagrant—as readily male as female.

When she impersonated a girl she described the boys as sex

Angela Carter, 1969.

objects; when she went in for cross-dressing she did it, she later remarked, with almost 'sinister' effectiveness: 'I was, as a girl, suffering a degree of colonialization of the mind. Especially in the journalism I was writing then, I'd—quite unconsciously—posit a male point of view as the general one. So there was an element of the male impersonator about this young person as she was finding herself.' That is one way to put it. Perhaps she adopted the male point of view also because, under the mask of the 'general', it was more aggressive, more licensed, more *authorial*. At any rate, the result is that in the early fiction her boys and girls look into each others' eyes and see—themselves. Then in 1969 she broke the pattern. She and her husband parted company, and she went to live with a Japanese lover, in Japan.

And there her size—and her colour—made her utterly foreign. She compounded her oddity when she stepped into the looking-glass world of a culture that reflected her back to herself as an alien, 'learning the hard way that most people on this planet are *not* Caucasian and have no reason to either love or respect Caucasians.' Her 1974 collection, *Fireworks*, contains three stories that, most uncharacteristically, are hardly fictionalized at all. She must have felt that their built-in strangeness provided sufficient distance, and it does:

> I had never been so absolutely the mysterious other. I had become a kind of phoenix, a fabulous beast; I was an outlandish jewel. He found me, I think, inexpressibly exotic. But I often felt like a female impersonator.
>
> In the department store there was a rack of dresses labelled: 'For Young and Cute Girls Only'. When I looked at them, I felt as gross as Glumdalclitch. I wore men's sandals . . . the largest size. My pink cheeks, blue eyes and blatant yellow hair made of me, in the visual orchestration of this city . . . an instrument which played upon an alien scale . . . He was so delicately put together that I thought his skeleton must have the airy elegance of a bird's and I was sometimes afraid that I might smash him.

Feeling a freak was a kind of rehearsal for the invention of her

lumpen winged aerealiste Fevvers years later. At the time, in
Tokyo, whatever she was looking for, she discovered the
truthfulness *and finality* of appearances, images emptied of their
usual freight of recognition and guilt. This wasn't, in other words,
old-fashioned orientalism, but the new-fangled sort that denied you
access to any *essence* of otherness. Tokyo offered cruel but
cleansing reflections. In another piece called 'Flesh and the Mirror',
she described an erotic encounter so impersonal it left no room at
all for soul-searching: 'This mirror refused to conspire with me.'

Self-consciousness had been her bane from the start, hence the
anorexia. But while most women come out the other side and learn
to act naturally, she somehow managed not to, and Japan is the
shorthand, I think, for how. She discovered and retained a way of
looking at herself, and other people, as unnatural. She was, even in
ordinary and relaxed situations, a touch unlikely on principle. Her
hair went through all the colours of the rainbow before becoming
white at the moment when decorum would have suggested a
discreet, still-youthful streaked mouse. Once, when I was staying at
her house, I discovered I had mislaid my make-up and she dug out
a paintbox from Japan, some kind of actor's or geisha's kit, which
was all slick purple, rusty carmine and green grease.

She escaped the character expected of the woman writer by
similar strategies. That is, she substituted work for inwardness.
She'd once wanted, in adolescence, to be an actress; when I
talked with her in 1977, she insisted that writing was *public*:
'Sometimes when you say to people you're a writer, they say,
"Have you had anything published?" Which is a bit like saying to
an actor, "Have you ever been on the stage?" Because if it's not
published it doesn't exist.' And the same point, made more
succinctly: 'I mean, it's like the right true end of love.'

Not that she stopped consulting the mirror. A small
allegory: Plotinus and later Neoplatonists suggested
mischievously that you could draw a subversive moral
from the fate of Narcissus—it's not self-obsession that destroys
you, but the failure to love yourself coolly and intelligently and
sceptically enough. If he'd recognized his own image in the water
he could have made a real beginning on knowing himself. Angela

looked into some dangerous mirrors—for instance, de Sade's (in *The Sadeian Woman*, 1979), but by then she'd stepped through the Japanese looking-glass and could say, 'Flesh comes to us out of history.' When she came back to England she had her career to build all over again, and that's what she did, with help from journalism and an Arts Council Fellowship in Sheffield. She was hard up and marginalized in ways she didn't at all relish. She had no secure relationship with a publisher—between 1971 and 1977 she moved from Hart-Davis to Quartet to Gollancz—she couldn't make enough money out of her fiction to live on and she didn't fit easily into the classic outsider role. She never accepted the madwoman-in-the-attic school of thought about the woman writer, particularly not about the Gothic or fantastical writer: freaks and fairies, she believed, were as much socially determined as anyone else; our 'symbols' are of course *ours*. Theory apart, however, she had a thin time during the 1970s, and she was painfully prickly about her reputation. When she filled in an author's publicity form for Gollancz (who published *The Passion of New Eve* in 1977 in their 'science fiction and fantasy' category), there was a section asking her to list her previous publications. Angela wrote simply '7 novels', without giving even the titles.

Some time before this, she wrote to me from Albert Road, Sheffield, about Virago, and her great friend and fan Carmen Callil's plans to *re*publish women. She was thinking hard about 'the woman writer', and meeting a pissed Elizabeth Smart at a party at Emma Tennant's had given her bitter food for thought:

> 'It is hard for women,' she slurred. Actually it was a very peculiar experience because she clearly wanted to talk in polished gnomic epigrams about anguish and death and boredom and I honestly couldn't think of anything to say. Except, I understand why men hate women and they are right, yes, right. Because we should set good examples to the poor things. (Was surprised to find Mary Wollstonecraft making exactly the same point, in a way.) . . . It was all very odd. I don't mean to sound hard. I mean, I'm sure her life has been astoundingly tragic. And I began to plot a study of

the Jean Rhys/E. Smart/E. O'Brien woman titled 'Self-inflicted wounds', which kind of brings me to the point, or anyway, a point.

I'm on the editorial committee of this publishing firm, VIRAGO . . .

From her point of view, Virago was meant—among many, many other things—to make money out of and for women's writing and to rescue it from the slough of passive suffering:

> The whole idea is very tentative at the moment, obviously. I suppose I am moved towards it by the desire that no daughter of mine should ever be in a position to be able to write BY GRAND CENTRAL STATION I SAT DOWN AND WEPT, exquisite prose though it might contain. (BY GRAND CENTRAL STATION I TORE OFF HIS BALLS would be more like it, I should hope.)

She herself was working on the Sade book at the time, and her ideas for Virago included some books by men (Sade's *Justine*, Richardson's *Clarissa*) which got at the roots of female 'pathology'. She feared and loathed and found hilarious the spectacle of the suffering woman. The Sade book was an exorcism of sorts, too. She needed to *theorize* in order to feel in charge and to cheer herself up, and that has left its mark marvellously on the fiction too, which is full of ideas, *armed* with them. (Desiderio in *The Infernal Desire Machines of Doctor Hoffman*, 1972, avoids being eaten by a tribe of river Indians, who are hoping magically to absorb his literacy, because he's a good enough anthropologist to rumble their plans. Like Angela, he's read his Lévi-Strauss. Much more recently, in *Nights at the Circus*, Fevvers escapes a murderous Rosicrucian by the same ploy, having this time read Frances Yates, I'd imagine.)

Anyway, with the Sade book and *The Bloody Chamber* in 1979, she rounded off the decade triumphantly. The fairy tale idea was a real breakthrough and enabled her to *read* with a new appropriateness and panache, as though she was *telling* these stories. She took to teaching creative writing too. In 1980 she went to the United States, to Brown University, where she substituted for John Hawkes: no one had read her, she said, but she enjoyed it enormously and had the company of her friends Robert and Pili Coover. Bit by bit, her earlier work would be republished (in Picador and King Penguin, as well as Virago); she would acquire a solid relation with Chatto & Windus, when Carmen Callil moved there; she would become a delighting globe-trotter, a visiting writer/teacher/performer; and her work would be translated into all the major European languages. In 1984 she was still broke enough to be tempted to come and teach on the creative writing programme at my university, East Anglia. I acted—apprehensively —as the go-between on this deal, well aware that she didn't see eye to eye with Malcolm Bradbury, who ran the course. Since he wasn't there when she was, this arrangement survived precariously until 1987, with the two of them alternating like the man and woman who forecast the weather. She chucked it in with relief, though students as different as Kazuo Ishiguro and Glenn Patterson had been rewards in themselves. I suppose the point to make about these years is this: she had to struggle hard to sustain her confidence, in the face of frequent indifference, condescension and type-casting. She was not, either, able to repose securely in the bosom of the sisterhood, since her insistence on reclaiming the territory of the pornographers—just for example—set her against feminist puritans and separatists. And of course she was in general an offence to the modest, inward, realist version of the woman writer. John Bayley, lately, in the *New York Review of Books*, contrived to imply that she had an almost cosy 'place' from the start: a magical realist, a post-modernist. This couldn't be further from the truth. Her work was unclassifiable in terms of British fiction, except as 'Gothic' or 'fantasy', throughout the whole difficult middle period of her career. If that situation has changed, it is largely because she refused to write 'fantasy' as (merely) alternative, 'in opposition', and because she made large demands on her readers.

B ad-tempered footnotes department:
Exhibit One: a letter undated, 'Tuesday':

Very bland place. At least, Toronto is . . . The son and

his father didn't miss me. But they seem glad to see me back. It seems we might well be going to Texas next spring; am awaiting letter. Am planning to write novel about sensitive, fine-grained art historian whose
PTO
life is totally changed by winning large, vulgar cash prize, she dies [sic] her hair green and wears leather trousers etc. Sniffs glue and turns into Kathy Acker . . .

Exhibit Two: a postcard from the States:

Have just heard about the Booker. I hope he drinks himself to death on the prize money (you know me, ever fair and compassionate). Will telephone soon—I keep meaning to write you the kind of letter people write in biographies, but there ain't time.

Ending

Because I simply could not have existed, as I am, in any other preceding time or place . . . I could have been a professional writer at any period since the seventeenth century in Britain or in France. But I could *not* have combined this latter with a life as a sexually active woman until the introduction of contraception . . . A 'new kind of being,' unburdened with a past. The voluntarily sterile yet sexually active being, existing in more than a few numbers, *is* a being without precedent . . .

Angela Carter, 'Notes from the Front Line', 1983

Angela made parenthood her theme in her last novel, *Wise Children*—parenthood of all sorts, literary, literal and lateral (twins as mirrors to each other). She'd also had her son, Alexander, at the last minute in 1983. Alex was perhaps partly responsible for the long gap between this novel and its predecessor (seven years), but it had always taken her a long time to 'gestate' the next because she *was* original, always moving on and changing. She didn't think there was anything Mythological about that: *Wise Children* in fact is all about coming from the wrong side of the tracks to claim kin with Shakespeare, traditionally one of the favourite examples of mythic fatherhood.

She had long before used pregnancy as a plot device, a way of ending a novel: first in *Heroes and Villains* (1969) and then in *New Eve* very elaborately indeed, so that it turns into an evolutionary re-run, with branches of the family tree for archaeopteryx and other intermediate beings missed out first time round. She had trouble with endings once she had taken to using the picaresque format of allegorical travels, and wanted them to stay 'open'. And it wasn't too different with her life. She and Mark Pearce had 'settled down' over the years, but in a most vagrant fashion. She travelled all over the place for jobs, residencies, tours; the Clapham house was always being changed around (her friend Christine moved out quite shortly), and was never finished. 'At home' they cooked, decorated, gardened, collected cats, kites, prints, paintings, gadgets, all piecemeal. The house became filled with the jetsam of their enthusiasms. Mark worked as a potter for a while and made plates that were beautiful but also enormous, so that they hardly fitted on the makeshift kitchen table and you felt like a guest at a giants' feast. The two of them took to wearing identical military surplus greatcoats outdoors, announcing their unanimity and accentuating their height. Domestically they communed in silence, which was very much Mark's speciality, though she was pretty good at it too. They conspired to present their relationship as somehow *sui generis*, like a relation between creatures of different species who both happened to be tall. They had nothing much conventionally 'in common' except that they were both eccentric, stubborn, intransigent, wordlessly intimate.

She didn't, I'm sure, study to conceive, but simply found herself pregnant and decided to go ahead with it. An aged *primagravida*, she joked, but obviously her condition underlined the difference in their ages and made her granny disguise all the more outrageous. That November, in her last weeks of pregnancy and on the day after she had helped to judge the Booker Prize (which went to J. M. Coetzee), she developed high blood pressure and was hospitalized. From hospital she wrote me a furious letter:

251

My blood pressure rating has not been improved by my second run-in with the consultant obstetrician. Every time I remember what she said, I feel raptly incredulous and racked by impotent fury. Although at the time I said nothing, because I could not believe my ears.

So she says: 'How are you feeling?'

'Fine but apprehensive,' I say, 'not of the birth itself but of the next 20 years.'

'How is your husband feeling?' she asked.

I paused to think of the right way of putting it and she said quickly: 'I know he's only your common-law husband.'

While I was digesting this, she pressed down on my belly so I couldn't move and said:

'Of course you've done absolutely the right thing by *not* having an abortion but now is the time to contemplate adoption and I urge you to think about it very seriously.'

That is *exactly* what she said! Each time I think about it, the adrenalin surges through my veins. I want to *kill* this woman. I want the BMA to crucify her. I want to rip out her insides.

Anyway, then she said: 'Its [sic] policy of the hospital to put older women into hospital for the last two weeks of pregnancy and I'll be generous, you can go home to collect your nightie & be back in an hour.'

Nobody had told me about this policy before & I feel she may have made it up on the spur of the moment. Needless to say, she then buggered off back to her private practice. Was she being punitive? Why didn't I kick her in the crotch, you may ask. Why didn't I cry, shreik [sic] & kick my heels on the ground, demanding she be forthwith stripped of her degrees & set to cleaning out the latrines. Why did I *come in*, after all that! Everybody else in this hospital is so nice & kind & sensible & sympathetic. There would have been a round of *applause* if I'd kicked her in the crotch. But, anyway, it turns out that I'm not in here for nothing—this ward

Photo: Eve Arnold/Magnum

is full of women with high blood pressure, swollen feet
& the thing they make you collect your piss for, the
dreaded protein in the urine. The doctor who looked at
me today said they all spent a lot of time patching
things up after my consultant, who is evidently famed
for making strong women break down. Evidently I can
agitate to go home again on Monday if my blood
pressure has gone down.

'What about the consultant's weekly clinic?' I said,
because I'm supposed to go to it.

'Dodge her,' the doctor said. The doctor is a slip of a
right-on sister young enough to be my daughter. The
consultant is a Thatcher-clone—evidently a Catholic,
I'm told—old enough to be my mother. I am the uneasy
filling in this sandwich.

A good example, this, of the way motherhood is used as a means
of denying a woman's own meanings, taking away her choices,
extruding her from normality's roster. Actually, the birth went all
right, and despite the seemingly inevitable hospital infection,
Angela was able to rejoice from the beginning in Alex's
Caravaggiesque beauty. But you can see how hard it was for her,
at times, to make up her life as she went along. The writing in
this letter belongs to a genre she disliked—the low mimetic, the
language that reproduces the world. Small wonder she preferred
surreal transformations, nothing to do with autobiography or
confession or testament. But that seeming impersonality was, I'm
arguing, entirely personal at base—a refusal to be placed or
characterized or *saved* from oneself. One of the last things she
wrote, *The Holy Family Album* (1992) for television, attacked
God the Father for the tortures inflicted on His Son in the name
of Love, but in the cause of Power: a piece of deliberate
blasphemy against the Almighty Author. And a plea for
mortality. *Flesh comes to us out of history*. Nothing stays, endings
are final, which is why they are also beginnings.

GELLHORN · CO **GRANTA** LIN THUBRON ·

GERMAINE GREER · JOHN BERGER · REDMOND O'HANLON · MARIO VARGAS LLOSA

MARTHA · DORIS LESSING · SAUL BELLOW · JOHN UPDIKE · ANDREI SINYAVSKY

"A stunning contribution to contemporary writing"—*Newsweek*

"Consistently worth reading"—*The Village Voice*

"If there is a document of our time, *GRANTA* is it."—*Spin*

"A courageous literary magazine"—Graham Greene

SUBSCRIBE & SAVE

Please enter my subscription to *GRANTA*. ❏ New ❏ Renewal

❏ 1 year $29.95 (4 issues) ❏ 2 years $57.95 ❏ 3 years $79.95

Name_____

Address_____

_____Zip_____

6203BH

$_____enclosed (cheque/cc). ❏ Bill me. I will pay later.

❏ Cheque ❏ Visa ❏ American Express ❏ MasterCard

Card No._____

Exp. Date_____Signature_____

Additional Foreign Postage Per Year: Canada, Mexico, South America: $5 surface, $15 airmail; Europe: $16 airspeeded; Rest of the World: $30 airspeeded.

Return to: Granta, 250 West 57th Street, Suite 1316, New York, NY 10107

· JAMES FENTON · GRACE PALEY · MARTIN AMIS ·

Notes on Contributors

Saul Bellow was born in Lachine, Quebec, in 1915. Two and a half years earlier, his father, Abraham (later 'Abram') Belo, had emigrated from Russia with his wife and three children—two boys and a girl. Abraham Bellows—the surname was the result of a customs official's error—chose Lachine because his sister, Rosa, had settled there along with another sister and brother. The family moved to Chicago in 1924 following a series of unsuccessful business ventures. 'Memoirs of a Bootlegger's Son', unusual among Bellow's work for being narrated by an older brother, was written in 1954, the year after the publication of *The Adventures of Augie March*, but was itself never published. Saul Bellow is currently working on a new novel. **James Atlas** began work on his biography of Saul Bellow shortly after writing an article for the *New York Review of Books* on Bellow's college friend, the writer Isaac Rosenberg. 'Dreams for Hire' is one of twelve stories that **Gabriel García Márquez** has been writing since 1976 about Latin Americans in Europe. The collection will be published in Spain this autumn, and by Jonathan Cape in Britain next spring with the title *Twelve Pilgrim Voices*. **Blake Morrison** has written two volumes of poetry: *Dark Glasses* and *The Ballad of the Yorkshire Ripper*. He is the Literary Editor of the *Independent on Sunday*. **Todd McEwen**, formerly an editor at *Granta*, lives in Palo Alto, California. His memoir of childhood 'My Mother's Eyes' appeared in *Granta* 39, 'The Body'. **Louise Erdrich**'s most recent book, written with her husband Michael Dorris, is *The Crown of Columbus*. *Low Life*, **Luc Sante**'s history of New York, appeared last year. The poet **Andrew Motion**'s biography of Philip Larkin will be published in April by Faber & Faber. **Richard Holmes**'s biography *Coleridge: Early Visions* was Whitbread Book of the Year in 1990. Since being rescued from the North Sea by an RAF Sea King helicopter last summer he has continued to work on eighteenth- and nineteenth-century lives. **Ian Hamilton**'s book *Keepers of the Flame* will be published in October by Hutchinson. He is currently editing *The Oxford Companion to Twentieth Century Poetry*. **John Banville** is Literary Editor of the *Irish Times*. His 'biographical' novels include *Kepler* and *Doctor Copernicus*. **Lorna Sage** teaches at the University of East Anglia. Her book, *Women in the House of Fiction*, a work of criticism, will be published next year.